THE DUAL EXECUTIVE

STUDIES IN THE MODERN PRESIDENCY

A series edited by Shirley Anne Warshaw

Studies in the Modern Presidency is an innovative book series that brings together established and emerging voices in modern presidential research, from the Nixon administration to the present. While works on the modern Congress abound, this series seeks to expand the literature available on the presidency and the executive branch.

Scholars and journalists alike are increasingly writing and reporting on issues such as presidential rhetoric, executive-legislative relations, executive privilege, signing statements, and so on. We are committed to publishing outstanding research and analysis that reaches beyond conventional approaches to provide scholars, students, and the general public with insightful investigations into presidential politics and power.

This series features short and incisive books that chart new territory, offer a range of perspectives, and frame the intellectual debate on the modern presidency.

A list of the books in this series can be found online at
http://www.sup.org/modernpresidency.

THE DUAL EXECUTIVE

UNILATERAL ORDERS IN A SEPARATED AND SHARED POWER SYSTEM

Michelle Belco and Brandon Rottinghaus

STANFORD UNIVERSITY PRESS

Stanford, California

Stanford University Press
Stanford, California
© 2017 by the Board of Trustees of the Leland Stanford Junior
University. All rights reserved.

Printed in the United States of America on acid-free,
archival-quality paper

Library of Congress Cataloging-in-Publication Data

Names: Belco, Michelle, author. | Rottinghaus, Brandon, author.

Title: The dual executive : unilateral orders in a separated and shared
power system / Michelle Belco and Brandon Rottinghaus.
Other titles: Studies in the modern presidency.
Description: Stanford, California : Stanford University Press, 2017. |
Series: Studies in the modern presidency | Includes bibliographical
references and index.
Identifiers: LCCN 2016051758 (print) | LCCN 2016052930 (ebook) |
ISBN 9780804799973 (cloth : alk. paper) |
ISBN 9781503601987 (e-book)
Subjects: LCSH: Executive power—United States. | Presidents—
United States. | Executive orders—United States. | Separation of
powers—United States.
Classification: LCC JK516 .B397 2017 (print) | LCC JK516 (ebook) |
DDC 352.23/50973—dc23
LC record available at https://lccn.loc.gov/2016051758

Typeset by Thompson Type in 10/15 Sabon

To Bea and Dan, who joyfully issue orders they expect others to obey.
                                        —M. B.

To B. J. and Ben, on whom no unilateral order would work.
                                        —B. R.

Contents

CONTENTS

List of Tables

List of Figures

Acknowledgments

THE SUBJECT OF THIS BOOK speaks to an important function of the presidency and a topic of current, heated debate—the use and abuse of unilateral powers. Whether the president is an "emperor" or a "clerk" is the subject of both academic and legal concern. We make the argument that presidents are a bit of both, serving in dual roles as both agenda setters and facilitators of the smooth function of government.

This project originally grew out of seminar discussions at the University of Houston and blossomed into a full-scale research project over the course of several years. Its creation, like all book projects, has been both tedious and rewarding. But after all the laboring in the vineyards, the book is a darn sight better for all the hard work.

But we couldn't have done it alone. Archivists at the National Archives at College Park, Maryland, and the George W. Bush, Carter, and Clinton Presidential Libraries were helpful in tracking internal White House discussion about unilateral orders. Presentations at Texas A&M University, Clemson University, Washington University in St. Louis, and the University of Georgia helped to sharpen and clarify our arguments. Special thanks to colleagues Jeff Cohen, Jim Pfiffner, Will Howell, Andy Rudalevige, Terry Moe, Adam Warber, Jeff Peake, Jeremy Bailey, and Jon Rogowski for constructive criticism and suggestions over the course of the project. Our most gracious thanks, however, are reserved for series editor and friend Shirley Anne Warshaw for her early championing of our project and her tireless efforts to revise and hone the manuscript. If it weren't for her, we would still no doubt be working on the book! Everyone at Stanford University Press has been a real joy to work with, especially editors Geoffrey Burn and Alan Harvey. Any errors are clearly our own. Portions of Chapter Six appeared in an article in Political Research Quarterly, "In Lieu of Legislation: Executive Unilateral Preemption or Support During the Legislative Process" in 2014 (Issue 67).

Michelle Belco would like to thank Gaby Briones and Zachary Brown for their tireless efforts.

Brandon Rottinghaus would also like to acknowledge the financial support of the University of Houston, National Endowment for the Humanities Research Fellowship and the National Science Foundation (SES # 1237627).

THE DUAL EXECUTIVE

CHAPTER ONE

Introduction

The Dual Executive and Unilateral Power

UNILATERAL ACTION IS OFTEN TREATED as an aggressive intrusion into the political system, with presidents issuing unilateral orders at their discretion in pursuit of their own policy goals. The use of unilateral orders as a powerful policy tool is, undeniably, an important aspect of the president's unilateral action. Conceivably, though, a picture of unilateral action does not have a singular nature. Instead, the use of unilateral power must be diverse enough to accommodate all of the president's needs. However, presidents do not always act in the role of commanders directing others to carry out their unilateral orders. Political and institutional circumstance may require them to act more in the role of facilitators, working together with Congress within the political system. In those instances, presidents are more likely to issue unilateral orders to carry out the affairs of government and the intent of the legislature.

The study of unilateral power has not considered fully how these dual roles shape the president's unilateral action. At times the president is *independent*, functioning as a leader in pursuit of his or her agenda, even if it creates an adversarial relationship with Congress. At other times, the president is an *administrator*, or clerk, who acts more as an ally in support of Congress. Richard Neustadt famously argued in *Presidential Power* (1990) that the difference between being a leader or a clerk is sometimes indistinguishable. He notes that "in form, all presidents are leaders nowadays," and "in fact, this guarantees no more than that they will be clerks." Presidents have the capacity to act as leaders, but, with both political and legal checks on the use of power, they may seem to act more as clerks. It is important that, whether acting as *independent* leaders or *administrator* clerks, presidents must be strategic in their decisions to issue unilateral orders.

PRESIDENT OBAMA AND THE DUAL EXECUTIVE

Examples from the Obama administration highlight these approaches. From one perspective, the nature of unilateral power affords presidents many opportunities to independently pursue their policy goals. On October 24, 2011, President Obama avowed that "without a doubt, the most urgent challenge that we face right now is getting our economy to grow faster and to create more jobs. We can't wait for an increasingly dysfunctional Congress to do its job. Where they won't act, I will." Under the banner of "We Can't Wait," the White House trumpeted its ability to act without Congress by issuing unilateral orders on combating domestic violence in the federal workplace, implementing a pilot program for workplace innovation, making it easier to refinance government-sponsored mortgages, making funding for Alzheimer's research more freely available, guaranteeing overtime pay protections for home care workers, and dozens more. The president openly claimed that he was bypassing lawmakers who disagreed with him, noting, "If Congress refused to act, I've said that I'll continue to do everything in my power to act without them." *New York Times* journalist Charlie Savage (2012) argued that this is not simply a short-term governing style but that the president's "increasingly assertive use of executive action could foreshadow pitched battles over the separation of powers in his second term, should he win and Republicans consolidate their power in Congress."[1]

President Obama continued to independently forge ahead, using unilateral power to alter public policy. In his 2014 State of the Union address, President Obama called on Congress to raise the national minimum wage from $7.25 to $10.10 an hour. He told Congress, "I'm eager to work with all of you, but America does not stand still—and neither will I. So wherever and whenever I can take steps without legislation to expand opportunity for more American families, that's what I'm going to do." Soon after his address, he signed Executive Order 13658, raising the minimum wage for new federal service contracts. Criticism focused on the imbalance of the separation of powers.[2] Republican opposition in Congress was quick to assert that this leadership tactic was both unprecedented and dangerous. Speaker of the House John Boehner (R-OH), warned the president that his executive order establishing the minimum wage for federal contractors was not a wise—or necessarily legal—tactic: "This idea that he's just going to go it alone, I have to remind him we do have a constitution. And the Congress writes the laws, and the President's job is to execute the laws faithfully. And if he tries to ignore this he's going to run into a brick wall."[3]

Functioning as an *independent* executive, President Obama was also accused of constitutional overreach and the aggrandizement of presidential power in the area of immigration reform (Shear 2014a). During his State of the Union address, President Obama remarked,

If we are serious about economic growth, it is time to heed the call of business leaders, labor leaders, faith leaders, and law enforcement—and fix our broken immigration system. Republicans and Democrats in the Senate have acted. I know that members of both parties in the House want to do the same . . . So let's get immigration reform done this year.

But legislation in the House was not forthcoming, and President Obama decided to act alone by providing deportation relief to illegal immigrants.[4] In response, Speaker Boehner stated,

The American people want both parties to focus on solving problems together; they don't support unilateral action from a president who is more interested in partisan politics than working with the people's elected representatives. That is not how American democracy works. Not long ago, President Obama said the unilateral action he just announced was "not an option" and claimed he'd already "done everything that I can on my own." He said it would lead to a "surge in more illegal immigration." He said he was "not a king" and "not the emperor" and that he was "bound by the Constitution." He said an action like this would exceed his authority and be "difficult to justify legally." He may have changed his position, but that doesn't change the Constitution.[5]

House Judiciary Committee Chairman Bob Goodlatte (R-VA) added, "The president's decision to recklessly forge ahead with a plan to unilaterally change our immigration laws ignores the will of the American people and flouts the Constitution."[6] Senator Jeff Sessions (R-AL) penned an opinion editorial in *USA Today* claiming that the president's failure to secure legislation to support his unprecedented act would "impose his rejected amnesty through the brute force of executive order," concluding that "apparently, America now has its first emperor."[7]

In another instance, President Obama decided to go it alone by unilaterally creating exceptions and waivers to requirements defined in law. In a speech from the White House, discussing his commitment to create waivers for states from the No Child Left Behind Act, President Obama promised:

Starting today, we'll be giving States more flexibility to meet high standards. Keep in mind, the change we're making is not lowering standards, we're saying we're going to give you more flexibility to meet high standards. We're going to let States, schools, and teachers come up with innovative ways to give our children the skills they need to compete for the jobs of the future. Because what works in Rhode Island may not be the same thing that works in Tennessee, but every student should have the same opportunity to learn and grow, no matter what State they live in[8]

On the same day, Arne Duncan, Secretary of Education, transmitted a letter to state school officers offering them the "opportunity to request flexibility on behalf of your State, your LEAs [Local Education Agency], and your schools, in order to better focus on improving student learning and increasing the quality of instruction."[9]

In contrast to an *independent* executive, unilateral orders can also be issued to support Congress's objectives and the legislative process. In this capacity, presidents function more as *administrators*. For instance, on March 24, 2010, President Obama issued Executive Order 13535, applying long-standing restrictions on the use of federal funds for abortion in the Hyde Amendment to the Patient Protection and Affordable Care Act of 2010 (PPACA).[10] Although issued from the White House, this was not unilateral policy making by the stroke of a pen; rather, following the legislative debate on health care in the House, this order implemented a deal led by Representative Bart Stupak (D-MI). Pro-life Democrats were concerned over the potential of federal funding for abortion because the bill placed "individual premium payments for the government-run public insurance plan into a Federal treasury account that may be used to pay for abortions."[11] The Stupak-Pitts amendment guaranteed that federal funds could not be used for abortion, and, although it had passed the House, it was not included in the Senate version of the bill.[12] To gain the commitment of Rep. Stupak and the bloc of pro-life Democrats, the president agreed to issue an executive order barring federal funding of abortion as a substitute for the language in the bill.[13] In his remarks on signing the PPACA into law, President Obama acknowledged the work of "leaders in each chamber who not only do their jobs very well but who never lost sight of that larger mission," noting, "They [chamber leaders] didn't play for the short term; they didn't play to the polls or to politics."[14] The next day, citing the PPACA as a justification for action, he issued the executive order enforcing restrictions against the use of federal funds for abortion by applying the Hyde Amendment and, consistent with the newly enacted law, ordering the lead agencies to create a model set of funding segregation guidelines for state health insurance commissioners.[15]

Consistent with his role as administrator, President Obama acted in accord with congressional goals even when the execution of law did not signify a win for the administration. In 2012, President Obama issued Executive Order 13626, implementing the Resources and Ecosystems Sustainability, Tourist Opportunities, and Revived Economies of the Gulf Coast States (RESTORE) Act, despite his objections.[16] Congress created the RESTORE Act in response to the Deepwater Horizon explosion to aid in the recovery along the Gulf Coast, but President Obama was not in complete agreement with the provisions of the bill. In a Statement of Administration Policy (SAP), Obama expressed his objections to the proposed mechanism for funding the recovery and conveyed his support for preserving the dedication of civil penalties from the Clean Water Act as a funding tool.[17] He also objected to the shift in policy control from the Gulf Coast Ecosystem Restoration Task Force, a joint state–federal council created under a prior executive order, to an independent Gulf Coast Restoration Council. However, consistent with his constitutional duty to execute the law, President Obama issued an executive order revoking his prior one and establishing, in its place, the Gulf Coast Restoration Trust Fund and the Gulf Coast Ecosystem Restoration Council.[18]

THE DIVERSITY OF EXECUTIVE POWER

President Obama's unilateral actions show how unilateral power, like executive power, is diverse (Black, Madonna, Owens, and Lynch 2007). As Mansfield (1989) argued, the word *executive* has two meanings. The executive serves both to carry out the will of the legislature and to enforce that will; therefore presidents must be able to exercise their own discretion. Scigliano (1989) notes that scholars have "embraced two conceptions of executive power: one makes the president subordinate to Congress, whereas the other allows him to be autonomous and self-directing within broad limits." Justice Marshall, in *Marbury v. Madison* (1803), wrote, "By the Constitution of the United States, the President is invested with certain important political powers, in the exercise of which he is to use his own discretion," but, as Marshall and later courts have recognized, "a ministerial act which the law enjoins" must also be carried out by the president.[19]

The diversity of executive power places theories of presidential action and tactics at odds with each other. Conceptually, presidents are boldly willing to act without Congress, and yet they also embrace their role within a shared system of power. The use of unilateral orders characterizes the dual nature of the executive. As President Obama's orders illustrate, unilateral action can be used to accomplish both a "go it alone approach" and one consistent with carrying out Congress's legislative goals to administer the responsibilities of the executive (Huetteman 2014). President Obama's executive order establishing a minimum wage for federal contractors shows how unilateral action can be used to pursue his administration's policy interests without congressional support. His executive orders implementing the PPACA and RESTORE demonstrate his commitment to administer laws passed by Congress. In this way, unilateral power is comprised of two parts, one that allows for expansive power and one that constrains power.

PRESIDENTIAL POWER IN THE
UNILATERAL CONTEXT

Befitting a system that requires both separate and shared powers, the scope of presidential unilateral action spans both cooperative and combative politics. Most studies of presidential power rightfully genuflect on the role Neustadt played in reshaping the discipline's views of how presidents exercise power. Neustadt's (1990) clerk-president has limited power and is "dependent on consent from other sharers" in government. Neustadt continued, because

. . . he [the president] needs them he must bargain with them [Congress], buttressing his share with his resources in their eyes of personal reputation and of public standing. The hallmark of presidential success is bargaining, not command, since the president's power may be inconclusive during moment of command but are always central when he attempts to persuade. Together with his powers, reputation and prestige become the sources of his power . . .

rather than some formal basis. Because presidential power is the power to persuade, presidents do not "obtain results by giving orders" because having formal power is no guarantee of success. Strictly unilateral uses of power are described by Neustadt as a "painful last resort" to be used expediently only after bargaining has failed.

Other scholars confront Neustadt's view of the president's dependence on Congress as being at odds with the formal powers presidents exercise when engaging in unilateral action (Howell 2003; Mayer 2009; Waterman 2009). Unilateral orders are powerful and often dramatic examples of the president's ability to command (Cooper 1986, 1997, 2002; Mayer 2001; Shull 1997; Dodds 2013). Cooper (2002) argues, "There is virtually no significant policy area in which presidents operate that has not been shaped to one degree or another by the use or abuse of these tools." Unilateral orders allow the president to "do what Congress could not or would not do" (Neighbors 1964). In the exercise of executive power, regulatory authority, budget authority, and civil rights, "the president's ability to move first, combined with Congress's relative inability to respond effectively, tilted competition in favor of the executive" (Mayer 2001).

According to Fleishman and Aufses (1976), executive lawmaking by unilateral order is powerful enough to undermine "democratic decision procedures, and threatens the rule of law" (Hebe 1972). The importance of unilateral action in the development of regulatory policy cannot be overstated. Presidents have the capacity to establish rules, norms, and policy consistent with their own preferences and without input from Congress. Presidents have carved a role for themselves in creating, reviewing, and implementing regulatory policy. Since President Nixon, there has been a process in place within the Office of Management and Budget (OMB) for presidential oversight of regulation.[20] President Carter issued Executive Order 12044, "Improving Government Regulations," as part of his goal to reform the administrative regulatory process. Carter's reforms included the introduction of cost–benefit analyses for all major regulations and established, within the White House, the Regulatory Analysis Review Group and the Regulatory Council (Mayer 2001).[21] In Executive Order 12866, President Reagan gave the Office of Information and Regulatory Affairs (OIRA), a Federal office within OMB, the authority to conduct regulatory impact analysis ensuring presidential control over all major rules.[22] When President Reagan issued Executive Order 12291, he centralized the authority for reviewing regulatory impact, implemented cost–benefit analysis, and established the requirement that a regulatory agenda be published annually.[23] According to Phillip Shabecoff, writing for the *New York Times*, "He transformed with a stroke of his pen what had been a useful economic tool into an imperative of Federal decision making."[24] The impact of Reagan's order was limited to major rules, an action that President Clinton reinforced in a subsequent executive order.[25]

SHORT-CIRCUIT OF THE SEPARATION OF POWERS?

The suggestion that unilateral orders are powerful policy tools that can be used at the president's discretion gave rise to the idea that they are used to short-circuit the separation of powers. By formal arrangement, the growth of institutional power, and the ambiguity of the Constitution, "Presidents can and do make new law—and thus shift the existing status quo—without the explicit consent of Congress" (Moe and Howell 1999). Unilateral orders allow presidents to act alone in an "efficient and alternative manner" compared to the legislative process (Krause and Cohen 1997; Deering and Maltzman 1999). The growth of unilateral action, chiefly during national emergencies, wars, or economic crises, is a direct consequence of the deference granted to presidents during these times by Congress (Cooper 1986; Howell 2005) and the opportunities they present for presidents to act alone (Howell and Pevehouse 2005). A muscular use of unilateral action in moments where the president perceives a political advantage in acting on his or her own begets further, smaller, seemingly innocuous expansions into a wide range of policy making, in both foreign and domestic policy (Moe and Howell 1999).

Based on the strategic model, presidents issue unilateral orders to bypass or evade Congress (Morgan 1970; Nathan 1983; Peterson 1990; Martin 1999; Fine and Warber 2012). Scholars have found support for the idea that the strategic use of unilateral action promotes the aggrandizement of executive power in the political system. In one of the first works that extensively articulated and tested this argument, Kenneth Mayer's *With the Stroke of a Pen* (2001) found that "the president—despite the checks and balances of the separation of powers—retains important advantages in struggles over institutional structure and process." According to Mayer (2001), presidents have these advantages because they can move first, with complete information, and leave "it up to the other branches to undo what has been done." His analysis of these orders over the last half of the twentieth century reveals that presidents use them when they are more likely to have trouble legislating or are politically weaker. His prediction is that "over time, presidents will use unilateral action to expand the reach of presidential authority and centralize power within the White House" (Mayer 2009). Building on this argument, William Howell in *Power without Persuasion* (2003) contends, "Modern presidents often exert power by setting public policy on their own and preventing Congress and the courts—and anyone else for that matter—from doing much about it." Presidents can act "first and alone"; therefore unilateral powers emerge from "specific institutional advantages within the office of the presidency itself: its structure, resources and location in a system of separated powers" (Howell 2003). He finds that presidents issue more orders when Congress is weaker but are less likely to issue significant orders when government is divided. Both of these findings suggest that the president acts strategically by taking advantage of congressional weakness while remaining cognizant of the political limitations on unilateral power. Put another way, "Presidents do as much as they think they can get away with" (Howell 2005).

SHARED POWERS IN THE UNILATERAL CONTEXT

A shared power arrangement is not anathema to the execution of presidential unilateral powers. Clearly, the president is not acting alone in all executive unilateral actions. The Constitution itself was designed to prevent placing too much power in one branch of government. In *Federalist 47*, Madison noted that "the accumulation of all powers, legislative, executive, and judiciary, in the same hands, whether of one, a few, or many, and whether hereditary, self-appointed, or elective, may justly be pronounced the very definition of tyranny." True as this may be, Madison acknowledged "the impossibility and inexpediency of avoiding any mixture whatever of these departments." The result was "instead of separated powers—shared powers" (Fleishman and Aufses 1976). The executive and legislative branches share power on a staggering range of items, including creating legislation, making bureaucratic and judicial appointments, establishing treaties, and responding to military hostilities and national emergencies.

This notion of shared powers as part of a linked interinstitutional arrangement applies even in the unilateral power context. The issuance of a unilateral order itself does not mean that the president is necessarily fulfilling his or her own agenda. In reality, the president may be executing the goals of Congress through prearranged policy or acting administratively to continue government functions with the tacit consent of Congress or in the context of congressional disinterest. Shull (1997) suggests that the issuance of unilateral orders is "influenced by interactions with Congress" and presidents "seldom act without input and constraint from others." He contends that because presidents often issue executive orders that are "highly supported by Congress, they [presidents] appear to be using them as a way of implementing legislation with which they agree or for routine matters rather than seeking alternative policy adoption." The influence on one type of action may alter the other (Cohen 2012). According to Dickinson (2008), the phrase *unilateral action* implies that presidents work alone, but this belies the fact that they must bargain with policy stakeholders inside and outside of the executive branch. President Obama's executive orders implementing the PPACA and RESTORE show an extended working relationship with Congress behind the facade of unilateral action.

Another way in which unilateral orders are integrated between the branches involves the source of authority on which presidents rely. Mayer (2009) writes, "Constitutional and statutory vestments turn out to matter a great deal, and give the president some decisive advantages in disputes over policy or control." He argues, "We might make more progress by looking at what happens before a president takes unilateral action, rather than after" (2009). The Constitution grants the president unilateral authority for executing law, the role of commander in chief, granting pardons, and the veto. With the exception of the pardon power, the president relies on authority from Congress if policy goals are to be achieved. The need for underlying authority from Congress suggests a form of congressional control (Moe 1998). In Howell's (2005) view, presidents justify their actions "on some blend of statutory, treaty or constitutional powers." Mayer (1999) argues that certain orders are "hybrid" because they "constitute a potential reservoir of independent authority, but one that presidents do not use without regard to circumstance or consequence." Warber (2006) finds that presidents are strategic about the source of authority they specify to lessen the likelihood of Congress to overturn their executive order. It is important that Congress's willingness to allow the president to act by delegating authority to him or her is directly related to the president's capacity to issue such orders.

A system of shared powers is critical to the president's decision to take unilateral action. The freedom the president has, at any moment, to unilaterally set public policy depends critically on how the other branches of government will respond. Moe and Howell (1999) argue that presidents are political animals and are keenly aware that extreme action taken in one policy domain may jeopardize their effectiveness in another. As a result, presidents may self-check, moderate their actions, and "take much smaller steps than their de facto powers would allow." Warber (2006) explores this possibility using a framework that evaluates the political cost to the president of acting unilaterally. He outlines the premise that executive orders are used by presidents to meet the demands placed on them by an uncertain political environment. Krutz and Peake (2009) suggest that the president and Congress are "interdependent parts of an adaptive system" that efficiently uses the shared power arrangement to enact policies on international trade. They reject the notion that presidents use executive agreements as a way to strategically evade the Senate's formal role in making international treaties. Instead, they argue the evasion hypothesis that has dominated the landscape of the literature on presidential unilateral action overlooks the "significant proportion of executive agreements that flow directly from statute or previously ratified treaties or require Congressional action in order to take legal effect." According to Krutz and Peake (2009), the executive and legislative branches reach a point of mutual accommodation and satisfaction by delegating and employing powers to accomplish their diplomatic and policy goals.

A NEW APPROACH TO UNILATERAL ACTION

The influence of a shared system of power needs to be incorporated into the study of presidential unilateral action. The study of the exercise of unilateral power is incomplete without an understanding of how and when unilateral orders are shared and integrated with Congress. The freedom the president has, at any moment, to unilaterally set public policy depends critically on how the other branches of government will respond. Howell (2003) argues that "institutional constraints lie at the heart of a theory of direct presidential action for they determine what presidents can actually accomplish." Mayer (2001) notes that "the dynamic between the presidency and Congress is too complex to be fully accounted for by a simple relationship between party differences and institutional collisions." In a later work, Mayer (2009) remarks that "the disparate and conflicting results [in prior studies] strongly suggest that we do not have a complete understanding of the interbranch dynamics of unilateral actions." Although Mayer did not necessarily have in mind that these powers were shared, an implication of his criticism is that the relationship between the issuance of unilateral orders and the president's shared and separated powers with Congress may be more interconnected than articulated to date.

The dual nature of the president needs to be considered in the context of unilateral power. It is important that this duality plays a larger role within the institutional dynamic between the two branches of government (see Marshall 2011). Presidents who exercise their unilateral power do so within a constitutional design of a separate and shared system of power. This approach changes the conception of the notion of presidential power in unilateral actions to show that *presidents exercise their dual executive functions in ways that allow them to dictate policy or share power.* As an *administrator,* a president issues unilateral orders working together with Congress, whereas as an *independent,* a president uses unilateral orders to aggressively pursue his or her own agenda. Presidents choose one of the dual executive roles—*independent* or *administrator*—at each stage within the context of legislative policy making. Presidents are eager to pursue their agenda and to act before legislation has been introduced. Once bills have reached Congress's agenda, the two branches bargain over the content and progress of legislation. After laws have been passed by Congress, presidents have the duty and authority to execute them. Changes in institutional arrangements and political conditions are also factors that need to be considered. The president's decision to take unilateral action is influenced by the source of authority, the extent of discretion delegated by Congress, the institutional strength of each of the branches, and the political conditions in Congress and between the branches. Identifying how these factors influence the president's decision at each of the three stages helps to better understand the dual executive at work in a system of separate and shared power.

As an *administrator,* a president acts together with Congress keeping the wheels of government oiled as a means to carry out executive functions. Presidents are more demure about using their executive authority when Congress has a stronger hand politically. They are especially mindful when Congress has expressed a preference on an issue through hearings and the introduction of legislation, especially bipartisan legislation, and in the use of congressional oversight when executing law. The modest use of unilateral powers in some contexts, though, *does not* preclude more muscular uses in others. As an *independent,* a president fulfills the expectation to advance his or her own policy objectives even if it is *against* Congress. Presidents are more likely to forge ahead with greater independence when the issue is on their agenda and they are less able to bargain with Congress. When the two branches are at political odds and

Congress is divided internally, presidents are more likely to pursue unilateral action consistent with their policy preferences. Relying on constitutional or delegated authority, unilateral action affords the president an opportunity to act first and alone, before and after legislation has been introduced, and laws have been passed.

Presidents can, and often do, act unilaterally with respect to their political position. They are able to act with dispatch, as the framers intended, and to work with Congress as a means to navigate and implement public policy. The presumption is that unilateral power allows them to act without restraint and when the need suits, despite scholarship showing that presidents act with anticipation of congressional or judicial response. Fears of an aggressive White House marauding over the constitutionally assigned window of responsibility delegated to the other two branches remain constant. Although motivation and opportunity may occasionally result in overreach, the unilateral actions of an assertive *independent* president are ultimately tempered by the shared nature of constitutional authority. A close look at the substance, tone, and timing of each order clarifies the use (and abuse) of executive power and helps to put some of these fears to rest.

PLAN OF THE BOOK

This book takes the next step in the study of unilateral power by quantitatively and qualitatively analyzing how the president's unilateral orders are part of a separate and shared power system. The chapters that follow explore both the prerogatives presidents undertake and obligations they fulfill with respect to their *independent* and *administrator* executive functions. It builds on several generations of scholarship on the presidency and draws from both public law and behavioral approaches (see Pious 2006). Debate over the use of unilateral orders suggests that a president's ability to act without the consent of Congress is largely unchecked by traditional institutional arrangements whereas others suggest that presidents are more likely to be restrained by Congress because many unilateral powers are justified with interbranch authority.

Chapter Two presents an organizational model to chart the process of when in the policy process a unilateral order is issued. This model conceptualizes the use of unilateral orders based on the dual roles of the executive at one of three stages in the policy-making process: at the agenda-setting stage before bills have been introduced into the legislative process, the president's bargaining with Congress after bills have reached the agenda, and implementing laws passed by Congress. This provides a basis for exploring the theoretical expectations derived from the institutional and power-sharing arrangements. Chapter Three describes the data collected and evaluates the trends over time. The data include executive orders and proclamations, the two most prominent types of unilateral orders. The data set includes a total of more than 2,400 unilateral orders issued from President Gerald Ford to President George W. Bush from 1974 to 2009. Chapter Four explores the president's sources of authority and how they are used. Presidents can rely on their constitutional powers or authority delegated by Congress. They may invoke statute-based and constitution-based sources of authority when issuing unilateral orders, although the variation is influenced by the different separate and shared power arrangements. The chapter examines the variation in the sources of authority the president cites, as well as when he or she invokes statute-based or constitution-based sources of authority and the influence of the extent of authority and discretion delegated by Congress.

Chapters Five, Six, and Seven analyze the president as *independent* and *administrator* at each of the three stages of the policy-making process. Chapter Five considers the unilateral actions of the dual roles of the president at the agenda-setting stage, before legislation has been introduced. At this stage, presidents have the incentive and ability to act as *administrators* by issuing routine orders or as *independent* presidents by issuing commands. This is the most familiar and potentially dangerous type of president—one who uses unilateral powers to manage the political system in a way that corresponds to his or her preferences and agenda. Because members of Congress are focused on deciding in committee the topics and direction legislation should take before adding it to the congressional agenda, presidents do not necessarily need to work with Congress; instead, they can act independently creating edicts, which they expect others to follow.

Chapter Six explores the unilateral actions of the president's dual roles after legislation is on Congress's agenda. At this stage, presidents decide whether to bargain with Congress over the formulation of legislation. Presidents are clearly interested in issuing unilateral orders that work to their advantage whether it is to prevent legislation from progressing or to facilitate legislative progress when it is otherwise slowed by collective action problems in Congress. *Independent* presidents use unilateral orders to preempt the lengthy legislative process, and *administrators* issue unilateral orders to support legislation. Presidents are more likely to use unilateral orders to preempt legislation when the issue is on their agenda, there is greater friction between the branches, Congress is internally divided, and presidents have greater discretion to act.

Chapter Seven investigates the dual roles of the executive after laws have been passed by Congress. At this stage, *independent* presidents issue unilateral orders to adapt legislation to suit their needs, and *administrators* to faithfully implement law. This is the final stage in the policy-making process where presidents have the duty to execute law; yet this is also their last opportunity to influence legislation. Presidents at the height of their powers take full advantage of this privileged place by shaping the outcome of legislation in their favor.

Chapter Eight concludes with the argument that, with respect to unilateral orders, presidents often have the authority to be independent but do not always act that way. *Independent* presidents engage their executive authority, and discretion, to act alone, whereas *administrators* exercise delegated authority and political will to work with Congress. The knowledge of how presidents use unilateral orders may help to dampen the fear that presidents are able to use their unilateral powers unchecked because of a congressional retreat. The circumstances where presidents act against Congress are selective. What remains is an understanding and awareness that the majority of unilateral orders are used to facilitate the needs of government. Concerns over an aggressive or overbearing president who pushes around an unsuspecting Congress may be overblown as presidents balance their political goals with their institutional responsibilities and duty to act.

CHAPTER TWO

A New Theory and Approach to
Studying Unilateral Orders

RECENT SCHOLARSHIP HAS PROVIDED IMPORTANT theoretical advances and empirical conclusions concerning how and when presidents issue unilateral orders. Cooper (2002) states some of the key ways presidents use the wide array of unilateral policy tools: to create significant policy initiatives, respond to emergencies, issue a statement that triggers a condition established by law, address routine administrative matters, direct agency action, enact or amend agency regulations, and establish or alter commissions for the purpose of studying and investigating policy objectives. When scholars study the genesis of a unilateral order, it is most often characterized as the president's direct action. What is sometimes less apparent is evidence of the linked executive–legislative relationship that shaped it. Unilateral orders are a unique blend of both executive policy making and shared power. Presidents issue unilateral orders as a policy-making tool reflective of their ideological preferences and based on their constitutional authority. They are presumed to have the power to act with dispatch, especially in emergencies, authority the framers of the Constitution recognized (see *Federalist* 69). Presidents also issue unilateral orders as part of a shared power system with express authority from Congress and in support of legislative goals. They act in concert with the design of the Constitution, which provides for carefully arranged power blocks and "connected and blended" distribution of powers (see *Federalist Papers* 37, 47 and 48; Fisher 1978).

Research has shown how the political environment shapes both the president's ability to use these orders effectively and the strategic considerations in issuing them. This is not surprising because both branches of government are concerned with solving national problems with each working to control policy creation and implementation. A closer look at the institutional dynamics between the two branches reveals opportunities for interaction with the potential to produce conflict and cooperation.

Each stage in the policy-making process provides an opportunity for consultation between the branches in the development of public policy. The president and Congress deliberate and negotiate while setting the agenda and during the legislative process, after bills are introduced. Once bills become law, both the president and Congress are involved in their implementation. This policy-making process creates a framework for explaining how presidents act strategically within a system of separate and shared powers.

THE EXECUTIVE'S DUAL ROLES

No one would suggest that presidents are only either clerks or leaders (in Neustadtian typology)—rather they evoke both interpretations of their power. Presidential action can, however, be categorized into two types: a clerk who acts in the role of an *administrator* and a leader who acts more *independently*. As an *administrator*, the president uses orders as a means to manage the affairs of government, about which he or she is either agnostic with respect to the issue or shares the views of Congress. In this capacity, the president fulfills a central, but largely benign, executive function of administering governmental maintenance by carrying out laws that have been passed or initiating the policy implementation process. With an *independent* president, unilateral orders are used to put his or her own issues on the agenda and to initiate policy goals consistent with an energetic executive (Rossiter 1956). This is the expectation of scholars who suggest that presidents use executive orders to set a policy agenda, act when Congress will not, and preempt an action Congress is considering of which the White House disapproves (Neighbors 1964). The scope of a president's unilateral action can be placed on a hypothetical scale ranging from *administrator* to *independent*, as illustrated in Figure 2.1. These two categories mirror the roles that presidents play in the exercise of power.

During the same week in February 2014, President Obama issued two executive orders of very different ilk. In his actions as an *administrator*, the president issued Executive Order 13657 changing the name of the "National Security Staff" to the "National Security Council Staff."[1] The order specifically states that it "shall not be construed to impair or oth-

FIGURE 2.1. Scale of presidential unilateral action.

erwise affect (i) the authority granted by law to an executive department, agency, or the head thereof; or (ii) the functions of the Director of the Office of Management and Budget relating to budgetary, administrative, or legislative proposals." Although created by the stroke of a pen, the order was issued to manage the affairs of government and attracted no attention from members of Congress. In his *independent* role, the president issued Executive Order 13658 ordering the Labor Department to establish the minimum wage for federal contractors and to revise overtime pay rules to "make millions more workers eligible for extra pay when they work more than 40 hours a week" (Joachim 2014).[2] After getting little traction on legislation, the president acted independently creating the order again by the stroke of the pen, but this time the order raised the attention and ire of both members of Congress and the business community.

SPECIFYING CONDITIONS ON INDEPENDENT AND ADMINISTRATOR ACTIONS

Because the two branches fortuitously share power in policy development, presidents have incentives to use both types of unilateral actions in different circumstances. The president is more likely to act as an *administrator* when the two branches have mutually agreeable objectives, when there is more support in Congress for the action the president is likely to take, and when Congress is disinterested in the outcome and relies on the expertise of the executive to act. If Congress and the president are more closely aligned either in terms of party or ideology (or both), it stands to reason that unilateral orders would be to their mutual benefit. As support, Mayer (1999) and Howell (2003) found that presidents issue more orders when government is unified. One reason may be because they generally have greater party support under a unified government (Gomez and Shull

1995; Shull 1997). Presidents may also have more flexibility from prior congressionally delegated authority to act (Shugart and Carey 1992; Sala 1998). However, when issuing routine orders to keep government running, the president's institutional responsibility should transcend partisan or ideological differences between the branches because Congress is more likely to be agnostic about the outcome.

When unilateral orders are a way to make policy, a president should use them more as an *independent* when it is less likely he or she will gain approval from Congress on a policy direction. Presidents are more likely to pursue their policy objectives with unilateral action when there is greater policy disagreement between the branches or within Congress, especially if the president is politically weaker (Krause and Cohen 1997; Deering and Maltzman 1999; Marshall and Pacelle 2005). When government is divided, presidents are less able to bargain and legislate. The opposition in Congress is less likely to support the president's initiatives and he or she may have greater incentive to pursue an independent and unilateral policy (Deering and Maltzman 1999). Presidents running for reelection, in the second half of their term, or during their second term are often busily trying to convince the legislative branch to work with them despite the fact that Congress is often unwilling to do so (Shafie 2013). Despite an anticipatory response, presidents are nonetheless willing to maximize power and act against a recalcitrant Congress to achieve their policy objectives (Moe 1994).

THE STAGES OF PRESIDENTIAL ACTION

Unilateral orders are often treated as monolithic, but they are used for different purposes at distinct moments in the policy process. Based on the nature and timing in the temporal, policy-making environment, unilateral orders can be classified into one of three distinct legislative cut points: direct action, legislative process, and executing law. Distinguishing the timing and type of unilateral order helps to reveal the conditions in which the president acts. In direct action, unilateral orders are the output of the presidential agenda. Presidents have an opportunity to act first on information obtained by the executive branch while Congress is still identifying and developing topics for legislation. During the legislative process,

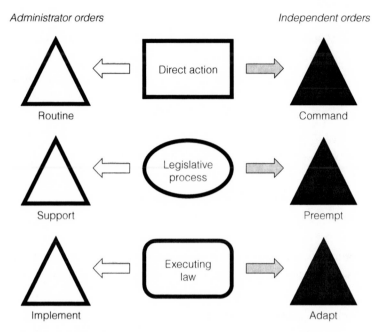

Administrator orders   Independent orders

Direct action

Routine   Command

Legislative process

Support   Preempt

Executing law

Implement   Adapt

FIGURE 2.2. Model of unilateral orders and three stages of the policy process. This figure illustrates when a presidents acts as an *administrator* or an *independent* within the three stages of the policy process: *direct action, legislative process*, and *executing law*.

presidents issue unilateral orders to influence bills on Congress's agenda. After laws have been passed, presidents issue unilateral orders to execute law. Presidents issue unilateral roles within each of these stages acting in one of their dual roles as *administrators* and *independents*.

Figure 2.2 illustrates when presidents act as *administrator* or *independent* within the three stages of the policy process: *direct action, legislative process*, and *executing law*.

Direct Action

A president who issues a unilateral order using direct action is exercising power when Congress is generally at the policy incubation stage (Rudalevige 2011). At this stage, the president can issue either a *routine* or a *command* order. Routine orders are primarily administrative or managerial in origin. The Obama administration's order changing the name of the National Security Council Staff is a clear example of this. This is the administrative presidency working to maintain the basic function of government and "keep the trains running." The topics of routine orders are not on the president's agenda. Instead, they are used to make internal organizational changes within the executive branch, such as altering a pay scale or job description. Routine orders are used to make necessary changes within the executive branch to comply with a judicial opinion, delegating authority to comply with recently enacted laws, or to reorganize agency responsibilities or reporting mechanisms to implement legislation. These are not orders that typically raise the ire of political opponents or constitutional purists.

The purpose of routine orders is generally, as Warber (2006) describes, "to accomplish a simple, noncontroversial, administrative task in the executive branch." Presidents use executive orders to create an investigatory board to solve labor disputes between union-represented employees and their employers pursuant to the Railway Labor Act (see Mayer 2001).[3] Similarly, presidents issue routine executive orders to establish succession for continuity of the operations of government in the event of a change in leadership. After the terrorist attacks of September 11, 2001, President Bush issued several executive orders providing for an order of succession within each executive department in response to this national emergency.[4] Although the response to the terrorist attacks was foremost on President Bush's agenda, the changes in succession were not specifically discussed as part of his public agenda.

Unilateral orders that command are distinguishable from those that administer routine functions because they stem *directly from the president's public agenda* and are used to fashion his or her own policy.[5] Command orders signal to Congress, or the public, the president's commitment to a larger initiative and, in some instances, set the agenda for the legislative branch to follow. President Carter acted quickly issuing a command to pardon Vietnam War draft evaders one day after taking the oath of office. Relying on constitutional authority and his role as commander in chief, Carter issued Proclamation 4483 pardoning the offenders and Executive Order 11967 directing the attorney general to take the necessary action to implement the pardon. He managed to fulfill both a campaign promise and an important topic on his agenda before members of Congress, who had been working on the issue during the prior session, could adopt legislation.

Presidents often use command orders to centralize policy in the executive branch by establishing a committee, task force, or commission giving the White House greater control over the policy development process. On his last day in office, President Carter had the gratification of issuing Executive Order 12285, which created the President's Commission on Hostage Compensation that would finally help resolve an issue that had dominated his heart and mind during his final year in office (Carter 1982). Sometimes a presidential commission is of particular importance, and presidents may use command orders to amend, extend, and shape the composition of committees and to continue them from one administration to the next, as President Reagan did when he expanded the authority and duration of the President's Commission on Hostage Compensation, under subsequent executive orders.[6]

The Legislative Process

When the president issues unilateral order to influence legislation, bills have already received a committee hearing and are on Congress's agenda. The president is attempting to influence floor action on the bill because of consensus or conflict between the branches over the content of policy or the use of legislation. At this stage the president can issue a unilateral order to either preempt or support legislation. The president can evade Congress through preemptive politics where Congress is poised to act but the president acts first (Mayer 2001; Howell 2003). Under this scenario, presidents are seen to act alone in an "efficient and alternative manner" compared to the legislative process (Krause and Cohen 1997; Deering and Maltzman 1999). The capacity to move first enables the president to preempt legislation or undercut Congress when an issue is within the legislative arena (Mayer 2001).

Presidents may preempt a policy because of a preference for administrative control over the issue or to shift policy closer when the bill is ideologically farther away from their ideal point (Howell 2003). When presidents preempt Congress, they may veto legislation before substituting their own policy. In 1989, both Congress and the president were concerned about the reaction of the People's Republic of China to the Tiananmen Square protests. Congress pursued its efforts in the legislative arena, culminating in the Emergency Chinese Immigration Relief Act of 1989. President George H. W. Bush vetoed the bill, determined instead to extend and broaden the same protective measures included in the bill but through executive rather than legislative action.[7] In 1990, President Bush and Congress were again at odds, but this time over the serious concerns posed by chemical and biological weapons. Congress presented the Omnibus Export Amendments Act of 1990 to the president for signature, but the content was not to his satisfaction. President Bush vetoed the bill because Congress had placed restrictions on the president's ability to cooperate multilaterally through the mandatory imposition of unilateral sanctions.[8] As his alternative to the bill, President Bush issued an executive order declaring the proliferation of chemical and biological weapons to be a national emergency and specifying the direction the administration would take without awaiting further legislative action.[9]

The president may take preemptive action to spur action in an internally gridlocked Congress. When this occurs, an order may be an end run around Congress with the president establishing policy that he or she could not otherwise compel Congress to pass or that Congress could not enact because of internal dispute (Howell 2003; Cooper 2002; Fleishman and Aufses 1976). President Carter was confronted with an impending statutory deadline to address the preservation of lands in Alaska, but because of internal gridlock Congress was unable to pass any legislation on the issue.[10] He was hopeful after the House finally passed the Alaska National Interest Lands Conservation Act, but no legislation appeared on the immediate horizon in the Senate (Carter 2010, 253).[11] Hampered by the gridlock in Congress, President Carter decided to take unilateral action by issuing presidential proclamations that preserved 56 million acres of land in Alaska and created fifteen new national monuments.[12]

Presidents may also invoke an order to support legislation. When Congress is considering major policy changes, rather than acting preemptively, the president's unilateral action may support the proposed policy. Presidents may establish a commission or task force to centralize policy development in the executive branch in order to maintain policy momentum while Congress is working on legislation (Warber 2006). President Bill Clinton used this strategy in an effort to jump-start his competitiveness plan, designed to establish a partnership between government and the high-technology industry. The Senate Commerce, Science and Transportation Committee approved the National Competitiveness Act of 1993 and reported to the full Senate soon after. The House meanwhile passed the National Competitiveness Act of 1994 and the National Information Infrastructure Act of 1993. The difficulty Clinton faced was that each chamber had its own priorities. Consequently, the bills were difficult to reconcile, and members were not eager to compromise.[13] In an effort to support legislative action in Congress and ensure that some progress would take place, President Clinton issued three executive orders, all of which reinforced his commitment to information infrastructure and national competitiveness and, for the interim, centralized policy making in the executive branch.[14]

Executing Law

Although Congress has the power to make all laws, the president has the constitutional authority to execute and enforce them. A president can choose to issue a unilateral order to faithfully implement the law, acting in concert with Congress by following the directions specified in the statute. Alternatively, the president can adapt the law by acting on his or her own. Signing statements can be a good indication of whether presidents are more likely to faithfully implement or adapt the law. When presidents faithfully implement law, they assume the role of Neustadt's (1990) clerkship because "no one else's services suffice." The type and extent of authority and discretion delegated in the law enable the president to faithfully execute Congress's intent. Presidents cite the specific statutory authority and attribute their unilateral action to the law in the statement or remarks accompanying the signing of unilateral order. Presidents may be faithfully implementing law even when it involves changing or enacting agency regulations, triggering a particular statutory action and responding to emergencies (Gleiber and Shull 1992; Shull 1997, 2006; Cooper 2002; Kerwin 2003). Sometimes presidents may use executive action to evoke multiple conditions as President Carter did when he issued an executive order in response to a natural gas emergency pursuant to the authority he triggered under the Emergency Natural Gas Act of 1977. Remarkably, he signed the law and issued the executive order on the same day.[15]

Presidents are generally expected to faithfully implement legislation using unilateral orders as complementary to the legislative process (see Gleiber and Shull 1992; Krause and Cohen 1997). Unilateral orders are a means by which presidents delegate the statutory authority granted by Congress to a division or agency within the executive branch or to the presidents themselves.[16] Congress may direct the president to designate a specific individual to carry out the duties under the law, as it did by specifying the secretary of defense as the presidential designee under the Uniformed and Overseas Citizens Absentee Voting Act.[17] Otherwise, the president generally decides to whom to delegate his or her authority as President Carter did in Executive Order 12101, when he designated and empowered "the Secretary of State to perform, without the approval, ratification, or other action of the President" his or her obligations under the Diplomatic Relations Act.[18]

Presidents do not always fully and faithfully implement law and, instead, issue unilateral orders that adapt law. Presidents may *interpret* laws differently than Congress or implement the general intent of legislation but not implicitly follow the direction of the law, or they may use different statutes or even their constitutional authority to adapt policy to meet their objectives. This undertaking is part of how presidents use their discretion (Rudalevidge 2014; Lowande 2014). President Reagan signed the Ethics in Government Act Amendments of 1985, which expressed the sense of the Congress that the government should "more aggressively use suspension or debarment of contractors convicted of crimes" but did not specify actions the government should take.[19] President Reagan's Executive Order 12549 followed the sense of Congress by addressing suspension and debarment but adapted law to achieve his policy objectives. Rather than acting pursuant to the statute as passed by Congress, he instead cited constitutional authority and the laws of the United States generally.[20] In his executive order, President Reagan created a government-wide system for debarment and suspension and established an Interagency Committee on Debarment and Suspension to oversee the implementation. These actions reflect both his policy goals and those prescribed by Congress but certainly tilt the balance of powers in the president's favor.

EXPECTATIONS FOR THE DUAL EXECUTIVE

This framework provides a structure for studying the dual roles of the executive within a system of separate and shared powers. At each stage, presidents still need to decide whether to act *independently* by exercising their separate formal powers, or as *administrators*, by working within a shared power system. Presidents are more likely to act as administrators because the structure of government demands it. They must bargain with Congress, the executive branch, and the public, if they want to achieve their goals. When bargaining is less likely because Congress is unwilling or unable to act, they are more likely to act as *independent* presidents. Because the decision to take unilateral action is not made in a vacuum, institutional and political conditions need to be considered. These include the scope of the president's authority, political and ideological differences within Congress and between the branches, and the two institutional agendas. These political and institutional arrangements will influence the type of order the president issues at each stage of the policy-making process.

Source of Authority

The source of authority presidents cite in each order reveals something important about their perception of power and their relationship to the political environment. The variation in citation provides insight into the executives' view of their institutional autonomy. The authority that presidents cite in an order can help to explain whether they cast themselves as *administrators* or *independents*. Presidents should be more likely to cite statutes when acting as *administrators* because they are more likely to be relying on authority delegated by Congress. Citing statute in an order may reflect the amount of discretion Congress has delegated to the president. Although broad discretion leaves room for independent action on the part of the executive, narrowed discretion may confer detailed instructions that constrain the executive to produce policy outcomes consistent with congressional objectives. A narrow avenue for discretion reduces policy uncertainty but gives the executive branch little room for independent action. As *administrators*, presidents narrowly constrained by Congress are more likely to cite statutory authority when they act.

A citation of statute, however, does not always imply compliance with Congress. Presidents are more likely to act as *independents* when they have been delegated broad discretion to act. Mayer (2009) reinforces the role of presidential authority and the likelihood of unilateral action, claiming, "Broad grants [of authority], ambiguity and the potential for swift action are a compelling combination." Marshall and Pacelle (2005) find that issuance of these orders are best explained by the fact that, having been delegated the responsibility to act, Congress is relying on the president to act. When presidents act with independence, they are more likely to cite the Constitution or executive authority and avoid entangling Congress. In a strategic sense, when presidents don't mention Congress, their perception is they have the authority to act on their own. They are less likely to cite statute when they prefer to have more control over how the order establishes or implements policy. Presidents are more likely to rely on their own authority when they prefer to act first and alone. These are times when Congress is less able or willing to act, such as when government is divided, there is polarization between the parties, or the size of the majority party is smaller.

Presidential Politics

Presidents are pressured to respond to their own unique political circumstances, and, in an election year, the decision of whether to be *independent* or to act as an *administrator* can influence whether they "look presidential in contrast to challengers who must overcome the threshold barrier of appearing to be of presidential caliber" (Mayer 2001). The rise of the permanent campaign has hastened the need to act quickly for legislative and political victories (Cook 2002). Incoming presidents can generally more effectively bargain with Congress, making it more likely they will act as *administrators*. Presidents are more effective in working with Congress earlier in their terms, during the first half of either their first or second term, which makes their role as administrators again more likely. During nonelection years, presidents are not faced with the need to draw attention to them and are generally more focused on working with Congress. Because the branches are in a more cooperative relationship during nonelection years, presidents are more likely to act as administrators.

Likewise, to appear more as leaders during an election year, presidents are more likely to act as *independents*. The growth of the public presidency has exponentially magnified the need for presidents to keep their promises (Light 1999). The legislative clock may run out before the president's policy preferences are translated into law, prompting him or her to issue a unilateral order to establish a stronger list of policy accomplishments to be bragged about to voters. Presidents need to act efficiently and in a timely way in the second half of their term or in their second term, to create policy to fulfill their agenda (Mayer 1999). As their terms draw to a close, bargaining with Congress is less likely to be effective (Howell and Mayer 2005). In the later stages of their administrations, presidents are more likely to act as *independents* when they issue unilateral orders.

Two Institutional Agendas

Light (1999) contends that presidents' agendas consist of those issues and topics they select from the country's most important problems. Although presidents have the capacity to create their agendas, Congress plays a significant role in determining whether their proposals and recommendations reach the legislative agenda. Kingdon (2003) acknowledges that "problem recognition, generation of policy proposal and political events can serve as an impetus or constraint" to the president's agenda. The president may transmit legislative proposals and initiatives in messages, the annual State of the Union Address, or a legislative package or program, or he or she may ask members to sponsor legislation, but there are no assurances that the president's legislative priorities will be placed on Congress's agenda. Presidents then may turn to unilateral action to meet their goals.

Presidents are more likely to act as *administrators* when the topic is not on their agenda. Because the policy is likely to be of only marginal interest, they may be more willing to negotiate the content. When government is unified, the branches are more aligned in their policy preferences and presidents are more likely to be amenable to the adoption of policy further away from their preference. Presidents have little incentive to act independently by challenging members of their own party. However, the notion that "the president proposes and Congress disposes," belies how the branches constantly skirmish over the control of the nation's agenda. *Independent* presidents are those who have a particular policy outcome for their agenda in mind or have made a campaign promise to the public they intend to keep and are more likely to take unilateral action at each stage of the policy process. The president may be more fearful of Congress adopting policy further away from his or her preference in a divided government when the differences in ideology may be greater. If the issue is on his or her agenda, the *independent* president is more likely to issue a unilateral order to forestall congressional efforts and create policy that meets his or her goals.

Executive–Congressional Conflict

When government is unified, presidents are assisting Congress in fostering and implementing legislation. Shull (1997) suggests that presidents issue more orders in unified government. This is consistent with Howell (2003), who argues and finds that larger, majority parties in Congress lead to fewer significant unilateral orders because the president is more able to get legislation of which he or she approves. Presidents are more likely to issue administrator orders when government is unified and larger, majority parties are in both chambers. Conflict occurs between the branches with Congress pulling in one direction and the president in another (Binder 1997). Differing policy and electoral interests reinforce institutional rivalries between the executive and legislative branches (Fiorina 1996). Lack of policy agreement usually prevails when there is divided government or when there is greater ideological disagreement between the branches. Divided government has a significant effect on the number of laws passed and a positive effect on the amount of legislative stalemate (Edwards, Barrett, and Peake 1997; Binder 2003; but see Krehbiel 1998; Mayhew 1991; Howell et al. 2000). This sets the stage for a classic case of why *independent* presidents take unilateral action.

The *independent* president wants policy closer to his or her preference and will issue unilateral orders to prevent congressional action that he or she opposes (Howell 2003) or when conditions do not favor legislative success (Krause and Cohen 1997). The lack of a majority in the president's party may reduce the likelihood of accord between the branches, but that doesn't stop the president from wanting his or her policy to be enacted. The distance in ideology between the branches may also influence the president's unilateral action. Deering and Maltzman (1999) find that the farther the ideological distance between the president and the median member of the House and Senate, the more likely the president is to issue an executive order. Fine and Warber (2012) find support for a president using important executive orders during divided government. *Independent* presidents, therefore, are more likely to take unilateral action when government is divided, the size of the majority party is smaller, or when there is greater distance in ideology between the branches.

Congressional Gridlock

The capacity of Congress to coordinate internally is strongly linked to the ability to effectively navigate the policy process, delegate power, hold committee hearings, and pass legislation. A homogenous party that has a shared ideology means party members in Congress are more likely to have mutual goals. Congress is less likely to be divided internally when the positions of Democrats and Republicans are less polarized. Presidents are more likely to act as *administrators* when Congress is able to function in its legislative role and policy making is able to progress. When they are faced with an ineffective Congress, they are more likely to act as *independent* presidents.

When the two chambers are internally divided by policy disputes over partisanship or ideology, Congress may become gridlocked in its ability to pass any kind of legislation (Binder 1999). Parties in Congress may be polarized with Republicans and Democrats unable to reach a policy agreement. Greater polarization within Congress causes greater conflict between the two parties on presidential initiatives (Andres 2005). When the parties are divided in their views, the gridlock interval become larger, and they are less likely to agree on a course of policy action (Krehbeil 1998). A party divided internally by differences in ideology creates heterogeneity within the party and makes it more difficult to reach a policy agreement. A president is more likely to act as an *independent* president when Congress is unable to act because of greater heterogeneity *within* the parties or polarization *between* them.

CONCLUSION

The dual nature of the presidency represents two facets of power. As articulated most clearly in Neustadt's work (Mayer and Price 2002), power can be comprised of "unilateral authority" or the "persuasive authority and agenda control." Examining the dual nature of the executive within a policy-making framework provides greater purchase on the question of when, and how, unilateral orders are used in a separate and shared system of power. Presidents may need to act with dispatch, as Alexander Hamilton argued in *Federalist* 70. An *independent* president's use of unilateral orders exemplifies a strong president and a muscular use of executive power. Consistent with most expectations, *independent* presidents use their constitutional and delegated authority to take unilateral action often without congressional consultation or approval. Using direct action, *independent* presidents issue orders that command. In the legislative process, with bills on Congress's agenda, *independent* presidents issue orders that preempt legislation. After laws have been passed, *independent* presidents issue orders to adapt legislation. These orders illustrate a strong president and a muscular use of executive power.

But all unilateral orders are not alike, and some have a closer link to the legislative branch than others. In Neustadt's (1990) view, the founders at the Constitutional Convention of 1787 "created a government of separated institutions sharing powers." To accomplish their goals, presidents need a closer link to the legislative branch. Thomas Jefferson believed that "if the members [of Congress] are to know nothing but what is important enough to be put in a public message . . . it becomes a government of chance, and not design" (Meacham 2012).[21] *Administrator* presidents are more constrained by Congress. This constraint is both legal, as defined by Congress's delegation of authority, and political. Often, the president's authority and capacity to act is related to political conditions, congressional preferences, and the ability of the Congress to function effectively. Perhaps Shull and Shaw (1999) put it best when they wrote, "They [the president and Congress] may not always work together but they can rarely work apart from each other."

CHAPTER THREE

The Presidents' Orders
Proclamations and Executive Orders

PIECING TOGETHER THE PUZZLE of how unilateral orders reflect the dual nature of the executive leads to an examination of the orders and how presidents have used them over time. There are a number of types of unilateral orders from which presidents can choose, ranging from executive orders to proclamations, agency directives, memoranda, security instruments, and findings. Proclamations and executive orders are the oldest, most frequently used, and most diverse.[1] Although they can be distinguished from one another, "the difference between executive orders and proclamations is more one of form than of substance."[2] This chapter explores the use of proclamations and executive orders generally and, importantly, how they reflect the dual roles of the executive in order to better understand the role unilateral power plays within a system of separate and shared powers.

PRESIDENTIAL PROCLAMATIONS

Proclamations can be either ceremonial or policy based. Ceremonial proclamations celebrate common history or collective national moments of pride (Tulis 1988; Mayer 1999, 2001; Howell 2003). These have a place in the political world by promoting the president's policy agenda and reaching out to constituency groups (Warber 2014; Rottinghaus and Warber 2015). Even more important, policy proclamations, because of their substance, reflect the distribution of power between the branches. Presidents use policy-based proclamations to make official "determinations" when a "statute or ratified treaty specifically authorizes the president to take action if specified events occur" (Cooper 2002). Cooper considers a presidential proclamation to be "an instrument that states a condition, declares a law and requires obedience, recognizes an event or triggers the implementation of a law (by recognizing that the circumstances in law have been realized)." This occurs because Congress has delegated authority for decision making to the president or because the president claims support for his or her action based on statutory interpretation.

Few would dispute that proclamations retain a central place in American political and constitutional development. Perhaps none is more famous than Abraham Lincoln's Emancipation Proclamation, which freed slaves in areas under Confederate control in 1863.[3] In foreign policy, George Washington's Proclamation of Neutrality in 1793 was important not only in determining that the United States would remain neutral in the conflict between England and France but, as suggested in the famous debate between Thomas Jefferson and Alexander Hamilton, in asserting the president's primacy in managing foreign relations (Dodds 2013).[4] Andrew Jackson's proclamation respecting the nullification laws of South Carolina was instrumental not only in undercutting attempts by the states to nullify federal laws and in laying out the understanding of the "Union" that the Whigs and, eventually, Abraham Lincoln would appropriate and expand in the decade leading up to the Civil War.[5] The constitutional bounds of presidential power was raised with each of these proclamations, whereas now these powers are an established part of the president's constitutional creed.

In more recent history, President Nixon used proclamations to implement wage and price control measures. Attempting to stem the swelling inflation ravaging the U.S. economy, relying on his authority to suspend the Davis-Bacon Act in the event of a national emergency, Nixon issued Proclamation 4031 to curb wage conditions in the construction industry (Cooper 2002; Howell 2003; Whittaker 2005).[6] In a later effort to improve the U.S. economic position in relation to its trading partners, Nixon seized on his authority under the Trade Expansion Act of 1962 to issue Proclamation 4074 declaring a national emergency as justification for imposing a supplemental import duty (Bowles 2005).[7] Presidents use policy proclamations to respond to particular conditions that arise, allowing the executive branch to address a crisis situation promptly and efficiently. President Reagan quickly retaliated to the expulsion of the U.S. ambassador and seven other U.S. diplomats from Nicaragua by issuing Proclamation 5887, prohibiting "officers and employees of the Government of Nicaragua and the Sandinista National Liberation Front" from

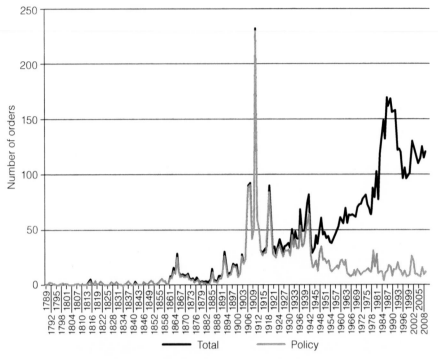

FIGURE 3.1. Proclamations over time. The x-axis charts the total number of proclamation of each type by year. Total proclamations include all proclamations (both ceremonial and policy based).

entering the United States as nonimmigrants.[8] Congress's broad delegation of power under the Immigration and Nationality Act and the president's own constitutional authority provided the support for his action.

Even though proclamations are an important part of the president's unilateral tool bag, they have received less scholarly attention than executive orders. Figure 3.1 shows the relationship of the number of policy proclamations to the total number of proclamations (ceremonial and policy) from 1789 to 2008. The total number of proclamations has progressed along with the growth of the government and the presidency. The trend of proclamations over time has risen steadily with two prominent peaks: one in the beginning of the twentieth century and one in the mid-1980s. Figure 3.1 shows that not all proclamations are ceremonial as often presumed—dozens of proclamations per year deal with substantive policy issues. The vast majority of the early-twentieth-century proclamations were substantive and not ceremonial. Policy-based use of proclamations dominated the total number of proclamations before 1945.

Ceremonial proclamations began a linear increase beginning in the 1950s. From 1945 onward, ceremonial or hortatory proclamations, according to Cooper (2002), are "by far the most numerous." The growth of political coalitions, especially following the New Deal and the growth of the middle class, created more possible constituencies to be courted by the White House. The number of proclamations briefly increased exponentially during the 1980s and early 1990s when the Reagan and George H. W. Bush administrations made a concerted effort to court conservative religious constituencies (Erickson 1985). Subsequent presidents followed suit and began to add their own specific constituencies to the rotating list of groups mentioned in these directives. Although President Obama is not included in the formal data on presidential proclamations, it is useful to compare these trends in his administration. From 2009 to 2015, President Obama issued an average of 130 to 142 total proclamations annually. The range includes a low of 127 ceremonial proclamations in 2009 and 142 in 2010. President Obama's use of policy proclamations is nearly nonexistent. On average, through 2014, he has issued about two per year, primarily on trade policy and the creation of national monuments. However, in 2015 as he neared the end of his last term in office, Obama issued six proclamations establishing national monuments and two on trade policy.

War

Although there are several variables that may predict the ebb and flow, times of war (especially the Civil War) seem to be a primary driving agent for the use of policy-based proclamations (Hart 1925). Substantiating this, the first major increase in these orders came in 1861 when President Lincoln issued a number of proclamations increasing the size of the volunteer army, naming the states in the "insurrection," warning potential enemy collaborators or spies, suspending the writ of habeas corpus, and establishing the movement of troops and military equipment and the starting or ending of blockades.[9] Presidents have expanded powers preparing for conflicts (Cooper 2002) or prewartime emergencies (Cooper 1986) where they are likely to issue more proclamations. Presidents are institutionally advantaged during wartime, both within the executive branch and with Congress (Howell, Jackman, and Rogowski 2013). For instance, during World War I, President Wilson issued several proclamations declaring a state of war and outlining the procedures for handling alien enemies, the seizure of private ships for public use, and instituting a selective draft.[10] President Franklin Roosevelt used proclamations during World War II to declare national emergencies, to begin war mobilization, and to prioritize resources on several occasions.[11]

Public Lands

An increase in the number of policy proclamations can be explained by their use to reserve public lands (Rottinghaus and Maier 2007). In the realm of public land law generally, the president has been delegated broad authority and wide discretionary power with few statutory ex ante controls or little congressional oversight. Although under the Constitution Congress was given the power to dispose of and to make all rules and regulations regarding property belonging to the United States, the president has been delegated much of this authority (Dodds 2013). Since the mid-nineteenth century, proclamations have been used by presidents to control the withdrawal and reservation of lands owned by the U.S. government. The president's authority to withdraw public lands was upheld on the basis of implied congressional acquiescence to withdrawals in the absence of statutory authority.[12] Beginning with the Forest Reserve Act of 1891, presidents have used their authority to withdraw and reserve land from the public domain through presidential proclamations.[13] Presidents Harrison, Cleveland, McKinley, and Theodore Roosevelt proclaimed nearly 80 million acres of national forests from 1891 to 1906. President Roosevelt issued a total of twenty-six proclamations in 1902 and eighty-nine in 1906, with the majority used to restore land to the public domain and establish forest reserves. In 1907, however, Congress decided to take some action to curtail presidential proclamation authority prohibiting the president from proclaiming forest reserves in six Western states.[14] This did little to limit future presidential action in the arena of public land withdrawals.[15]

Trade Policy

Presidents have frequently used proclamations in trade policy. Under the Constitution, Congress is charged with regulating commerce with foreign nations, but the executive branch ensures that the laws Congress enacts are faithfully executed. Trade policy was delegated to the president in the late nineteenth century, subject to varying degrees of congressional oversight. An increase in the number of policy proclamations can be explained by their use in trade policy. There are two spikes in the number of proclamations in Figure 3.1. President Harrison issued twenty-eight in 1892, and President Taft issued 230 in 1910; a significant number of these were on the subject of trade. President Harrison's trade proclamations were issued under the Tariff Act of 1890 (McKinley Tariff Act) which granted the president significant authority to protect domestic industries from foreign competition. President Taft acted under the Payne–Aldrich Tariff Act of 1909, using his authority to liberalize trade. Taft announced in his Second Annual Message to Congress that he had issued 134 proclamations liberalizing trade by applying the minimum tariff of the United States universally.

Just after World War II, policy proclamations were used to create trade policy. In 1948, Congress began to limit the president's nearly unfettered discretion by providing for agency participation and direct congressional involvement in executive decision making regarding import relief to domestic interests (O'Halloran 1994; Pastor 1980). The president's role in trade was redefined in the 1974 Trade Act, but although the president was delegated greater involvement in international trade, Congress retained its role in the process. Congress imposed ex post procedural and substantive constraints on the president's discretionary authority and continued to give greater involvement in the decision-making process to independent agencies (Milkis and Nelson 1993). An elaborate system of advisors enabled members of Congress to follow the actions of the executive branch and for the White House and Capitol Hill to know which constituents would be hurt by and likely oppose a proposed trade agreement. The number of proclamations related to trade declined.

National Monuments

Relying on the Antiquities Act of 1906 as their source of authority, presidents issue proclamations to designate national monuments. Between 1906 and 1943, presidents proclaimed eighty-two national monuments. The march toward American preservation ended with the New Deal; after World War II, the National Park Service moved away from the creating new monuments toward maintenance and conservation of those already proclaimed. Only five national monuments were proclaimed between 1943 and 1970. A surge occurred between 1970 and 2006 when nearly forty national monuments were proclaimed. Nineteen of the forty were proclaimed by President Clinton between 1996 and 2001 (Belco and Rottinghaus 2009).

EXECUTIVE ORDERS

Executive orders are the most commonly discussed type of unilateral order (Dodds 2006). Unlike proclamations, executive orders are directed internally rather than externally to private individuals (Cooper 2002). Executive orders are "generally directed to, and govern actions by, government officials and agencies" (U.S. Congress, 1957). Like proclamations, executive orders reflect the sharing of powers. Executive orders "can range from transferring certain authority from one department to another over a policy matter, reorganizing organizational structures in federal agencies and executive departments, increasing the number of positions within the executive schedule, delegating authority to specific executive branch officials to implement provisions of a statute" (Warber 2006). Figure 3.2 shows the number of executive orders issued from 1936 to 2008.

The range and scope of executive orders makes them a critical tool for presidents in managing the executive branch, centralizing power, and establishing specific policies in fields generally conceded to the president by Congress (Mayer 2001; Cooper 2002). Executive orders were used more routinely with the expansion of the federal government during the New Deal programs of President Franklin Roosevelt, making this a good start-

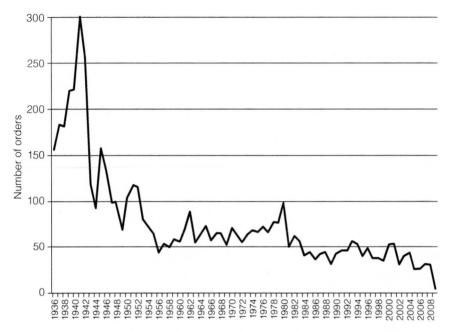

FIGURE 3.2. Executive orders over time. The x-axis charts the total number of executive orders by year.

ing point for analysis (Cooper 2002; King and Ragsdale 1988). Figure 3.2 shows an increase in executive orders between 1941 and 1942, when the Roosevelt administration was busy preparing for war (Mayer 2001). Just after World War II ended, there was another spike as President Truman rescinded previous orders governing wartime regulations (Mayer 2001).

After a brief increase early in the Eisenhower administration due to the rise of delegated powers in foreign and defense policy, "the number of orders dropped permanently" to an average of sixty orders per year (Mayer 2001). They peaked again during the Carter administration to implement a comprehensive reorganization within the executive branch, adopt energy policy, and address foreign policy flare-ups in Afghanistan and Iran. During the Reagan and George H. W. Bush administrations the number of executive orders dropped. One explanation for the secular decline in executive orders may be that neither president used executive orders to reorganize government or to implement major policy reform as

Carter had. The number of orders rose again briefly during the Clinton administration and immediately following the terrorist attacks of September 11, 2001, during the George H. Bush administration.

Although President Obama is not included in the formal data analysis presented here, it is useful to compare these trends to his administration's use of executive orders. From 2009 to April 2015, President Obama issued 213 executive orders ranging from a high of thirty-nine in 2009 and 2012 to a low of twenty in 2013 and only seven from January to April, 2015. His executive orders span the substantive range of policy action, from the weightier to the mundane bureaucratic ones. On the weightier side, Executive Order 13491 revoked a previous executive order issued by President George W. Bush concerning detention or interrogation of detained individuals. President Obama's order aligned the policy of the United States with the Convention against Torture by the United Nations and Geneva Convention by limiting interrogations to specified and acceptable guidelines. The order outlawed torture as a means of interrogating detainees, effectively undoing a controversial Bush administration policy. Executive Order 13490 required every executive agency employee to pledge to a family of obligations, including a gift ban from lobbyists, an agreement not to lobby for two years after leaving their positions, and a commitment to hiring qualified employees. On the bureaucratic side, several orders from the Obama White House created or extended specific internal White House offices of councils, including establishing a White House Council on Women and Girls, a White House Office of Health Reform, and a White House Council on Automotive Communities and Workers. President Obama's total use of executive orders is low, in part because this White House has used executive memoranda more extensively than past presidents (Korte 2014). Memoranda are used narrowly for agency directives and do not require a citation of authority, making them less comparable to other unilateral orders but meaningful in how President Obama has used his unilateral authority.

TESTING THE THEORY: CREATING THE DATA SET

The data set begins with President Ford and ends with President George W. Bush's second term in office. This time frame was selected because

Presidents Gerald Ford and George W. Bush represent extremes in presidential power. President Ford was sworn into office when presidential power was at an all-time low. President Nixon's resignation came as a result of the Watergate scandal stemming from a 1972 break-in at the Democratic National Committee offices at the Watergate office complex in Washington, DC. Ford noted in his inaugural remarks, "As we bind up the internal wounds of Watergate, more painful and more poisonous than those of foreign wars, let us restore the golden rule to our political process."[16] Even though he had been able to remove the traces of President Nixon from the White House, any honeymoon he may have experienced ended after he issued Proclamation 4311 granting a presidential pardon to President Nixon (Brinkley 2007).[17] Calabresi and Yoo (2008) consider that "after the Nixon pardon, congressional power vis-à-vis the executive branch began to grow enormously, continuing a trend that had started in the Johnson and Nixon administrations." The George W. Bush administration stands at the other extreme of presidential power. The Bush administration fought vociferously to protect the independence of the executive. After the terrorist attacks of 2001, the president became a staunch supporter of the unitary executive and opposed congressional attempts to limit the exercise of presidential power (Fisher 2010; Genovese 2010a).

The data set of presidential executive orders and proclamations was compiled from several sources, including the *Codification of Presidential Proclamations Disposition Tables*, the *United States Statutes at Large*, the United States *Federal Code*, the *CIS Index to Presidential Executive Orders and Proclamations*, the United States *Federal Register*, the *Public Papers of the Presidents*, and the White House website of President George W. Bush. The data consist of 1,704 executive orders and 441 policy proclamations for a total of 2,145 unilateral orders. Figure 3.3 shows the number of orders issued by individual presidents. President Carter, who served only one term in office, was as prolific in issuing unilateral orders as President George W. Bush, a two-term president. When considered in relation to other one-term presidents, President Carter issued double the number of orders than either President Ford or President George H. W. Bush, both of whom may have resisted the

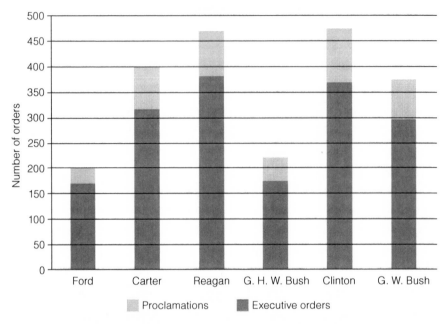

FIGURE 3.3. Executive orders and proclamations by the president. The figures correspond to the total proclamations or executive orders by the president.

draw of unilateral action after having served in Congress. Ford used executive orders and proclamations more frequently to implement laws enacted by Congress and less as unilateral policy tools (with the exception of the Nixon pardon and the inflationary impact statement). Notably, President George H. W. Bush may not have issued a large number of orders during his one-term presidency, but he used executive orders to assert control over his administration and to take significant policy action in the area of fetal tissue banks, the Tiananmen Square protests, and export controls. Overall, President Clinton issued the most unilateral orders, followed closely by President Reagan, and President Ford issued the fewest. This is not surprising given that both Presidents Reagan and Clinton made extensive use of their unilateral powers to shape the administrative state (Moe 1985; Kagan 2001). Both used executive orders more frequently than policy proclamations, cementing the status of executive order as the preferred unilateral tool among presidents during this time period.

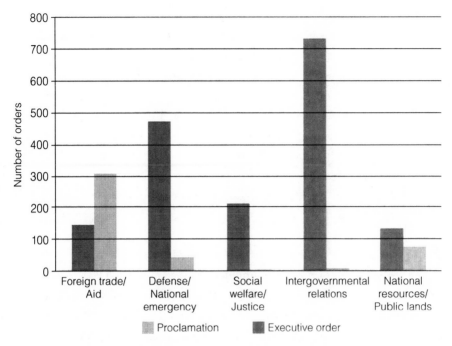

FIGURE 3.4. Executive orders and proclamations by policy area. The figures correspond to the total proclamations or executive orders by the president.

UNILATERAL ORDERS BY POLICY AREA

One way to better understand how unilateral orders are used is to consider them within the context of policy areas. Unilateral orders can be classified into five policy areas: intergovernmental relations, national defense and emergencies, foreign aid and trade, social welfare and justice, and natural resources and public lands. Figure 3.4 shows the distribution of the 2,145 executive orders and policy proclamations within our data set according to these areas.

Intergovernmental Relations

The highest number of unilateral orders issued is in the area of intergovernmental relations. Intergovernmental relations include governmental relations within the executive branch, between the branches, and between the federal, state, and local governments and territories of the United States. Intergovernmental relations are generally managed using executive orders, as indicated by the more than 700 issued in this category. An example of intergovernmental relations within the executive branch is Executive Order 12221, "Improving Government Regulations," issued by President Carter on June 27, 1980, which continued existing procedures for improving government regulations in anticipation of the passage of regulatory reform legislation. Although policy proclamations are rarely used for this purpose, an example is Proclamation 5207, "Application of Certain United States Laws to Citizens of the Northern Mariana Islands," issued by President Reagan on June 7, 1984, which exempted the applicability of certain laws of the United States to citizens of the Northern Mariana Islands.

Defense and National Emergencies

The second largest area where unilateral orders are issued is defense and national emergency. This includes the declaration of national emergencies and the imposition of economic sanctions, immigration controls, and other types of limitations and sanctions in response to national emergencies, export controls, troop deployment and management, domestic insurrections, declarations to begin and end war, and foreign invasions. These policies are primarily executed by executive orders. From 1974 to 2009, presidents issued 517 executive orders compared to only fifty proclamations. Traditionally, presidents use executive orders to declare national emergencies and to order troops to active duty. In response to the "Iraqi interference in the conduct of U.N. weapons inspections crisis," Secretary of Defense William Cohen announced that "he needed the reservists to fill gaps in combat support and logistics operations."[18] In response to Secretary Cohen's request, President Clinton issued Executive Order 13076 of February 24, 1998, ordering "the Selected Reserve of the Armed Forces to Active Duty" invoking the authority granted by Title 10, section 12304 of the United States Code.[19]

Presidents rely on executive orders for the management of export controls, an integral part of both national defense and emergencies generally used to manage the "exports of sensitive equipment, software and technology as a means to promote our national security interests and foreign policy objectives."[20] Historically, presidents seek to expand export control authority, whereas Congress actively works to limit executive authority, often forcing presidents to take unilateral action relying on expired statutory authority. To preserve export control, President Reagan issued Executive Order 12451, "Continuation of Export Control Regulations," on December 20, 1983, citing expired statutory authority. Congress sparingly extended Reagan's authority in an amendment to the Export Administration Act from December 5, 1983, through February 29, 1984. Proclamations are used to manage domestic insurrections and unrest. Although most proclamations that addressed insurrection were issued in the eighteenth and nineteenth centuries, a twentieth-century example is Proclamation 6427, "Law and Order in the City and County of Los Angeles, and Other Districts of California," issued by President George H. W. Bush on May 1, 1992. The proclamation was issued in an attempt to curb the rioting that occurred primarily in Los Angeles following the acquittal of police officers on trial for a police brutality incident against Rodney King.

Foreign Trade and Aid

The third largest category includes orders involving foreign trade and foreign aid. This area includes the adoption and implementation of foreign trade and foreign aid agreements, decisions to deny trade or aid, and the adoption of tariffs, quotas, and other tools of trade policy. Presidents issued 300 proclamations compared to 150 executive orders. Generally, the implementation of trade agreements is executed through proclamations rather than executive orders. President Reagan issued Proclamation 5340, "Modification of Import Quotas on Certain Sugar Containing Articles," on May 17, 1985. Meanwhile, executive orders are generally used to issue waivers and exemptions from specific statutory requirements under the Trade Act, enabling countries to trade with the United States. Executive Order 12772, "Waiver under the Trade Act of 1974 with Respect to Romania," was issued by President Bush on August 17, 1991, and waived requirements for Romania to comply with Section 402 of the Trade Act. This section prohibits the granting of most favored nation status (MFN), government credits or investment guarantees, or the negotiation of a commercial agreement with any communist country if that country does not allow its citizens the freedom to emigrate. Section 402 permits the president to waive this prohibition for limited periods of time if he or she determines that doing so will promote freedom of emigration.

Social Welfare and Justice

In the area of social welfare and justice, presidents issued 210 executive orders and no proclamations. This area includes health, welfare, education, civil liberties and civil rights, and social, employment, and economic equality. One of the most renowned unilateral actions in this category is Executive Order 12806, issued by President George H. W. Bush on May 19, 1992. Despite being the subject of controversy in Congress, President Bush directed the Secretary of Health and Human Services to establish a human fetal tissue bank for research.

Natural Resources and Public Lands

In the category on natural resources and public lands, presidents issued 150 executive orders and eighty proclamations. This includes the withdrawal, management, and designation of public lands and national monuments; control of natural resources; establishment of territorial boundaries; protection and development of energy sources; and management of interstate compacts and agreements. An example of an executive order within this category is Executive Order 12996, for the Management and General Public Use of the National Wildlife Refuge System. The order, issued by President Clinton on March 25, 1996, established the mission and goals of the National Wildlife Refuge System and identified the management principles for the Secretary of the Interior. Proclamations issued to establish national monuments fall within this category. One of the best known is Proclamation 6920, which established the Grand Staircase–Escalante National Monument. The proclamation was issued by President Clinton on September 18, 1996, to the outrage of members of the Utah delegation and the governor of Utah (Belco and Rottinghaus 2009).

UNILATERAL ORDERS IN THE POLICY PROCESS

Unilateral orders can also be categorized into one of three stages of the policy process: direct action, legislative process, and execution of law.

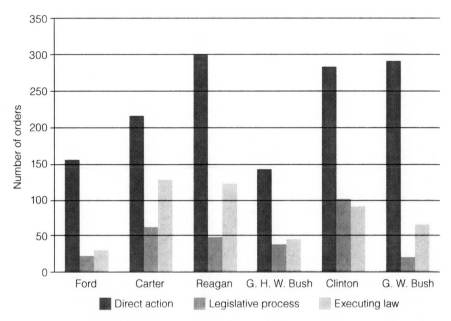

FIGURE 3.5. Stage of unilateral action by the president. The figures correspond to the total proclamations or executive orders by the president in each category.

The category of direct action, where the president routinely fulfills an administrative duty or acts first to command action rather than waiting for Congress, includes 1,382 unilateral orders. The category of the legislative process, where presidents decide to work with or against Congress on proposed legislation, includes 287 unilateral orders. The category of executing law, where presidents decide to adapt or implement law recently enacted by Congress, includes 476 unilateral orders. Figure 3.5 shows the number of orders issued by president in each of these stages. Each president issued significantly more unilateral orders in direct action than in relation to the legislative process or executing law. This suggests that presidents are more likely to use direct action to issue unilateral orders for routine matters and as a means to harness their first-mover advantage when Congress is contemplating legislative action. They are less likely to intervene in the legislative process, perhaps because of the potential for conflict with Congress, which at that stage is more visible and has greater potential to affect executive-legislative relations.

President Reagan issued the most unilateral orders using direct action, followed closely by President George W. Bush and President Clinton—all two-term presidents. This is understandable because Presidents Reagan and Clinton made extensive use of their unilateral powers to shape the administrative state, whereas President George W. Bush had a penchant for using unilateral power to flex his unitary executive powers. President George H. W. Bush and President Ford issued fewer orders using direct action than President Carter—all one-term presidents. Because President Ford served in the aftermath of Watergate and in the era of a resurgent Congress, fear of congressional reprisal from a strengthened Congress and the weakened state of the presidency may have contributed to the Ford White House's decision making. Figure 3.2 shows that President Clinton was significantly more active in the legislative process than any of the other presidents. President Carter and Reagan are tied in the number of orders issued in executing law.

DISTRIBUTION OF PARTISAN INSTITUTIONAL POWER

An important factor directly related to the data is the extent of party control in government during the time a president served. Table 3.1 shows party control by legislative session for each president in the data set. The differences from President Ford to the second President Bush allow for a viable test of questions concerning the use of unilateral orders in divided and unified government and the influence of variation in heterogeneity within a party as well as polarization between the parties. Although President Carter was favored with unified government, the differences in ideology within the Democratic Party complicated his bargaining strategy. President Reagan, on the other hand, was afflicted by divided government, but the same ideological differences in the Democratic Party that limited President Carter's bargaining ability helped President Reagan to gain cross-party votes from conservative Democrats.

THE BATTLE FOR THE AGENDA

The creation of policy in a system of separated and shared powers justifies an examination of the relationship between the agendas of the presi-

TABLE 3.1.
Party control, 93rd through 110th legislative sessions.

Congressional session	President	President's party	Dominant party in senate	Dominant party in House
93rd	Ford	Republican	Democrat	Democrat
94th	Ford	Republican	Democrat	Democrat
95th	Carter	Democrat	Democrat	Democrat
96th	Carter	Democrat	Democrat	Democrat
97th	Reagan	Republican	Republican	Democrat
98th	Reagan	Republican	Republican	Democrat
99th	Reagan	Republican	Republican	Democrat
100th	Reagan	Republican	Democrat	Democrat
101st	G. H. W. Bush	Republican	Democrat	Democrat
102nd	G. H. W. Bush	Republican	Democrat	Democrat
103rd	Clinton	Democrat	Democrat	Democrat
104th	Clinton	Democrat	Republican	Republican
105th	Clinton	Democrat	Republican	Republican
106th	Clinton	Democrat	Republican	Republican
107th	G. W. Bush	Republican	Republican/ Democrat*	Republican
108th	G. W. Bush	Republican	Republican	Republican
109th	G. W. Bush	Republican	Republican	Republican
110th	G. W. Bush	Republican	Democrat	Democrat

Note: Shaded areas signify Congresses with divided government.
*Denotes split party control: Republican January 20 through June 6, 2001, Democrat from June 6, 2001 through November 12, 2002.

dent and Congress. A topic may be pursued by the president or Congress, and in some cases a topic may be on the agendas of both branches.[21] The president's agenda provides a master list from which his or her future administrative and legislative accomplishments are drawn, and, not surprisingly, many of the topics of unilateral orders are also issues of congressional concern (Deering and Smith 1997). Members of Congress may be discussing the topic in committee hearings before the president takes unilateral action. These hearings are held for oversight, investigations, and gathering information to aid in determining whether legislation is needed and, if so, the direction it should take. When the topic is still under discussion in committee and subcommittee hearings Congress may

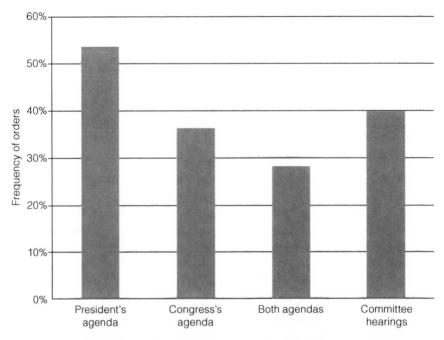

FIGURE 3.6. Unilateral orders and the two agendas. The figures indicate
the percentage of the total cases where the issue was on the agenda of the
president, Congress's legislative agenda, or both, or the subject of a committee
hearing.

be more willing to accept the president's agenda. The president's unilateral action may also relate to bills on Congress's agenda. That requires
that a bill be, first, introduced by a member and, second, a committee
hearing must be held to discuss the proposed legislation. If presidents are
interested in the topic or it is on their agenda, then they may introduce a
unilateral order to influence subsequent committee and floor action on
the bill. Figure 3.6 shows the frequency of unilateral orders issued when
the topic is on the president's agenda, Congress's agenda, or both agendas, and when the topic of an order relates to a committee hearing before
legislation has been introduced.

More than half the time, the order issued by the president was *only* a
topic on his agenda. The issue was *only* on Congress's agenda 36 percent
of the time. For fewer than 30 percent of the orders issued, the topic was

on the agenda of both institutions. The relationship between the agendas and congressional hearings can be used to explain one way in which the branches use their separate and shared powers. For almost 40 percent of all unilateral orders, Congress held hearings on the topic *before* the president issued an order.

The timing of when to use unilateral action to pursue a topic on the president's agenda can be perplexing even for the White House. In an internal planning memorandum during the Clinton administration in 2000, Karen Tramontano and Thomas Freedman created a list for John Podesta, Chief of Staff, of several "best" executive orders from the Cabinet Affairs Office, the Domestic Policy Council, and agency heads, for issuance by the president.[22] The list included prominent agenda items for the administration and outlined specific ways to announce these orders to the public. In the category of water, the possible orders included a clean water rule and implementation of the Safe Drinking Water Act by the Environmental Protection Agency and a review by the Department of the Interior of all federal dams. On hate crimes, the chief of staff was encouraged to use the Hate Crime Reporting Study (May 2000) or the Hate Crimes Prevention Media Campaign (April 2000) as a launching point. Earlier in the term, Bruce Reed, Clinton's domestic policy advisor, wrote a memorandum to Elena Kagan (then Associate White House Counsel) listing his top ten most needed executive orders, which included applying patient protections in federal health plans, requiring welfare recipients to work within two years, ordering a reduction of 100,000 federal pensions, banning federal funding for human cloning, and requiring federal employees to pay child support.[23]

The genesis of the president's agenda may reach back to a first-term campaign promise by a president already in his or her second term. In 2008, candidate Barack Obama made an ambitious pledge to help alleviate poverty in an age of rising economic inequality by increasing the minimum wage by 2011. Other policy priorities pushed raising the minimum wage off the agenda for much of the president's first term. Increasing pressure to act before leaving office spurred the White House to put the minimum wage increase back on the table in 2014, when President Obama's State of the Union address renewed his push to get Congress to consider legislation. Unsuccessful in Congress, the president followed through on his agenda through an executive order (Lowery 2014).[24]

At other times, presidents find that they are not alone in their efforts to accomplish their policy goals. During the 100th session, President Reagan and Congress used both executive orders and legislation to effectively promote the commercialization of federally funded inventions and encouraging the public and private cooperation and partnership. The transfer of science and technology was a topic on the president's agenda as well as being the subject of committee hearings and bills.[25] President Reagan had the privilege of seeing his work with Congress as well as his own federal initiatives in the form of an executive order and legislative messages culminate in the Steel and Aluminum Energy Conservation and Technology Competitiveness Act.[26] The law provided for a public–private partnership to undertake scientific research as developed under his executive order, which President Reagan cites in the statement on signing the act.[27]

CONCLUSION

Unilateral orders are not all equal. Disaggregating them provides a broader perspective on their diversity and how they are used over time and across policy issues. Proclamations in particular have not been systematically understood as an important unilateral tool. Their importance rests in their ceremonial significance. Edwin Corwin described presidential proclamations as "the social acts of the highest official government." The Thanksgiving Day Proclamation first issued by George Washington has continued as a tradition each Thanksgiving since (Corwin 1957). Presidential proclamations are not simply ceremonial or rhetorical—they carry important substantive policy power that is critical to defining the scope of power of the history of the American presidency. Cooper (2002) argues that proclamations have a "more significant and complex nature than it might appear." Proclamations and executive orders are recognized by scholars as being critical to understanding modern presidential powers because they virtually define how contemporary presidents behave (Mayer 2001; Howell 2003). Importantly, these two types of unilateral orders are used in different policy areas. Executive orders may dominate in one and proclamations in another, but in many instances, they are both used by presidents to create policy. Examining these orders reveals the richness of their history and the differences between the leadership styles of presidents. Presidents issue unilateral orders at each of the three stages of the policy process. Some prefer direct action before Congress can act, some will fearlessly enter the legislative process, and others prefer to execute law in the wake of Congress's action. Knowing when presidents act leads to an understanding of how and why they act.

CHAPTER FOUR

The Source of Authority and Delegation of Powers

Audience member: So, Mr. President, please use your executive order to halt deportations for all 11.5 million undocumented immigrants in this country right now.

The President: What we're trying—

Audience member: We agree that we need to pass comprehensive immigration reform. At the same time, we have a—you have a power to stop deportation for all—

The President: Actually, I don't.[1]

PRESIDENT BARACK OBAMA'S EXCHANGE with a heckler during a speech on immigration illustrates the limited ability of the president to act unilaterally. Frustrations from several camps within the president's party pressured him to act on immigration reform. After responding to the heckler, the president added, "The easy way out is to try to yell and pretend like I can do something by violating our laws. And what I'm proposing is the harder path, which is to use our democratic processes to achieve the same goal that you want to achieve—but it won't be as easy as just shouting. It requires us lobbying and getting it done." As the president implied in his response, a source of authority is required to cement the legal basis of an executive's unilateral power. Presidential action is meaningless unless ratified by an underpinning authority to act.

One year later, still frustrated with Congress's lack of legislation to reform immigration, President Obama announced a major expansion of an executive branch program: "Now, I continue to believe that the best way to solve this problem is by working together to pass that kind of common sense law. But until that happens, there are actions I have the legal authority to take as President—the same kinds of actions taken by Democratic and Republican Presidents before me—that will help make our immigration system more fair and more just."[2] To reinforce the strength of his action, the president's specific source of authority was presented in a thirty-three-page memorandum from the Department of Justice explaining the law and judicial precedent for his action.[3]

Understanding the ways that presidents justify their authority can tell us something about how they strategically merge their powers with those of Congress but also act autonomously. The legal justification for each order is of nontrivial importance (Pious 2006). Warber (2006) argues that the heterogeneity in the "goals and domains" of executive orders spans constitutional, statutory, and other sources of authority, and "it is important for presidency scholars studying unilateral powers to be aware of the multidimensionality found" in these orders. For example, presidents rely on authority delegated from Congress (Mayer 2009). Citing Congress through statute often provides more clearly defined authority and limitations. Citing inherent presidential power may give the executive more leeway in establishing or interpreting policy or administrative rules. For instance, in an internal White House memorandum in the Carter Administration, the Department of Energy (DOE) objected to draft language of an executive order that would have required agencies to consider the environmental effects of federal actions in other countries. DOE objected because the executive order could be read as tethered to congressional authority rather than the president's power. Specifically, the DOE review counsel recommended that the order be structured so the decisions rest "expressly on the inherent authority of the President and not tied to" Congress under the National Environmental Policy Act.[4]

The strategic use of the source of authority as part of the president's orders, however, has not been fully studied. Historically, there has been variation in how presidents justify their executive actions. The invocation of executive authority for President Harry Truman's order to desegregate the armed forces and President Andrew Jackson's Nullification Proclamation demonstrates that presidents often willfully approach the source of authority strategically. President George Washington explicitly chose not to consult Congress before issuing his Neutrality Proclamation, acting first and alone, or as Alexander Hamilton put it, "establish[ing] an antecedent state of things that ought to weigh in the legislative decisions" (Hamilton and Madison 2007). President Abraham Lincoln's Emancipation

Proclamation easily ranks as the most important of all policy proclamations in U.S. history, but he looked to his power as commander in chief and not authority delegated from Congress to emancipate slaves as a military necessity.

The way the president treats the source of authority is part of his or her political calculation. A president who decides to issue a unilateral order must decide whether to cast that action as executive driven or shared with Congress. As scholars of executive prerogative have long argued (Wilmerding 1952; Schlesinger 1973; Mansfield 1989; Pious 2011), the justification for a president's order has implications for the durability of his or her actions and constitutional practice (Sollenberger and Rozell 2012). Presidents know that their orders will become part of the public record and eventually be scrutinized by citizens, political officials, and the courts. This is particularly true of orders that give rise to legal controversies: Because there are winners and losers—individuals who will be arrested, lose land, be deported, or be denied access to courts—presidents are certain that the legal and political basis of their orders will be examined and contested. In one instance, the Obama White House was embroiled in weighing decisions about how to justify unilateral authority to execute strikes inside Syria in 2013. Without a self-defense rationale, the administration had difficulty determining whether the president should seek congressional authorization. In past situations, presidents have acted unilaterally without congressional limits to bind them, but this action would set a new precedent. Responding to questions prior to the action being undertaken:

Kathryn Ruemmler, the White House Counsel, said the President believed a strike would be lawful, both in international law and domestic law, even if neither the Security Council nor Congress approved it. But the novel circumstances, she said, led Mr. Obama to seek Congressional concurrence to bolster its legitimacy. The move is right, said Walter Dellinger, who led the Justice Department's Office of Legal Counsel in the Clinton administration, because the proposed attack is not "covered by any of the previous precedents for the unilateral use of executive power." "That doesn't mean it couldn't become another precedent," Mr. Dellinger added. "But when the president is going beyond where any previous president has gone, it seems appropriate to determine whether Congress concurs." (Savage 2015)

The decision to act first and alone, then, is not a trivial one. Legitimacy and institutional legacy are at stake for both presidents and Congress.

LEGAL AUTHORITY AND THE SOURCE OF ACTION

Presidents use multiple sources of authority when taking unilateral action. The legal basis for their authority to act is either authorized by Congress or the foundation of the Constitution (Rudalevidge 2014). Because unilateral orders issued by the president have the force of law, they are sometimes considered to be tantamount to the president legislating by fiat. The president's power in these cases, though, is not limitless. Congress may place express limits on the president's authority to act by restraining his or her discretion, specifying certain parameters or circumstances (Shugart and Carey 1992). With the delegation of specific policy functions through statute, Congress builds its preferences into executive branch decisions (McCubbins and Schwartz 1984; McCubbins, Noll, and Weingast 1987, 1989; Calvert, McCubbins, and Weingast 1989; Lupia and McCubbins 1994; Lindsay 1994). Likewise, even when presidents are acting under the auspices of their constitutional authority, their power is only as broad as the Constitution allows. These two sources of authority are also tempered by the president's interpretation and the constraints of the judicial branch. Ultimately, both political conditions and the extent of actual or perceived discretion reveal much about the decision-making process within the context of unilateral power.

The relationship between the sources of authority invoked, the delegation of authority, and the political and institutional conditions under which presidents issue unilateral orders reveals much about their separate and shared nature. The political environment should influence when the president is more likely to issue an order that cites specific statutory authority or that cites constitutional and executive authority. Specifically, when a president uses a unilateral order in cases where the branches are more likely in agreement, the source of authority is more likely to be the authorizing statute. But a president who issues an order to establish his or her own policy or to pursue his or her own agenda should rely more broadly on executive prerogative or his or her constitutional authority. The joint effect of presidents' assumptions about their legal authority and the political conditions they face reveals much about how presidents choose to use their unilateral powers. Through the delegation of authority and discretion, Congress plays enabling and restraining roles in the president's decision to exercise unilateral action. The shared nature is further imposed on presidents when Congress incorporates statutory constraints into their exercise of discretion.

SOURCES OF AUTHORITY AND UNILATERAL ACTION

Examining the relationship between the sources of authority cited in a unilateral order establishes a sound basis for studying the president's dual roles. The following two examples illustrate the different ways presidents accomplish the same objective:

BY VIRTUE of the authority vested in me by the Constitution and Statutes, and in order to effectuate the purposes of the Reorganization Act of 1939, Public No. 19, Seventy-sixth Congress, approved April 3, 1939, and of Reorganization Plans Nos. I and II submitted to the Congress by the President and made effective as of July 1, 1939, by Public Resolution No. 2, Seventy-sixth Congress, approved June 7, 1939 by organizing the Executive Office of the President with functions and duties so prescribed and responsibilities so fixed that the President will have adequate machinery for the administrative management of the Executive Branch of the Government, it is hereby ordered as follows . . .

Executive Order No. 8248 (1939)

As President of the United States of America, I direct each Executive Agency to adopt procedures to improve existing and future regulations.

Executive Order No. 12044 (1978)

These authorizing texts of two executive orders directing the executive branch illustrate the importance of the source of authority in unilateral action. The first order, from 1939 by President Franklin D. Roosevelt, created the Executive Office of the President to help the president control his growing administrative duties. The second order, from 1978 by President

60

Jimmy Carter, instituted new rules for agencies, proposing new regulation with "an annual effect of $100 million or more," shifting the "terms of debate from inflationary impact, to whether a proposed regulation was worth its cost" (Dodds 2006). Both orders brought about vast changes in the administration of law and increased the president's power in terms of control the regulatory apparatus (Milkis and Nelson 1993; Mayer 2001) and were issued by the stroke of pen. But, as the preceding excerpts reveal, there is an important difference between the two. President Franklin Roosevelt's order explicitly links his authority to act to Congress, while President Carter's does not.

The literature on the exercise of unilateral power is split with respect to when presidents act, some scholars argue that the political environment constrains presidential action, whereas others suggest a more unfettered ability to act. The authority presidents invoke as a justification for each order helps to expand on the explanation for their unilateral actions.[5] Presidents often operate under very specific delegated guidelines from Congress to exercise executive functions (Fisher 2007), but they may have a free hand to pursue orders in other circumstances. A president who issues a unilateral order generally turns to a plethora of sources ranging from his or her powers expressed in the Constitution to statute established by law and inherent and implied authority (Waterman 2009). Each provides a source of authority, although some provide a more adequate basis for withstanding a constitutional challenge than others. The divergence in the source of authority adds to an understanding of the separate and shared nature of unilateral power.

PRESIDENTIAL PREROGATIVE
POWER, LINKED TO CONGRESS

Each institution in government has partial agency to act within a permissible structural authority. The president's prerogative authority, as outlined by constitutional structures, allows the executive to take certain legally justified actions to enforce policies (Cash 1963; Fisher 2000). James Madison articulated a view in *Federalist* 47 and 51 that protected the prerogative of each branch of government and powers that were both separated and blended. The use of prerogative can be soft or hard, where under a soft prerogative presidents act unilaterally to resolve an issue but claim that this was done under the cover of statutory authority (Pious 2011). The Constitution and subsequent intraexecutive interpretations provide for some flexibility, but the president's discretionary powers on executive matters are "subordinate and ministerial" to the legislative power of Congress (Langston and Lind 1991). Ultimately, the framers intended that the "president was authorized only to act on the basis of law, and never against it" but that "all prerogatives are not equal" (Genovese 2010b). Presidents toggle between two political and legal realities: one that allows them to function independently based on necessity and one that tethers their actions to congressional and constitutional limitations.

Although scholars who study the unilateral presidency have generally not considered citation patterns (see Warber 2006 for an exception), scholarship on presidential power has long examined how presidents ground their use of executive power. This is particularly true for normative and interpretative explanations of executive prerogative. Within the public law approach, Fisher (2003) has documented the importance of Franklin Roosevelt's appeal to "the law of war" rather than "Articles of War" in his proclamation limiting the access to courts for the Nazi saboteurs. Sollenberger and Rozell (2012) trace how the expansion of the use of presidentially appointed "czars" goes back to Woodrow Wilson's expansive reading of the Overman Act, a reading that allowed Wilson to create what Sollenberger and Rozell regard to be the constitutionally suspect practice of appointing czars outside the Senate confirmation process. Within the scholarship on the prerogative power, there has been continued interest in the way presidents justify prerogative (Wilmerding 1952; Schlesinger 1973; Mansfield 1989; Langston and Lind 1991; Pious 2011), and scholars continue to distinguish Hamiltonian, Jeffersonian, and Lincolnian approaches to presidential strategy with respect to defending prerogative (Arnhart 1979; Schmitt 1988; Thomas 2000; Bailey 2004; Fatovic 2004; Kleinerman 2005). As Mayer (2009) notes, both the literature in the empirical study of unilateral power and the literature with respect to constitutional authority would benefit from consideration of the other.

To be sure, what a president says about source of authority does not reveal in a precise way whether that president is adhering to congressional authority on acting on his or her own. The decision to cite a source of authority is typically made by the attorney general as part of a review process that was initiated to standardize the process for creating executive orders and policy proclamations.[6] The formal process, which has evolved over time, includes the coordination by OMB general counsel with interested agencies and White House staff. The proposed order is sent to the Department of Justice Office of Legal Counsel (OLC), which issues an opinion on legality and form on behalf of the attorney general. Once comments have been received, the order is then circulated within the White House staff by OMB for consistency with policy and the president's program. The director of OMB, the attorney general, or one of the White House advisors transmits the order along with one memorandum attesting to the legality of the order, and a second one requesting the president's signature.[7] Tobias Gibson (2006) conducted interviews with OLC staff to explore this issue. In his interview with John Harmon, former Assistant Attorney General in the OLC during the Carter administration, Harmon responded to a question on the importance of the source of authority:

The point there is that the executive order must be found in either statutory authority that has been given to the president and the executive branch, or in constitutional authority. They had to be cleared by the OLC before they could be issued by the president. Yes there would be modifications to make sure they strictly complied, that there was legal authority for a particular executive order that was being issued.[8]

David Stockman, President Reagan's director of OMB, attested in a memorandum to the legality of the Executive Order 12488 and the president's source of authority:

Section 218 of Title 18 of the United states Code, enacted in 1962, authorizes agency heads, under regulations promulgated by the President, to declare void any transaction entered into by the government for which there has been a final conviction for violation of the bribery, or corruption provisions of the Federal criminal code. This proposal, which was submitted by the Department of Defense, would implement that statute for the first time by authorizing the head of each Executive Department and agency to exercise this power.[9]

Policy proclamations receive the same interagency review process for the content and legality as executive orders. Ronald A. Kienlen, OMB Associate General Counsel, transmitted a memorandum to Robert J. Lipshutz, Counsel to the President, attesting to the legality of the proclamation and the president's authority:

> As the President was advised, attorneys in the Department of Justice had previously reviewed this proposal and advised, in the limited time available for review, that while there was no doubt of the President's authority to waive the fees, the President's authority to remove the duties was not free from doubt. At their suggestion however, we have added a sentence to the end of the preamble to the proposed proclamation. This sentence asserts that the action being taken is consistent with the statutory requirement to adjust imports so as to avoid a threat to the national security.[10]

It is possible that the OMB, OLC, or the attorney general could invoke a statute incorrectly. Presidents too, may decide to act against their recommendations in order to achieve their own ends.

Presidents may decide not to cite a specific statute and instead refer to general laws of the United States. They may cite their executive authority vested in the Constitution when they are relying on what Congress understands to be delegated power. Andrew Jackson relied on his own executive authority when issuing the Nullification Proclamation, instead of citing the 1807 Insurrection Act as he and other presidents had done in other instances of domestic resistance (Vladeck 2004; Bailey and Rottinghaus 2013). Presidents and their advisors work to operate within the boundaries of the law, a dilemma President Obama faced when 2014 advocates of immigration reform called on him to make changes in deportation policy. The White House agreed with the proposal, but the president "would not suspend deportations because his advisers did not believe that such a move would be legal" even though inaction meant inert policy progress (Shear 2014b). President Obama subsequently decided to take executive action, and, as noted before, the Department of Justice issued a thirty-three-page legal memorandum on the president's authority.[11] The legality of unilateral action and the legal interpretation of the facts and laws are left to the courts.

WHEN PRESIDENTS CITE DIFFERENT
SOURCES OF AUTHORITY

The source of authority cited by presidents in the face of the order should vary according to the political environment. Presidents should generally cite statute because, like all executives, they know that, despite incentives, they cannot act without the support of the Constitution or law. This expectation is supported by no less than Supreme Court Justice Robert Jackson's famous "practical grouping" of presidential power.[12] When presidents act under authority delegated by Congress in addition to their constitutional authority, presidential power is at its maximum and is safe from judicial sanction. This is confirmed by recent scholarship, which has shown that even during wartime the Supreme Court usually casts itself as an auditor of process, checking to see if Congress has delegated authority to the president, rather than as an umpire of zero-sum contests between executive power and individual rights (Pildes and Issacharoff 2004). Presidents *do not* always cite congressional authority. One common critique of Vice President Richard Cheney's approach to executive power was the lack of reliance on Congress. According to Jack Goldsmith (2007), the former head of the OLC, Cheney consistently advised President George W. Bush to *avoid* reliance on Congress completely, and, in Goldsmith's opinion, this strategy ultimately backfired. Had President Bush cultivated congressional support, Goldsmith argues, he would have been more successful in building the muscular executive the vice president wanted because congressional backing is less circumspect than relying solely on executive power.

Why don't presidents just cite all possible sources in each order? There are several potential reasons why a president might choose to go alone in this way. Some are practical. There might be several laws, rather than one law, that provide the president with sufficient legal authority. Creating new law could take time, and the president may wish to move quickly. External crisis, such as wartime, may require presidents to act timely and with authority. There are also strategic considerations. Presidents might lack the ability or desire to bargain, or to appear to bargain, with Congress. When presidents believe their own legal authority is clear, they want to protect the historical prerogatives of the executive branch (Mayer 2001). Presidents might not want to rely on congressional authority when they think they can, or should, go alone. The actions of the Bush administration reinforced executive power, and they highlight how presidents protect their institutional turf from Congress (Goldsmith 2007). From the perspective of retaining executive power, a simple gesture in the present may become binding precedent in the future. Presidents cite executive authority when they consider themselves most free to act, particularly when their party controls both chambers of Congress or when their authority originates in the Constitution, such as in matters of control over foreign policy or over the executive branch. Marlow (2011) noted that in President Obama's first executive order, he expanded the authority of the incumbent president with regard to executive privilege, citing the "authority vested in me by the Constitution and laws of the United States of America," and not the Presidential Records Act or prior Supreme Court cases as in President George W. Bush's prior order.[13]

Presidents may be timid about citing statutory authority when he or she has a weak legal justification, especially if opposition to executive action is high. In an internal memorandum circulated during the Clinton administration in August 1995, several staff members considered issuing an executive order that would have required federal contractors to pay a minimum wage of $5.15 an hour, an increase over the prevailing minimum wage at the time.[14] The reasoning was that higher wages would lead to more efficient workers. The memorandum proposed the Federal Property and Administrative Services Act as the source of authority delegated to the president in 1949 "to provide for the Government an economical and efficient system of procurement and supply." The authors of the memorandum cautioned against this approach as being "unprecedented," noting that it would generate considerable congressional backlash and that the economic ideas on which the legal justification was based were only a theory and would invite scrutiny from the courts. Although President Clinton's administration decided against issuing such an executive order, President Obama moved forward, establishing a minimum wage for federal contractors on February 12, 2014, despite the potential for congressional backlash.[15] Citing "the authority vested in me as President by the

Constitution and the laws of the United States of America, including the Federal Property and Administrative Services Act, 40 U.S.C. 101 *et seq.*," which relates to concerns about efficient management, President Obama issued the order, and on October 7, 2014, the Department of Labor issued a final rule raising the hourly minimum wage paid by contractors to workers performing on or in connection with covered Federal contracts to $10.10 per hour.[16]

TRACKING THE SOURCE OF AUTHORITY OVER TIME

As history and law have borne out, presidents must rely on either the Constitution or Congress for an executive order or proclamation to have the force of law as sanctioned by the Supreme Court. To analyze the varying sources of authority, the enabling clause of each unilateral order in the data set was examined, and each policy-based proclamation and executive order was coded according to whether the text mentioned Congress (resolution, joint resolution, or statute) or a presidential-based power (Article II of the Constitution, "executive authority").[17] Orders that invoked both sources of authority were coded as Congress-based authority, although an analysis of the role of joint authority is included in Table 4.3 later in this chapter. Unilateral orders are most often justified using constitutional and congressional authority. Almost all proclamations issued from President George Washington to President George W. Bush were justified using statute. However, of the 166 policy proclamations that did *not* mention Congress, more than two-thirds were issued by early presidents. For most executive orders, presidents are more likely to justify an executive order citing congressional authority rather than their own authority. The ratio of statute to nonstatute is higher for proclamations than for executive orders, but both reveal the dominance of statutory-based orders.

Figure 4.1 examines these trends more closely by year by tracking policy proclamations that are both statute and nonstatute based. The data include the course of the modern presidency, from President Franklin Roosevelt to President George W. Bush (1936 to 2009), to gain greater perspective on the trends in the data. The proclamations are again separated by Constitution-based authority (references to inherent presidential authority or constitutional authority only) and statute-based authority

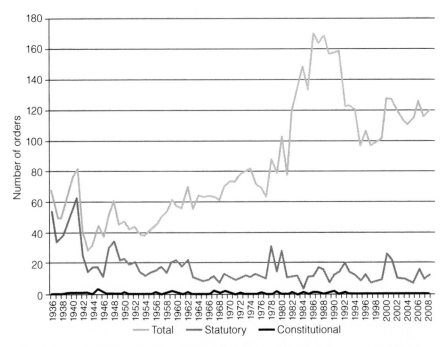

FIGURE 4.1. Proclamations by source of authority. The figures represent the total proclamations in each category by year.

(any reference to statute only). After World War II, presidents averaged about thirty statute-based proclamations a year, primarily supported by a range of policy issues that Congress delegated to the president, especially in trade, foreign policy, and rule making. There are modest increases between 1977 and 1978 and after 2001, related to trade, immigration, and financial sanctions or restrictions on nations or groups of individuals in the case of terrorism. The United States had ongoing political disputes with Iran during President Carter's administration and with Afghanistan and the Taliban during President George W. Bush's administration. In these moments of foreign conflict, presidents tend to issue more proclamations invoking their own authority. There are not many nonstatute proclamations per year, and that number declines to only a handful per year beginning in 1985. At this point, presidents began to justify their authority based on statute because Congress had delegated many of these powers to the executive (Marshall and Pacelle 2005). Presidents rarely

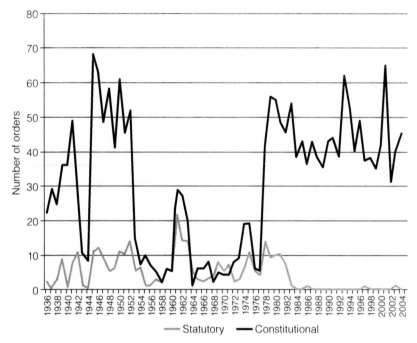

FIGURE 4.2. Executive orders by source of authority. The figures represent the total proclamations in each category by year.

cite inherent or constitutional authority exclusively; instead they marshal these moments for when they really need them.

Figure 4.2 shows that executive orders are primarily statute based. Three periods tend to dominate the increases in the use of statute-based executive orders: 1937 to 1943, 1946 to 1955, and 1978 to 1990. The first period (1937 to 1943) is clearly characterized by the expansion of the executive branch under the New Deal and the onset of World War II. The Brownlow Committee's recommendations suggested that the executive could be managed more effectively, and Congress reluctantly gave the president the authority to create, distribute, and shift power within the executive branch (Waterman 1989). The second period (1946 to 1955) corresponds to the growth of the president's delegated power to manage foreign policy and national security, as well as the fear of citing presidential authority in the wake of the Supreme Court's ruling in *Youngstown Sheet & Tube Co. v. Sawyer* (1952), also known as the steel seizure case.

The final period (1978 to 1990) clearly marks the beginning (and continuation) of the administrative presidency. Presidents rarely relied on an exclusive grant of constitutional authority (Warber 2006). Instead, they attempted to *politicize* or *presidentialize* the bureaucracy to their own ends (Nathan 1983). In particular, President Reagan (and most presidents who followed him) used executive orders to establish and amend rules or regulatory review procedures. These actions were at times directly authorized by Congress, although the president relied generally on the "laws or statutes of the United States."

In 1961, the Democratic Party had been out of the White House for eight years, and the incoming Kennedy administration used their authority and laws of the United States to amend previous executive orders. Although seemingly benign, one executive order furthered the president's policy agenda by consolidating a presidential commission into one dedicated to evaluating the principle of equal opportunity in government:

The President's Committee on Government Employment Policy, established by Executive Order No. 10590 of January 18, 1955 (20 F.R. 409), as amended by Executive Order No. 10722 on August 5, 1957 (22 F.R. 6287), is hereby abolished, and the powers, functions, and duties of that Committee are hereby transferred to, and henceforth shall be vested in, and exercised by, the President's Committee on Equal Employment Opportunity in addition to the powers conferred by this order.[18]

President Kennedy relied on his Constitution-based authority and Congress for the establishment of the President's Commission on the Status of Women:

WHEREAS a Governmental Commission should be charged with the responsibility for developing recommendations for overcoming discriminations in government and private employment on the basis of sex and for developing recommendations for services which will enable women to continue their role as wives and mothers while making a maximum contribution to the world around them.[19]

From 1978 on, it is rare to find an executive order that cites constitutional authority alone. Presidents are less likely to cite inherent or Constitution-

based authority alone and begin to justify their authority based on statute in part because Congress has delegated many of these powers to the
executive. They are more likely during this time frame to jointly cite statute and constitutional authority.[20] The total number of presidency-based
orders rarely exceeds more than ten per year.

EXPECTATIONS OF CITING A
SOURCE OF AUTHORITY

There is variation in the source of authority cited in unilateral orders, but
the goal is to understand the relationship between the president's dual
nature and the source of authority presidents cite. The expectation is that
presidents will cite statute under conditions different than those when they
cite constitutional authority. First, *administrator* presidents will evoke
the authority of Congress in an order (such as legislation through statute,
public law, or joint resolution) when they consider themselves *less* free to
act because of fear of being challenged or overturned. The president will
appeal to Congress (cite a statute) when Congress is stronger. That is, the
president should be more likely to issue unilateral orders citing statutes
when the majority party in Congress has large and cohesive majorities.
When presidents believe they have less authority in a policy domain in
which they are considering using unilateral action, they are more likely to
monitor and consult with Congress (Howell and Kriner 2008). Presidents
will be more likely to cast their actions as consistent with Congress when
it is stronger and the president is cognizant of the limitations. Presidents
will want to appear cooperative when they see that the majority party in
Congress is strong, and they should be more eager to share power and use
the authority delegated by Congress. Specifically, the larger and more unified the majority party in Congress—signaling a stronger Congress—the
more likely the president is to issue orders based on statute.

Independent presidents believe they have more freedom or have a desire
to act alone, and they should be more likely to cite their own authority
(the Constitution, the commander in chief clause, or executive authority).
Believing they have the authority to act without Congress, presidents may
want to press their agenda or need to act expediently and are willing to
take their chances if the other branches disagree. Presidents should be

more likely to issue unilateral orders justified by their own inherent or constitutional authority when the majority party is smaller and fragmented. This expectation builds on the findings of Howell (2003), who argues that unilateral activity is related to the power of the majority party in Congress and to the size and unity of the congressional majority. Howell's president is more likely to use unilateral power when the majority party is small and divided. When presidents desire to act "first and alone" in a strategic sense (Moe 1998; Mayer 1999), they are more likely to cite their own inherent or constitutional authority and avoid entangling Congress.

Independent presidents should cite constitutional and executive-based authority in their orders when they need to act expediently or when executive prerogative is greater. This includes incoming presidents, in the second half of a term, the second term, and times of war. In each instance, presidents should have more incentives to act on their own when they need to act quickly. The clearest example among these is wartime. War presents the president with all sorts of advantages, and among these is more attention to foreign policy. Scholars have long documented presidential success in the foreign policy arena relative to domestic politics (Wildavsky 1966; Canes-Wrone, Howell, and Lewis 2008). Howell, Jackman, and Rogowski (2013) find that war helps the president achieve policy victories that would not have happened during peacetime, but they find that this is not true of all wars.

Hybrid unilateral orders are those that cite presidential, constitution-based, and statute-based authority. These represent a presidential middle ground. Mayer (1999) argues that certain orders are "hybrid" because they "constitute a potential reservoir of independent authority, but one that presidents do not use without regard to circumstance or consequence." The inclusion of presidential authority (any executive justification) to the list of cited sources of authority has the benefit for presidents of carving out and preserving a presidential claim on the policy area in question, but it adds some uncertainty because it invites potential scrutiny from a Congress wary of executive claims of authority. The mention of inherent executive or constitutional powers may raise a red flag to Congress and cause greater attention to the content of the order. Accordingly, presidents are not acting wholly as either *independents* or *administrators*. They rely on multiple sources of authority in conditions in which presidents are less cautious or in moments when the institutional need to act is greater but *not* when they totally act alone. Divided government should produce fewer such orders; presidents should be wary of challenging Congress by including any kind of odious justification when Congress can more easily restrict the president's use of a particular type of order. Substantiating this, Howell (2003) shows that divided government results in fewer executive orders, or, put another way, presidents possibly issue more orders in unified government because the president and Congress are more likely to negotiate a mutually agreeable outcome (see Fine and Warber 2012). Moments where quick, decisive action is paramount for the president, such as timing in wartime, should encourage more citations using executive, constitutional, and statutory authority because presidents seek to preserve some of their own prerogative.

DATA AND METHODS

Several measures of institutional and political conditions are used to test these expectations.[21] First, the size of the majority (*Majority Size*), which is used by Howell (2003), examines assertions pertaining to whether the size of the majority party influences the president's invocation of constitutional sources of authority. The variable calculates a ratio of the total number of seats held by the majority party in each chamber by dividing the total number of seats in each chamber for each congressional session.[22] Second, unity within the majority party is an important consideration because it influences the legislative potential for policy change (LPPC). Howell (2003) utilizes the LPPC scores from Cooper, Brady, and Hurley (1977) because they capture moments where the majority party is large, unified, and "faces minimal opposition from the minority party." The variable (*LPPC Ratio*) is calculated by multiplying the percent majority size by party unity and dividing by the percent minority party size multiplied by party unity.[23] Third, a divided government (*Divided*) can influence the president's decision to exert his or her own authority or to rely on Congress. The variable is created using a dichotomous measure to indicate when government is divided between the branches or between the chambers. Fourth, four dummy variables are used, to measure significant moments in the president's administration. The variable *New President* measures when a president of a new party enters office. The variable *Second Half* measures the second half of the president's first or second term in office. The variable *Second Term* measures the president's second term in office. The variable *War* measures significant conflicts during the presidential administration, including the Vietnam War (1964–1973), the Persian Gulf War (1991–1992), the Afghanistan War (2001–2009), and the Iraq War (2003–2009).

The data span the period from 1973 to 2009. Each policy proclamation and executive order was examined to identify every source of authority cited for the actions taken within the order. The sources of authority were coded into three categories. The first category is Congress (*Statute-based*) and indicates when authority is attributed to Congress through resolution, joint resolution, specific statutes, or laws of the United States generally. The second category is presidential-based power (*Constitution-based*) and indicates when the president's constitutional powers or executive authority under Article II of the Constitution is invoked. The third category is joint authority and includes when both constitution-based and statute-based sources of authority are invoked. The unit of analysis is the congressional session, from the 93rd to 110th Congress. A series of count models (a Poisson or negative binomial) was used to conduct the regression analysis because linear regression models may result in inefficient and biased estimates for the count of events, and it is "much safer to use models specifically designed for count outcomes" (Long and Freese 2006). Count models estimate the number of occurrences of an event within a fixed period and consider other factors. Substantively, the focus is the number of orders of each type issued per legislative session, making a count model with each congressional session the appropriate unit of analysis.[24] The estimated results are interpreted with respect to the percent change in the dependent variable.[25]

WHEN PRESIDENTS VARY THE SOURCE OF AUTHORITY IN THEIR ORDERS

The results in Table 4.1 demonstrate, as expected, that there is variation in how and when presidents cite either statute or constitutional sources

TABLE 4.1.
Count models for proclamations and source of authority.

	Source of authority		
	All[†]	Statute[‡]	Constitutional[‡]
Majority size	−0.023 **	0 .036 ***	−.0143 **
	(0.012)	(0.011)	(0.083)
Second term	0.060	0.120	−0.547
	(0.128)	(0.126)	(0.808)
Second half	0.059	0.245 **	0.381
	(0.111)	(0.112)	(0.789)
War	−0.131	−0.193 ***	−1.38 *
	(0.100)	(0.103)	(0.906)
New president	0.209	0.115	0.663
	(0.146)	(0.145)	(0.913)
N (Congresses)	18	18	18
LR Chi^2	6.09 *	18.4 ***	7.38 *
Pseudo R^2	0.031	0.137	0.195
Log likelihood	−213.4	−57.9	−15.2
Ln(α)	100.2 ***	0.84	0.0

Note: Dependent variables are the count of policy proclamations from the 93rd Congress to 110th Congress for: **All** (joint sources of authority), **Statute** (specific statute and laws generally), and **Constitutional** (president's constitutional sources of authority).
[‡] Models are Poisson models.
[†] Models are negative binomial count models.
*** Indicates statistical significance at $p < 0.01$
** Indicates statistical significance at $p < 0.05$.
* Indicates statistical significance at $p < 0.10$.
Tests are two-tailed tests.

of authority for policy proclamations.[26] As the size of the majority party increases, presidents issue *more* proclamations that cite statute but *fewer* orders citing their constitutional authority. The substantive effects for these two models are graphed in Figure 4.3. The figure shows that as the size of the majority party increases from a simple majority (50 percent of the chamber) to a supermajority (67 percent of the chamber), the number of proclamations citing statute increases, whereas the number citing constitutional authority decreases.

Holding all of the other variables at their mean, the number of predicted statute-based proclamations increases from just over twenty per congressional session to almost forty per session. For constitution-based proclamations, the magnitude of expected counts decreases. Holding all

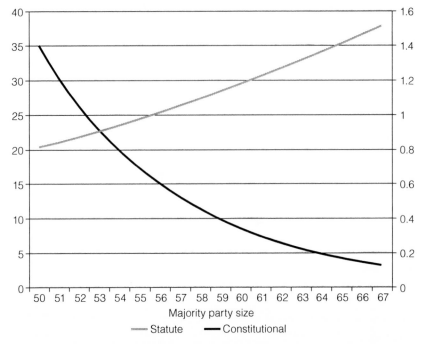

FIGURE 4.3. Predicted probabilities for proclamations. These are predicted probabilities for models in Table 4.1. The probabilities were created holding all other variables at their mean. Constitutional proclamations are graphed on the right axis. Statute-based proclamations are graphed on the left axis.

of the other variables at their mean, the number of predicted constitution-based proclamations decreases from approximately one per congressional session to almost zero. It is important to note that the number of proclamations citing only the Constitution as the source of authority never exceeds three in a single congressional session, making any reduction to nearly zero substantively important. The results suggest that when presidents issue policy proclamations, they are concerned with the capacity of the majority party in Congress to grant them the authority they need or to challenge the exercise of their authority. This reinforces the conclusion that the creation of policy proclamations is often shared between the branches.

The results in Table 4.1 indicate that the coefficient for the source of authority is not statistically significant for new presidents. However, as

TABLE 4.2.
Count models for executive orders and source of authority.

	Source of authority			
	All EOs [†]	Statute [†]	President [‡]	C-in-C [‡]
LPPC ratio	0.037	0.995 **	−2.23 ***	−1.95 ***
	(0.306)	(0.424)	(0.525)	(0.605)
Second term	−0.101	−0.145	−1.04 **	−0.530 **
	(0.189)	(0.268)	(0.281)	(0.330)
Second half	0.087	0.223	−1.03 ***	−0.087
	(0.176)	(0.246)	(0.276)	(0.100)
War	−0.293 *	−0.635	0.157	0.698 ***
	(0.163)	(0.226)	(0.224)	(0.289)
New president	0.106	0.416	−1.44 ***	−1.21 ***
	(0.220)	(0.319)	(0.324)	(0.451)
N (Congresses)	18	18	18	18
LR Chi^2	4.04	10.6 *	41.7 ***	33.4 ***
Pseudo R^2	0.0023	0.058	0.193	0.331
Log likelihood	−85.4	−85.1	−87.0	−33.7
Ln(α)	97.1 ***	109.2 ***	85.1 ***	0.33

Note: Dependent variables are the count of executive orders from the 93rd Congress to 110th Congress for: **All** (all executive orders), **Statute** (specific statute and laws generally), **President** (executive authority), **C in C** (commander in chief).
[‡] Models are Poisson models.
[†] Models are negative binomial count models.
*** Indicates statistical significance at $p < 0.01$.
** Indicates statistical significance at $p < 0.05$.
* Indicates statistical significance at $p < 0.10$.
Tests are two-tailed tests.

the honeymoon wears off, presidents later in their terms are more likely to issue a proclamation citing statute. This change amounts to about seven more per year. Presidential activity during this time may reflect the need to work with Congress to facilitate legislation in advance of elections. These trade-offs are found when presidents weigh their strategic options to issue an order or attempt to legislate (Cohen 2012; Dickinson and Gubb 2016). When the country is involved in foreign conflict, the results in Table 4.1 indicate that presidents are less likely to issue proclamations citing statute-based or Constitution-based authority.

In Table 4.2, the results for executive orders further demonstrate that, as expected, there is variation in how and when presidents cite either statute or constitutional sources of authority. The coefficient for the variable that measures Congress's ability to legislate (the *LPPC Ratio*) indicates that presidents issue more orders citing statute-based authority when the ability of Congress to legislate increases. This suggests that presidents are more likely to appeal to Congress when congressional majorities with a shared ideology have a more influential say in the policy-making process. Holding the other variables constant, as Congress's capacity to legislate increases by one standard deviation, the expected number of statute-based orders increases by seven. An increase in Congress's ability to legislate indicates that presidents are less likely to issue constitutional-based orders that cite his or her authority as commander in chief or as president. When the *LPPC Ratio* increases by one standard deviation, the expected number of constitutional-based orders decreases from approximately four to two, holding the other variables constant.

Presidents are generally less likely to cite their authority as the executive or commander in chief in their second terms and in the second half of their first or second terms, contradicting the expectation that presidents are more independent later in their term. Newly elected presidents of a different party than their predecessors are less likely to issue orders citing authority as the executive or commander in chief, reinforcing the expectation that they are more likely to take advantage of the honeymoon by working with Congress instead of acting unilaterally. Presidents are more likely to cite their authority under the commander in chief clause of the Constitution during times of war. This corresponds to Young's (2013) finding that the amount of unilateral activity spikes during wartime.

Another way to examine how presidents change their strategy in citation patterns for executive orders is to examine when presidents cite *both* statute and constitutional sources. When presidents cite both sources of authority, they are making *some* claim of executive authority because they include executive power as part of the justification, but not as much as when citing *only* presidential authority. They are taking more risk than they would be in citing Congress alone. Table 4.3 includes count models for executive orders and policy proclamations orders combined that cite both statute and constitutional sources of authority, using as the unit of analysis. The coefficients for divided government and majority size are negative for each model in Table 4.3. Presidents are less likely to challenge

TABLE 4.3.
Logistic regression models for both sources of authority.

	Model			
	(1) † Executive statute	(2) † Executive statute	(3) ‡ Constitution statute	(4) ‡ Constitution statute
Divided government	−0.364 ** (0.172)	—	0.067 (0.122)	—
Majority party size	—	−0.023 ** (0.013)	—	−0.074 *** (0.010)
Second term	1.59 *** (0.263)	1.31 *** (0.271)	1.43 *** (0.177)	1.03 *** (0.184)
Second half	0.613 *** (0.167)	0.613 *** (0.165)	0.158 (0.119)	0.276 ** (0.123)
War	1.52 *** (0.336)	1.45 *** (0.347)	2.15 *** (0.245)	1.65 *** (0.253)
New president	0.685 *** (0.222)	0.738 *** (0.222)	0.403 *** (0.152)	0.452 *** (0.156)
N (orders)	2,145	2,145	2,145	2,145
LR Chi²	113.8 ***	112.1 ***	257.6 ***	311.4 ***
Pseudo R²	0.089	0.088	0.118	0.142
Log likelihood	−580.2	−581.1	−962.3	−935.4

Note: Models are logistic regression. The dependent variable is proclamations and executive orders for each category from 1974 to 2009.
† (1)(2) are president's executive authority-based and statute-based orders.
‡ (3)(4) are Constitution-based orders and statute-based orders.
*** Indicates statistical significance at $p < 0.01$.
** Indicates statistical significance at $p < 0.05$.
* Indicates statistical significance at $p < 0.10$.
Tests are two-tailed tests.

Congress when they cite both executive and congressional sources of authority along with statutes. Presidents are risk averse in that the inclusion of presidential citation of authority lessens when they face potential rebuke from Congress. For orders that cite statute-based and executive-based authority, presidents will issue two fewer joint orders per session when government is divided and one fewer order as the size of the majority party increases. For orders that cite statute-based and constitution-based authority, presidents will issue one fewer order per session as the size of the majority party increases, but the coefficient for divided government is not statistically significant.

Temporal variables that illustrate the need for the president to act quickly are, as expected, positive and generally statistically significant. For each model, presidents in their second terms, the second half of their terms, or when new to office are more likely to issue orders citing both types of authority. In each case, this amounts to about one more order per year. Periods of war are strong positive predictors of the likelihood of issuing an order citing both types of authority. The latitude presidents have in moments of crisis such as war give them incentives to empower themselves with their own source of authority, presented here as citation of executive or constitutional authority in the order. In second terms and in the second half of their terms, presidents are more risk seeking when including citations of executive authority for fear that the clock will run out on their term in office. When citing both types of authority, presidents are using the belt and suspenders approach, breaking the usual pattern of citing only Congress.

DISCRETION AND THE BOUNDARY
OF UNILATERAL ACTION

Integral to the source of authority cited to justify the president's unilateral order is the extent of authority and discretion delegated by Congress to the president. The delegation of authority is important to consider in the study of unilateral power because it allows for assessment of the distribution of power between the branches. The degree of discretion delegated by Congress has an influence on the president's use of authority (Fenno 1958). Research on unilateral orders tends to focus on when presidents choose to exercise their power *against* the will of agencies and Congress. Unilateral orders have the force of law when issued under authority delegated from Congress, and these powerful presidential directives are seen as an alternative to legislation. Howell (2003) argues that "presidents have always made law without the explicit consent of Congress, sometimes by acting upon general powers delegated to them by different Congresses, past and present, and other times by reading new executive authority into the Constitution itself."[27] Jones (2005) contends that—in a system that separates and shares powers—presidents, Congress, and the Courts often agree on the delegation of power, the appropriate balance of the use of this power, and the duration of that authority. Congress is often overlooked as an actor who participates in the creation and exercise of unilateral power.

When studies aggregate all unilateral orders, they may undercount the degree to which a president works with Congress, making the act of issuing an order a shared, rather than individual action (Johnson, Gibbons, and Gibson 2010). Delegation is generally nested within the principal–agent relationship where principals (Congress) delegate authority to agents (the president or the executive branch) to develop and implement policy (Mitnick 1973, 1975; Waterman and Meier 1998; Bendor and Meirowitz 2004). Under optimal conditions, by delegating its authority to those with knowledge and expertise, Congress reduces high levels of technical uncertainty and information asymmetry; in exchange, it receives enhanced information concerning policy alternatives and outcomes (McCubbins 1985; Gilligan and Krehbiel 1987; Kiewiet and McCubbins 1991; Epstein and O'Halloran 1994; Bawn 1995). Delegation enables Congress to absolve itself of the costs of policy making, which are borne instead by the president and the executive branch.

Congress, though, does not always have perfect knowledge about the partisanship and ideological preferences of the executive branch (Spence 1999). In enacting legislation, the sitting Congress does not have the capacity to foresee the outcomes of future presidential elections or changes in administration (Spence 1999; Bendor and Meirowitz 2004). The costs versus gains of the uncertainty about delegation shape presidential–congressional relations (Polsby 1964). Congress relies on the delegation of broad or narrow authority to ensure that its will is ultimately reflected (Moe 1987). By delegating broadly, members of Congress can claim credit for the benefits of policy outcomes without having to bear the costs because decision making is borne by the president, who has the freedom associated with a unitary actor (Fiorina 1982; Epstein and O'Halloran 1999). Fiorina (1986) refers to this as "shifting responsibility," where Congress delegates policy implementation specifically to the executive either to avoid blame or because of the policy expertise of the executive. It can be a strategic move on the part of Congress to gain an advantage over the executive by giving him or her an opportunity to act as the first mover

(Bendor, Glazer, and Hammond 2001). Mayer (2009) reinforces the role of presidential authority and the likelihood of unilateral action, claiming "broad grants [of authority], ambiguity and the potential for swift action are a compelling combination." Marshall and Pacelle (2005) find that issuance of these orders is best explained by the fact that Congress had already delegated the responsibility to act, suggesting that Congress is relying on the president to act.

After determining the extent of authority to delegate to the president, Congress must identify the type of discretion to be placed on the executive (Krehbiel 1991; Volden 2002; Whittington and Carpenter 2003). Narrowed discretion may confer detailed instructions, which constrain the executive branch to produce policy outcomes consistent with congressional objectives, leaving the executive branch with little room for independent action (Fleishman and Aufses 1976; McCubbins, Noll, and Weingast 1987, 1989; Moe 1990; Bawn 1997). The most common forms imposed within a statute are substantive (or express) limits, ex ante controls, and ex post controls (McCubbins and Page 1987; Epstein and O'Halloran 1999; Huber and Shipan 2002; Moe 2005). Substantive discretionary limits are linked to the level of detail that Congress includes in the statute, specifying the extent and type of action required (Epstein and O'Halloran 1999). Broad or complete discretion occurs with few or no detailed instructions, whereas when Congress includes limits, there is less room for independent action (Huber and Shipan 2002). Ex ante provisions are sometimes referred to as structural controls because they determine the procedures that must be followed by bureaucratic agencies when developing policy. Ex ante constraints can specify how and when the president must seek advice from agencies and input from the public. Ex post measures—a means by which the legislative branch maintains final control over executive decisions—are concerned with the approval of agency policy and, in some cases, presidential decisions. Some ex post controls used to exercise oversight have withstood judicial scrutiny, such as those providing Congress with progress updates and reports and requirements for congressional committee review and approval or authorization of executive action. Others, like the legislative veto—where Congress can overturn the president's order by a one-chamber, joint, or concurrent resolution, post-*Chadha*—have not (Fisher 2005).[28]

MEASURING DISCRETION

Discretion forms the boundary of acceptable (legal) presidential action as presidents rely on statute for the source of authority. Researchers have developed different methods for measuring discretion (Fiorina 1986; McCubbins and Lupia 1994; Epstein and O'Halloran 1999; Huber and Shipan 2002). The two most common forms of discretion are substantive, which measures numerical limits imposed by statute, and procedural, which measures ex ante and ex post controls (Epstein and O'Halloran 1999). For this analysis, the intention was to analyze more fully the type and extent of statutory constraints placed on a president's ability to exercise discretion.[29] The type of discretion is identified first by compiling the relevant provisions in each statute for the executive orders and policy proclamations within the data set. The relevant portions of each statute were obtained from the *U.S. Statutes at Large*. Second, each provision was coded according to three categories of discretion, which include: (1) substantive, (2) ex ante procedural control, and (3) ex post procedural control. Each of these broad categories was defined more narrowly to reflect how discretion is delegated in law.

For substantive discretion, general *substantive* limits are generally placed on the president in three ways. First, the president may be delegated authority that has little to no discretion. The legislation may require only that the president proclaim an act of Congress, as President Dwight D. Eisenhower proclaimed Alaskan statehood in Proclamation 3269 and Hawaiian statehood in Proclamation 3309. Second, the statute may require the president to adhere to a specific numerical limit or guideline that gives the president limited discretion. Presidents are granted the discretion to increase or decrease the level of tariffs under reciprocal trade agreements, but Congress establishes the percentage of change allowed, as well as the procedure that the president must follow. Third, the president may have broad or complete discretion under the law, such as when the president was granted authority under the Antiquities Act to withdraw land from the public domain for the purpose of proclaiming national monuments without any limits placed on executive authority (16 USC § 431–433).

The second category of discretion captures ex ante procedural controls placed on the president. The level of discretion was divided into three types. First, if no controls were imposed, then the president was not subject to a limitation. Second, in limited discretion, Congress frequently recommended (but did not require) that the president consult with an agency prior to issuing an order or proclamation. An example of recommended agency consultation is under Section 22 of the Agriculture Adjustments Act of 1935, where the president was required to consult with the Tariff Commission, but the final decision to make adjustments to import quotas was subject only to presidential discretion. Third, when Congress chose to exert greater control and made consultations mandatory, the president was required to follow the agency's recommendation, as in the escape clause in the Trade Act of 1974 (19 U.S.C. § 2251–2254), which is designed to provide domestic industries with relief from injurious imports. Before taking action, the president must first seek advice from the International Trade Commission, secretary of commerce, and secretary of labor. The third category of discretion captures ex post procedural controls placed on the president. Discretion becomes dichotomous in this category because Congress does or does not retain authority to approve or disapprove (override) each executive action.

Table 4.4 shows the variation in the category and type of discretion between and within the policy areas for the executive orders and policy proclamations in the data set.[30] The results reveal an important and interesting pattern with respect to how unilateral powers can be used. Presidents are granted, and often act in accord with, greater discretion as delegated by Congress. Presidents are afforded a great deal of discretion on public lands and defense and national emergency issues, although Congress is more restrictive (at various points in time) on foreign trade and foreign aid. Presidents have nearly complete discretion with respect to ex post decisions on public lands, meaning Congress has no provision to override the president's decision. Presidents have virtually no restrictions placed on their discretion in the area of social welfare and justice. In the area of trade policy, one implication is that Congress is more likely

TABLE 4.4.
Cross tabulations of type of discretion by policy area, 1974–2009.

	Foreign trade/ aid	National defense/ emergencies	Social welfare/ justice	Governmental relations	Public lands/ resources
Substantive (statutory guidance)					
Narrow discretion (President carries out orders)	1	1	1	5	0
Limited discretion (president follows guidelines but has authority over outcome)	345	15	3	47	9
Broad discretion (president has authority over process)	111	501	210	689	207
Ex ante (agency restrictions)					
No discretion (consultation mandatory)	261	7	0	1	0
Limited discretion (consultation recommended)	64	4	0	2	7
Complete discretion (not subject to limitation)	132	506	214	738	209
Ex post (congressional restrictions)					
No discretion (congressional override allowed)	117	4	0	0	0
Complete discretion (no congressional override)	340	513	214	741	216

Note: Each number represents the number of orders presidents issued under each type of discretion for each order they issued (at the time it was issued) on these policy issues. A single order can be coded into substantive, ex ante, and ex post discretion. See the text for details about coding definitions.

to try to restrain the president before he or she acts, not after. Government management and executive organizational issues fall somewhere in between, with presidents acting with some limited discretion but having more ex ante or ex post discretion. The role of discretion is tested more completely in Chapters Five, Six, and Seven.

DISCRETION AND THE HISTORICAL REACH OF LAW

Do outdated laws create a limit on presidential discretion? One criticism (of many) concerning President Obama's unilateral use of military force in Iraq and Syria in 2015 centered on his reliance on the 2001 Authorization to Use Military Force (AUMF) on al-Qaeda and the 2002 AUMF regarding Iraqi insurgents to wage war against the terrorist group Islamic State (ISIS). In the 2001 AUMF,

The President is authorized to use all necessary and appropriate force against those nations, organizations, or persons he determines planned, authorized, committed, or aided the terrorist attacks that occurred on September 11, 2001, or harbored such organizations or persons, in order to prevent any future acts of international terrorism against the United States by such nations, organizations or persons.[31]

In the 2002 AUMF,

The President is authorized to use the Armed Forces of the United States as he determines to be necessary and appropriate in order to (1) defend the national security of the United States against the continuing threat posed by Iraq; and (2) enforce all relevant United Nations Security Council resolutions regarding Iraq.[32]

President Obama asked Congress in 2015 for new authority authorizing the use of military force against ISIS, which would place strict limits on the types of U.S. ground forces that could be deployed but would keep current ground troops in place and would "sunset" after three years (a clause not present in the 2001 or 2002 AUMFs).[33] At the same time, President Obama sought to repeal the 2001 AUMF.[34] This raises two very important questions regarding the president's discretion. First, do outdated laws provide a boundary on presidential discretion? Second, how far back do presidents go in their search for discretion to exercise unilateral authority?

Presidents in their quest for unilateral authority may rely on the stability of past statutes to unilaterally initiate or tweak current policies. Capturing the historical reach of presidential statutory-based authority

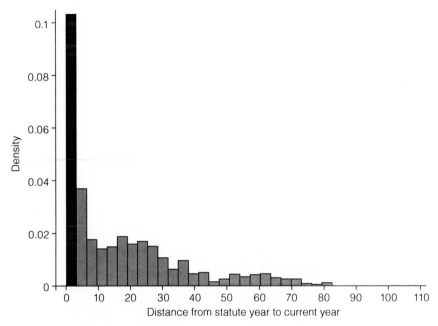

FIGURE 4.4. Histogram of statute enactment and the issuance of orders, 1933–2009. The data collection process is described in the text. Orders include only those citing statute alone.

requires examining the individual orders and the specific citation used to justify them. The data for this examination started with compiling the statutory citations from congressional statute for executive orders and proclamations from 1933 to 2009. The relevant portions of the statues and changes were compiled from the *United States Code* and the *U.S. Statutes at Large*, to ensure that the law was captured as it was for the correct time period. A larger span of time was included to capture the ability of presidents to reach farther back in time. If multiple statutory citations were included in an order, the controlling legal citation that was most central to the function of the order was coded. If the statute was amended, the most recently amended date was used. This process left 2,266 orders for which a year from a statute could be located.[35] The distance between the origin of the statue and the use by the president in an order is graphed in Figure 4.4. Most orders wherein presidents cite a statute as the primary basis of their order are cited in the same year in which they are enacted.

In 251 of the cases, the citation in the order referenced a statute that was passed or amended in the same year; in 656 cases, orders cited statutes that were within two years of the enactment of the legislation. Presidents do reach back to cite statutes that are years and sometimes decades old. In 44 percent of the cases, presidents cite statutes that are between ten and sixty years old. They rarely cite statutes that are more than eighty years old, with the exception of eleven cases.

Presidents reach back in law for a source of authority that suggests that they are more likely to seek a broad delegation of discretion. Given broad authority and the political disadvantage posed to the White House from the potential for greater political friction and less opportunity to achieve legislative victory, presidents should be more likely to rely on broad authority for issuing a unilateral order. To test this expectation, a dependent variable was created to operationalize the delegation of broad and narrow discretion in law. The variable *Discretion* is coded 1 when the president was granted broad substantive discretion and 0 otherwise. The data set is limited to only those cases where presidents cited statute. The key independent variable is the distance in years (*Distance*) from when Congress authorized a statute to when the president cited it in a unilateral order. A second independent variable is divided government (*Divided*), which indicates when government is divided between the branches or within Congress. The distance variable is interacted with divided government (*Distance*Divided*) to determine whether the president alters his strategy based on possible friction from Congress. A logistic regression model is used to conduct the analysis.[36] The results of the regression analysis are shown in Figure 4.5.

The results show that even though presidents do reach back into time for their authority, they are less likely to seek laws that provide for the exercise of broad discretion. As a stand-alone variable, the distance in years from the original statute date to the unilateral order issuance has a 72 percent reduction in the discretion employed by presidents. This suggests that presidents rarely use greater discretionary authority for statutes that reach back in history. In other words, as statutes age, presidents rely on them less for their discretionary authority. Divided government by itself has only a small positive statistically significant effect on the president's

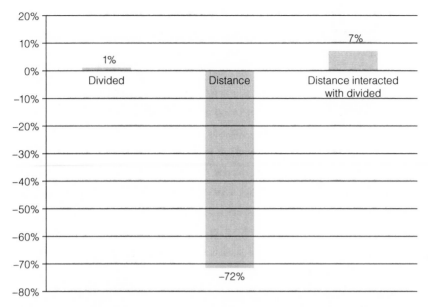

FIGURE 4.5. Predicted probabilities for the use of discretion in the historical reach of law. The dichotomous dependent variable is coded 1 if broad substantive discretion was used and 0 otherwise. "Distance" is measured as the number of years from the year in which the statute was authorized to the time the order that used that statute was issued. Predicted probabilities for logistic regression model were created holding all other variables at their mean.

use of greater discretion in a unilateral order. The effect is substantively rather small at a 1 percent increase. Yet, as statutes age, presidents are somewhat more likely to cite older statutes that rely on substantive discretion when government is divided. Presidents are 7 percent more likely to issue orders with substantive discretion when government is divided and the date of the original statute is further back in time. The pressure to act for presidents and the inability to get Congress to update or amend new statutes to give presidents more authority to act may lead to the executive branch reaching to justify their current actions as they search for legal standards to meet current policy needs.

CONCLUSION

The reach of presidential unilateral power is expansive but has clear limitations. The merging of authority between the legislative and executive branches creates confusion and complications. Congress is not merely a backstop to the president's exercise of authority. A key variable in explaining unilateral action is the source of authority presidents use to justify their actions. The ways that presidents justify their actions materially matters to explaining unilateral orders. Presidents are both strategic actors and participants in politically integrated activities with Congress. Unilateral orders are not uniformly used for one selective purpose or the other, nor are all orders dictated by the same type of political events—presidents vary their strategy depending on the nature of the political environment they face. These concerns are not strictly political in origin but are a meaningful combination of the institutional conditions presidents face and the authority with which they have to act (see Mayer 2009). This realization formalizes one of the legal and political building blocks necessary for the study of unilateral orders.

Acknowledging the role of delegation and discretion is another step toward sorting out the competing explanations that have characterized the president's dual nature. First, there is variation in the institutional conditions under which these are used, based on the source of authority. Presidents vary their strategy to act using unique types of authority based on the size and strength of Congress and on their own strategic need to act. Second, scholars have suggested that presidents act out of fear of Congress and in anticipation of interbranch sanction (see Deering and Maltzman 1999; Howell 2003). This is correct, but presidents are not always adversarial with Congress. They are not simply looking for ways to evade Congress; they are, in some instances, looking for ways to potentially work in tandem with Congress, especially when they cite statute as a means to implement orders or pursue jointly agreed-on action. Presidents do rely on their own authority to act in circumstances when they are political disadvantaged. They think politically, even when they are acting alone. The authority of the president (via the Constitution) is constantly changing through this and other political conflicts and constitutional contestations (Kleinerman 2009).

Although presidents act "first and alone" and cause the other players in the system to react, other actors significantly shape the process of when and under what conditions presidents issue unilateral orders prior to the issue being ordered. The reality is often more detailed than can be explained by the mere presence of a unilateral order. The type and extent of delegated authority has an influence on the way in which presidents use unilateral orders. Presidents often invoke statute or the Constitution when issuing unilateral orders. Governing this variation is the range and scope of the powers Congress delegates to the president. His or her powers change with respect to the willingness of Congress to provide the president with that power (Epstein and O'Halloran 1994). As Kiewiet and McCubbins (1991) note, "Principals can be highly successful in using delegation to pursue their interests, yet appear passive and ineffectual, relative to their agents." Reaffirming the work of Jones (2005), presidents and Congress often agree on a delegation of power, the appropriate balance of the use of this power, and the duration of that authority in a system that separates shared powers.

This is a first step in approaching unilateral orders from a different vantage point, although it reveals much about how presidents understand their power, the role of Congress, and how the branches distribute and share power. This helps to unravel our assumptions about the president's dual roles and unilateral orders. At a minimum, presidents are strategic in the way they cast their power. At a maximum, a linked interbranch process is the trigger. Through Congress's delegation of power, unilateral orders are often simply the lynchpin that initiates a previously agreed-on arrangement. This is not to suggest that unilateral orders are always issued with Congress's interest or consent. Presidents are able to act as *independents*, using their own authority to leverage their information and first-mover advantages. As *administrators*, presidents may work jointly with Congress to carry out legislation and the execution of policy.

CHAPTER FIVE

An Independent President or Administrator?
Command and Routine Orders

A TENSION HAS HISTORICALLY WEIGHED on the president's dual nature. Presidents must balance the need to aggressively push their agenda with the challenge of executing the routine affairs of government without riling up Congressional opposition. The hallmark of *independent* presidents is the ability to issue unilateral orders to set the agenda, thereby shifting policy to their preferences before legislation has been introduced in Congress. The capacity to act with dispatch gives presidents a significant advantage over Congress early in the policy-making process. Mayer (2001) notes, "The president's ability to move first, combined with Congress's relative inability to respond effectively, tilted competition in favor of the executive." Presidents, though, must balance acting first and alone at this stage in the policy-making process, with the other facet of power that is more mundane. An *administrator* president, on the other hand, is charged with ensuring the wheels of government are kept well oiled and turning. A significant enthusiast of presidential power, Clinton Rossiter (1960), noted that both the Constitution and Congress have "recognized his [the president's] authority to supervise the day-to-day activities of the executive branch." These two roles are reflected in the unilateral orders they issue.

The *independent* president's unilateral order may notably resemble a command for executive branch action, as did the executive orders President Obama issued to fulfill his campaign promise to the electorate to close the base at Guantanamo Bay. In 2007, Barack Obama promised, "As president, I will close Guantanamo, reject the Military Commissions Act, and adhere to the Geneva Conventions. Our Constitution and our Uniform Code of Military Justice provide a framework for dealing with the terrorists."[1] Immediately after his inauguration, the newly elected president issued three executive orders in quick succession: ensuring lawful interrogations, establishing procedures for effectuating the disposition of detainees and closure of Guantanamo Bay, and creating an interagency task force on the disposition of detainees.[2] Chastising the prior administration for its reckless military actions, which undermined the integrity of ethical military conduct, the incoming president acted quickly and with determination. Rather than share power with Congress or wait for Congress to act, President Obama took the view that executive authority resided with him and he did not need the consent of Congress to act. President Obama's executive orders to close Guantanamo show an *independent* president, a "unitary" actor for whom all executive capacity should be instilled (see Calabresi and Yoo 2008). Presidents set the tone of the discussion or agenda to enact incremental change on an issue or to prime the public for action on the issue. In one respect, these are the most worrisome types of presidential orders because the power of the executive seems virtually unrestrained.

Yet, the least worrisome but programmatically essential unilateral orders are issued by presidents acting as *administrators*. Unilateral action in this context can appear almost circumspect. Many routine orders enact jointly agreed-on law without fanfare or interbranch skirmishes. Warber (2006) argues that executive orders are used "to implement routine, bureaucratic matter or to accomplish symbolic acts"; between half and one-third of all executive orders since President Nixon have been routine. Mayer (2001) finds that the categories of executive branch administration and civil service executive orders, or routine orders, account for about half of all orders issued. Light (1999) notes that "the executive option is generally reserved for routine decisions; it is not perceived as a suitable alternative for major initiatives." These routine orders are banal, the argument goes, because they are not significant enough to alter the balance of power or determine the extent of policy-making advantages for one branch or the other. Consider President Obama's commitment to the Gulf Coast recovery after Hurricanes Katrina and Rita. Although the Office of the Federal Coordinator for Gulf Coast Rebuilding was established under President George W. Bush in Executive Order 13390, President Obama extended the office's life twice before shutting its doors permanently in March 2010. In Executive Order 13504, Obama extended the work of the Coordinator of Federal Support for the Recovery and Rebuilding of the Gulf Coast Region from February 28, 2009, to September 30, 2009, and, in Executive Order 13512, from September 30, 2009, until April 1, 2010. When the office closed in March 2010, even Sen. Mary Landrieu (D-LA) agreed, "It is no longer necessary to continue the Office of Gulf Coast Rebuilding."[3] President Obama's two orders were routine actions that continued the aid and resources of the federal government to those in need, but they did not change the balance of power or create a policy-making advantage for the executive branch.

Presidents do, however, have a great deal of control and influence over the executive branch, and an active administration can transform routine unilateral action into something more substantive (Rudalevige 2012). Neustadt notes (1990) that "the transformation of his routine obligations testifies to their dependence on an active White House." Mayer (2001) argues that "even purely administrative decisions can have dramatic effects on the public," and this type of unilateral control by the president "reaches far beyond agency boundaries." For example, President Obama issued two executive orders to expand the membership of the National Economic Council and the Domestic Policy Council.[4] A change in the number and expertise of persons within a president's advisory councils can appear to be simply a routine matter, but it is important to the administration of the president's inner circle. Presidents can gain expertise and policy acceptance as the White House navigates the policy process. The day-to-day functionality of these orders illustrates the separation of powers in practice.

The two executives are at work when using direct action. Depending on their political circumstances and structured policy needs, presidents seek to pursue one of their two facets of power. Presidents exercise direct action when Congress is uninvolved in the issue or before legislation has been introduced. Presidents can initiate their policy goals from their stated political agenda in a unilateral fashion or jointly manage the affairs of government. Because Congress is more malleable on the issue, presidents work with a more or less willing Congress. The puzzle is to determine when this duality is reflected in the routine or command unilateral orders the president issues.

THE TWO EXECUTIVES

Reaching back to the example of George Washington, although the first president "respected the separate powers allocated to each branch," he nonetheless "assertively exercises his clearly executive powers" (Cronin 1989). Thomas Jefferson, who violated his own principle that "the execution of the laws is more important than the making of them" (Bailey 2007), negotiated the purchase of the land that became known as the Louisiana Purchase largely without Congress. Jefferson was reluctant to prioritize presidential power in this way, but he recognized the need for a strong and unified executive (Goldsmith 1974; Balleck 1992). The history of the development of presidential institutional power is in part due to the executive's ability to use autonomous policy innovation, where "independence of action" is valued by the design of the Constitution (Whittington and Carpenter 2003).

Attempting to bridge the gap between their formal power and expected action, presidents have historically realized the limitations of their own power and the advantages of administrative power. Moe (1985) argues that, with greater expectations to create, interpret, administer, and modify public policy, "the modern president is driven by these formidable expectations to seek control over the structures and processes of government." Presidents accomplish this by looking at the corpus of statutory work, resolving conflicts by balancing any competing requirements, and exercising discretion as a way to impose their own priorities on government (Moe and Wilson 1994). James (2009) argues that use of unilateral powers to centralize authority is at the heart of the "administrative presidency" and that the question concerning the president's dual role as "executive" traces back to the founders:

Faithfulness to what: the statutory letter of the law, the best interests of the nation, or the higher law obligations enshrined in the Constitution? Faithfulness to whom: the intent of the originating Congress, the political sentiment of the current Congress, the judgment of experienced bureaucratic experts, the current climate of public opinion, or the mandate of the last presidential election? And what about the president's own conscience and discretionary judgment as an elected leader responsible to the nation at large?

The expansion of administrative authority puts the presidency, or more specifically the president, at the center of the administrative state (Moe 1985; Weko 1995).

Looking at the duality of the executive, *independent* presidents are proactive agents who are supposed to design and initiate public policy. In the *Federalist Papers*, Alexander Hamilton favored a strong executive and wrote in *Federalist* 70 that "energy in the executive" is critical to good government (see Laski 1940). He wrote that "decision, activity, secrecy and dispatch" are key to how a president should act to festoon the working of good government. In terms of policy making, Corwin (1957) noted, "By virtue of his duty to inform Congress as to the State of the Union the President himself participates in legislative power." Presidents are authorized in Article II to recommend measures to Congress that the president "shall judge necessary and expedient." There is sufficient room for the constitutional role of *administrator* presidents. In Rossiter's (1960) view, because issues of public policy are too complex for Congress to handle, "The president alone is in a political, constitutional and practical position to provide such leadership, and he is therefore expected, within the limits of constitutional and political propriety, to guide Congress in much of its lawmaking activity."

INDEPENDENCE AND COMMAND OR *ADMINISTRATOR* AND ROUTINE

As the preceding examples make clear, presidents can act with two types of orders in this phase of the policy process. *Administrator* presidents issue *routine* orders to manage the affairs of government rather than pursue topics on their agenda. Following Warber's definition (2006), routine orders may be used for "updating the specific wording within an existing directive, providing new guidelines for retirement or financial benefits for federal employees, or closing down the federal government during a holiday." Routine executive orders are also used to confirm changes to reconcile retirement and disability within the various federal agencies.[5] For instance, they are issued to manage personnel schedules as President Clinton did by issuing Executive Order 13068, excusing executive department and agency employees from work for the days before and after

Christmas Day, and as President George W. Bush did by issuing Executive Order 13343 giving employees of "executive departments, independent establishment and other government agencies" the day off to mark respect for the death of Ronald Reagan.

A primary distinguishing characteristic of routine orders is that presidents fulfill their duties as part of a shared system of power. The president may rely on authority delegated by a prior Congress to execute managerial functions, such as the awarding of various military awards or military officer promotions. Similarly, the president has been granted emergency powers to help settle labor disputes that routinely occur.[6] Presidents are expected to address fluctuations in the demand and supply of imports and exports under authority granted by Congress. Members of Congress rely on the executive branch to take action, but the decision to act is not the president's alone. Congress imposes ex ante procedural and substantive constraints on the president's discretionary authority in the majority of laws governing trade policy (see Chapter Four).

For instance, the process for deciding whether to adjust the quantity of a specific product involves consultation among several agencies and an investigation into unfair trade practices by the U.S. International Trade Commission (USITC). Presidents can follow the recommendation of the USITC or deviate from it if they determine it is not in the national economic interest.[7] In 1978, the USITC was conducting an investigation into whether foreign imports of clothespins were causing an injury to the domestic industry.[8] The topic was not part of President Carter's policy agenda, but he had to decide whether to adjust quotas as a means of import relief. After President Carter received a report and recommendation from the USITC, he consulted with the Departments of Commerce and Labor and decided to take a less restrictive approach. In February 1979, Carter issued Proclamation 4640, granting a temporary quantitative limitation on plastic and wooden clothespins and, as required by the Trade Act of 1974, transmitted his decision to both chambers of Congress the same day.

On the other side of the spectrum, *independent* presidents issue *command* orders, a term that refers not to the president's authority as commander in chief but to the use of unilateral action to execute his or her policy agenda. Specifically, these orders may be used to signal Congress or the public about the president's commitment to a larger initiative. In 1999, trade expansion was a priority for President Clinton. The House and Senate were holding hearings to consider trade priorities, trade expansionism, and the need for increasing the president's authority to respond more effectively to foreign protectionism, in anticipation of the administration's participation in the upcoming World Trade Organization (WTO) meeting.[9] Ambassador Charlene Barshefsky was scheduled to chair the WTO meeting, and, shortly before she left the United States, President Clinton issued Executive Order 13116, committing the administration to an annual review of its trade expansion priorities, monitoring of compliance with U.S. trade agreements and specific enforcement actions to protect U.S. rights under those agreements.[10]

Orders that command can be used to centralize power in the White House, especially when they serve as an extension of the president's agenda. Centralizing efforts across the executive branch provides for greater legislative success, making this effort a major payoff for presidents when navigating the political process (Rudalevige 2005a). A foremost and infamous example of this type of command is President Reagan's Executive Order 12291, which further centralized control over regulatory initiatives within the OMB, requiring executive departments and agencies to gain clearance from OMB regarding congruency with White House initiatives. This executive order made sure that government regulations were consistent with the president's political promises and philosophy but allowed for greater centralized executive control over proposed future regulations (Nathan 1983). This accomplished twin objectives for the president: to streamline government and to centralize political power in the White House.

Command orders are also used to implement the president's foreign policy agenda. In 1982, President Reagan issued a policy proclamation to address the actions by the military dictatorship in power in Poland that had declared "Solidarity," the organization of the working class of Poland, illegal. The topic was important enough to President Reagan that he discussed it in his State of the Union Address, a news conference, a statement on the situation in Poland, and a radio address to the nation on "Solidarity and United States Relations with Poland." In the radio address Reagan remarked, "Yes, I know Poland is a faraway country in

Eastern Europe. Still, this action is a matter of profound concern to all the American people and to the free world." President Reagan's Proclamation 4990 restricted U.S. trade with Poland's martial law government by suspending the country's most-favored-nation status.[11]

Presidents also use command orders concerning issues of national security and national emergencies. In 1975, President Ford responded to the Middle East oil embargo by placing a fee on imported oil, which increased the revenue derived from custom collections. The administration argued that "a 'fee' on imported materials need not be legislated," and the Supreme Court agreed.[12] President Reagan faced the unanticipated refusal of Fidel Castro to honor a 1984 immigration agreement with the United States, after Voice of America's Radio Marti began broadcasting to Cuba.[13] In a plea to the nation not to become complacent and to increase funding levels for national security, President Reagan noted that "the only guarantee of peace and freedom is our military strength and our national will. The peoples of Afghanistan and Poland, of Czechoslovakia and Cuba, and so many other captive countries—they understand this."[14] Reagan was resolved to continue radio broadcasts to Cuba as a way of allowing democracy to reach the country's citizens (Walsh 2012). Rather than end the broadcasts, in response to Castro's actions, President Reagan issued Proclamation 5517, suspending immigration from Cuba "disrupting normal migration procedures between the two countries."[15] Presidents similarly use command orders to implement sanctions during national emergencies, as President Carter did with Iran over the Iranian hostage crisis, President Reagan during the Nicaraguan conflict, and President Clinton during the crisis in Haiti.[16]

ROUTINE AND COMMAND ORDERS OVER TIME

Figure 5.1 charts the individual instances of the use of command and routine orders over time by individual presidents. Presidents serving about the same number of terms appear to issue approximately the same number of total orders using direct action over time. Two-term presidents like Reagan, Clinton, and George W. Bush each issued about 300 orders, with Clinton and Bush using 307 and 309 respectively. One-term presidents like Ford, Carter, and George H. W. Bush used between 150 and 200 such orders.

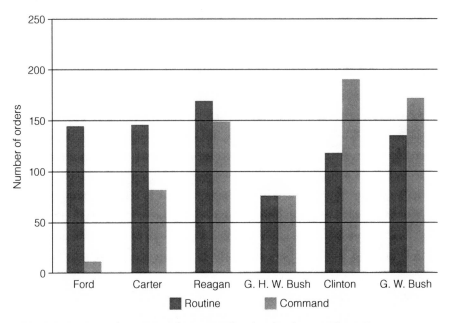

FIGURE 5.1. Use of routine and command orders by the president. Figures represent total orders in categories of routine and command by the president. Definitions are available in the text.

The number of orders Presidents Ford and Bush issued differed by only three orders. One implication to this commonality is that all presidents appear to have a consistent need to use their unilateral power to exercise executive control and maintenance of government. Given that the orders in this category are the most frequently used, this stage is the most important for study of the use of unilateral power.

Although the number of orders issued by presidents during the direct action phase is similar, the use of command or routine orders is distinct. Command orders tend to be more frequently used in eras where Congress is institutionally stronger than the president, often when the branches are divided but also when the parties are heterogeneous and less presidential influence is possible in a divided party. This effect is most apparent in the number of command orders President Ford issued. During his administration, a Republican president faced off against Democratic control of both chambers. President Ford's power was challenged as well by a resurgent

Congress following the resignation of Nixon (Calabresi and Yoo 2008). His journey began as a House minority leader, moving next to vice president, and then president. But even after assuming office, Ford remained committed to working with Congress. In his first address to Congress, President Ford remarked:

Minutes after I took the Presidential oath, the joint leadership of Congress told me at the White House they would go more than halfway to meet me. This was confirmed in your unanimous concurrent resolution of cooperation, for which I am deeply grateful. If, for my part, I go more than halfway to meet the Congress, maybe we can find a much larger area of national agreement.[17]

President Carter had the benefit of a unified government but did not offset the institutional strength of Congress or the friction found within his own party. He issued fewer command orders than later presidents, in part because he had to be wary of a Congress committed to checking the leanings of a too powerful president (Sundquist 1981). President George H. W. Bush, too, issued fewer command orders than his successors. He served in a moment when Congress was resurgent, following several Reagan administration scandals and a backlash against strong executive power from a Democratic-controlled legislature. President Bush, however, is an outlier, not only for the low number of command orders but for his patrician insistence on working closely with Congress to find common ground on legislation. He remarked in his 1989 inaugural address:

To my friends—and yes, I do mean friends—in the loyal opposition—and yes, I do mean loyal: I put out my hand. I am putting out my hand to you, Mr. Speaker. I am putting out my hand to you, Mr. Majority Leader. For this is the thing: this is the age of the offered hand. And we can't turn back clocks, and I don't want to. But when our fathers were young, Mr. Speaker, our differences ended at the water's edge. And we don't wish to turn back time, but when our mothers were young, Mr. Majority Leader, the Congress and the Executive were capable of working together to produce a budget on which this nation could live. Let us negotiate soon and hard. But in the end, let us produce.[18]

The use of command orders is, with the exception of the George H. W. Bush years, linear in use—presidents use these orders more prominently over time. As presidential power swelled during the Reagan, Clinton, and George W. Bush eras, so too did the use of command orders. Perhaps, not surprisingly, the use of command orders appears to be highest when government is divided. This is especially true for President Reagan, who issued 149 command orders, and President Clinton, who issued 191, making the most frequent use of these orders.

EXPECTATIONS FOR COMMAND ORDERS IN DIRECT ACTION

The expectations from Chapter Two contend that the president commands when he or she acts first by setting policy unilaterally before Congress takes action on legislation. The advantage for the president is that he or she does not have to share power by negotiating and compromising with Congress. In the direct action phase, the battle for agenda control means that the president acts before legislation is introduced. But presidents can anticipate legislation by acting first when the topic of their unilateral order relates to the subject of committee and subcommittee hearings in the current session or the content of bills from the prior session. In both cases, the president wants to set policy before Congress does. The length of the president's term in office is likely to influence his or her unilateral action. Presidents are more likely to act with greater independence as they lose the capacity to negotiate with Congress later in their second term or the second half of their first terms. The source of authority presidents cite in their orders to justify their action will influence *when* presidents issue orders that command. Specifically, the president is more likely to rely on the Constitution for issuing a command order because he or she is acting more clearly under his or her own prerogative. Similarly, presidents acting with greater discretion should yield a higher probability of a command order.

Gridlock within Congress and between the branches will influence presidents when deciding whether to work alone or with Congress. In general, presidents are more likely to issue command orders when they are more at odds with Congress, specifically when the ideological distance is greater between the president and key members in the House and Senate. They are also likely to take advantage of conflict *within* Congress by issuing more command orders when Congress is weaker and less able to act. Congress will be weaker when there is greater ideological distance between the most liberal and conservative members within each of the parties, within one party, or with greater ideological distance between the medians between the parties, which will cause party members to disagree among themselves. As a result, a party is less able to reach an agreement within the party and or between the parties. Congress is weaker when parties are polarized in this manner, and presidents should issue more command orders when they want to act with dispatch and Congress is less able to legislate.

DATA AND METHODS

Scholars generally classify all unilateral orders as direct action because the president is acting alone without Congress. The majority of unilateral actions are argued to consist of routine orders used to execute the president's administrative duties (Schramm 1981; Warber 2006). But within the context of our conceptualization of the shared unilateral process, direct action means presidents issue unilateral orders before legislation has been introduced but the issue is under discussion in committee and subcommittee hearings or was on the prior Congress' legislative agenda. Using direct action, presidents may issue command orders to fulfill their promises or priorities before Congress can take action on legislation. The topic of a command order is not yet on Congress's agenda, but it is on the president's agenda, which means he or she discussed it in a message, statement, speech, or public address. The topics of routine orders are not on the president's agenda.

Presidents *command* when they act first by setting policy unilaterally before Congress can act. The advantage to presidents is that, while the topic is on their agenda, they do not necessarily share power with Congress. The topic of a unilateral order may have been a topic of a congressional committee hearing unrelated to legislation in the current legislative session (*Congressional Hearing*) or the subject of a bill on Congress's agenda in the prior session (*Prior Congressional Agenda*).[19] *Routine* orders are not on the president's current political agenda but may also be the topic of congressional hearings or legislation from the prior session.

To operationalize direct action (*Direct Action*), a binary categorical dependent variable was created and coded 1 for commands and 0 for routine orders, which is the base case.

Several presidency-centered variables are included because the president has some degree of control over the timing of an order with respect to political or temporal conditions. First, "*Second Half*" is coded as the second half of a president's term (either first or second term). Second, "*Second Term*" is coded as the second term for a president (the data include Presidents Reagan, Clinton, and George W. Bush as second-term presidents). *Second Half* and *Second Term* are interacted to form a variable that operationalizes the lame duck presidency (*Second Half, Second Term*). Third, "*Election Year*" is coded as any full year in which there is a presidential election. Two variables are included to operationalize the source of authority that presidents cite in their orders to justify their action. A binary categorical variable (*Statutory Authority*) measures when an order cites a statute, and a binary categorical variable (*Constitutional Authority*) measures when an order cites the president's constitutional authority. A binary categorical variable is included as a dichotomous measure of the president's broad substantive discretion (*Substantive Discretion*).

Several explanatory variables are included to operationalize the degree of conflict between the branches and within Congress.[20] First, *intrabranch* gridlock, or the measure of disagreement *between* and *within* the parties for each chamber, is operationalized in two ways. Partisan polarization measures the distance in ideology *between* the two political parties in the House and Senate. Polarization is a shorthand way of determining how likely it is that the parties in Congress can get along well enough to pass legislation; greater polarization implies less cooperation, whereas less polarization implies more potential cooperation. Two variables (*Party Polarization House/Senate*) were created by calculating the absolute value of the difference of the CS-NOMINATE scores for the median member of each party, for both the House and Senate (Poole and Rosenthal 1991, 1997; McCarthy and Poole 1995). Two variables (*Party Heterogeneity House/Senate*) were created to measure the ideological distance *within* each party in each chamber by calculating the absolute value of the difference between the CS-NOMINATE scores for the extreme members (most conservative member and most liberal member) within each party for both the House and Senate.

Second, *interbranch* gridlock between the president and Congress is operationalized in three ways. Two variables are created to measure the ideological distance between the president and the median member of each chamber (*Distance between House/Senate Median and President*). These are created by calculating the absolute value of the difference in the CS-NOMINATE scores for the president and the median member in each chamber (see Deering and Maltzman 1999). The size of the majority party is operationalized by using a continuous variable of the total number of seats held by the majority party in the House and Senate (*Majority Party House/Senate*). The third variable measures the ideological distance between the president and the Senate filibuster pivot (*Distance between Filibuster and President*). The variable is created by sorting each senator within each session using the CS-NOMINATE scores and calculating the absolute value of the difference in the CS-NOMINATE scores for the president and the filibuster pivot.

Because the dependent variable is a binary categorical one, a series of logistic regression models, a generalized linear model for a binomial regression, are used to test the hypotheses.[21] This method allows us to predict a binary probabilistic response from a dichotomous variable based on the predictor (independent) variables. Because the estimated parameters from the equation do not directly provide useful information, the marginal change is used to estimate the effect and relative importance of each coefficient (Long and Freese 2006).

WHEN PRESIDENTS ISSUE ROUTINE AND COMMAND ORDERS

Presidents issue more routine orders than commands, which suggests that they act more often as *administrators* rather than *independents*, yet it is instructive to learn when presidents act more independently in this phase of the process. The dependent variable is coded to explain when presidents are more likely to act as independents. A positive coefficient indicates they are more likely to issue a command order, whereas a negative coefficient indicates they are less likely to issue a command and, instead, act consistently with the base case, which includes routine orders.[22] The results in Table 5.1 show four models to estimate the effect of the institutional and temporal variables on the use of command or routine unilateral orders. In each of the four models, presidents are more than 60 percent likely to issue a command order when it relates to the subject of a current congressional hearing. This suggests that presidents use information from congressional hearings to act first to adopt policy in which Congress has an interest.

For instance, one of President Clinton's campaign promises (and a topic on the 1992 Democratic Party platform) was to reduce the activities and actions that contributed to ozone depletion and, on a larger scale, to address global warming. Congress was also interested in the topic of ozone depletion and global warming. On March 10, 1993, the House Committee on Energy and Commerce's Subcommittee on Energy and Power held a hearing on global warming to listen to the administration's views.[23] Later that month, the House Committee on Science, Space and Technology Subcommittee on Space held a hearing to address the Global Change Research Program (USGCRP).[24] President Clinton, aware of Congress's interest in the issue, was able to act first to implement a policy goal on his agenda. On April 21, 1993—Earth Day—President Clinton announced and signed three executive orders signifying his commitment to energy conservation and combating global warming by establishing procurement standards within the executive branch of ozone-depleting chemicals, alternatively fueled vehicles, energy-efficient computers, and computer equipment.[25]

Presidents are more likely to issue a command order when the topic was on Congress's prior legislative agenda. Column 4 in Table 5.1 shows that presidents are more than 32 percent likely to issue a command order when the topic relates to legislation on Congress's agenda from the prior session. The president may anticipate that, because Congress considered the issue in the prior session and it was not adopted into law, members will introduce it again. Congress may or may not approach the issue in line with the president's preferences. To guarantee that policy will reflect his or her position, the president acts first. During the last half of President Reagan's first term in office, Congress was considering regulatory

TABLE 5.1.
Issuing routine and command orders: Institutional measures

	Statutory authority	Constitutional authority	Substantive discretion	Prior congressional agenda
Second term	0.240 (0.223)	−0.065 (0.224)	0.250 (0.225)	0.352 (0.228)
Second half	0.754 *** (0.181) [18.6%]	0.570 *** (0.185) [14.0%]	0.798 *** (0.182) [6.2%]	0.800 *** (0.187) [8.7%]
Election year	−0.715 *** (0.195) [−17.3%]	−0.625 *** (0.201) [−15.0%]	−0.726 *** (0.197) [−17.6%]	−0.594 *** (0.202) [−14.5%]
Second half, second term	−0.154 (0.304)	−0.055 (0.306)	−0.206 (0.314)	−0.206 (0.314)
Congressional hearings	3.13 *** (0.154) [64.2%]	3.00 *** (0.158) [62.9%]	3.15 *** (0.156) [64.5%]	1.39 *** (0.165) [61.8%]
Statutory authority	−0.530 ** (0.272) [−13.1%]	—	—	—
Constitutional authority	—	1.99 *** (0.263) [40.2%]	—	—
Substantive discretion	—	—	0.793 *** (0.173) [19.8%]	—
Prior congressional agenda	—	—	—	1.39 *** (0.165) [32.8%]
N	1,468	1,468	1,468	1,468
Pseudo R²	0.305	0.341	0.314	0.340
Log-likelihood	−703.8	−667.0	−694.6	−668.8
Likelihood ratio χ²	619.5 ***	693.0 ***	637.0 ***	689.5 ***
Reduction in error	57.2%	57.9%	57.2%	60.2%

Note: Dependent variable: Presidents issue a command order (dichotomous).
*** Indicates statistical significance at $p < 0.01$.
** $p < 0.05$.
* $p < 0.10$.
Standard errors are in parentheses. The percentage of expected change is in brackets (holding all other variables at their mean). Tests are two-tailed tests.

reform legislation to provide for more advance notice and transparency in rulemaking.[26] After being elected to a second term in office, President Reagan acted quickly on the topic by issuing Executive Order 12498 to address the regulatory planning process before Congress could introduce legislation. [27] The president anticipated the reintroduction of regulatory reform legislation from the prior session and incorporated some of Congress's objectives directing agencies to prepare a yearly agenda containing all contemplated regulatory actions for the coming year (Mayer 2001).[28]

Two of the temporal variables—election year and second half—in Table 5.1 are particularly noteworthy in all four models. Presidents are more likely to issue a command order in the second half of their terms (either first or second terms), suggesting that presidents act with some urgency in these moments as expected. However, the joint effect of a president's second half and second term is not statistically significant in any of the models, nor is the effect of the president's second term. Presidents are also less likely to issue a command order in election years, contradicting expectations. They may want to act presidential in election years but clearly find other ways to demonstrate this rather than issuing a command. These temporal findings are as curious for what they show as for what they do not show. Although presidents are expected to act presidential, or with greater dispatch, in times when they are in greater need for expedient action, these findings suggest that this is not always the case. Presidents are more likely to issue a command order when it is late in their terms, or when Congress has failed to act in past legislative sessions on their political agenda. For instance, in 2014, President Obama, serving in the latter half of his second term, faced an opposition Congress who had failed to pass climate legislation in the prior legislative session (Baker and Davenport 2014).[29] Rather than wait for a second chance at legislation, in the second half of his second term President Obama acted quickly, issuing Executive Order 13689 to enhance national climate protection efforts in the Arctic because "over the past 60 years, climate change has caused the Alaskan Arctic to warm twice as rapidly as the rest of the United States, and will continue to transform the Arctic as its consequences grow more severe."

In a unilateral order, citations to the source of authority are revealing. The first three models in Table 5.1 examine the source of authority the president cites to justify the order and the amount of discretion Congress has delegated to them on that issue. The marginal effect of the coefficient for the statutory source of authority, which is negative and statistically significant, indicates that presidents are 13 percent less likely to cite a specific statutory basis of authority when they issue command orders. This suggests that presidents are more likely to cite statutory authority when they issue routine orders. However, when the source of authority cited is constitutional, presidents are more likely to issue (40 percent more) a command order. Given the nature of the command orders, this is logical. Because these orders are commonly used to subsidize executive power, presidents rely on an internal source of authority to justify their actions. This conforms to expectations that presidents, when issuing command orders, are generally fulfilling their role as autonomous executive agents. They are less concerned with accommodating Congress, at least with respect to justifying their authority on an order. That is, when presidents go alone and issue command orders as part of their political agenda, they are less likely to involve Congress, at least in the text of the order. This corresponds to the findings from Chapter Four and other work that suggests that presidents are less likely to cite congressional authority when they have a political incentive to avoid entangling Congress (Bailey and Rottinghaus 2013).

The third model in Table 5.1 considers the effect of delegated discretion on the president's decision to issue a "command" order. In general, greater substantive discretion leads to a greater probability (about 20 percent more likely) that presidents will issue a command order. With broader discretion, the president has the added authority to act in ways that may deviate from legislative intent. For instance, in Executive Order 13689, President Obama not only relies on "the authority vested in me as President by the Constitution and the laws of the United States of America"; he states that his authority includes the duty "to prepare the Nation for a changing Arctic and enhance coordination of national efforts in the Arctic." President Obama's command order is consistent with the theory and findings from the aggregate models. President George H. W. Bush also exercised his broad presidential discretion when ordering the selected reserve of the Armed Forces to active duty in Iraq following the invasion of Kuwait.[30] The conflict was the topic of committee hearings in both chambers of Congress regarding the emergency and necessary

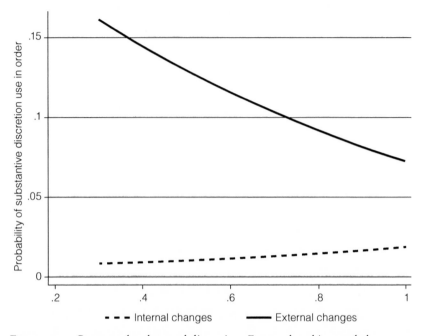

FIGURE 5.2. Command orders and discretion: External and internal changes. Dependent variable: The dichotomous variable is coded 1 if discretion was used in an order making an internal change to the executive branch and 0 otherwise.

action, but the president acted first, relying on broad discretion delegated under prior law.[31]

Another way to identify the frequency and amount of discretion used in command orders to manage the executive branch is to consider it visually. A dichotomous dependent variable was created to operationalize command orders to organize the internal executive branch or to direct external agents outside the executive branch. Figure 5.2 graphs the probability that presidents will invoke greater substantive discretion for orders that issue internal or external commands. The results show that presidents use greater discretionary authority when making internal changes to the executive branch rather than when issuing edicts for other external actors to follow. For instance, Executive Order 12291 (referenced earlier) shows how President Reagan, relying on broad authority, established a system for internal regulatory review. The statistical effect is large, but the substantive effect is modest. Nevertheless, the results demonstrate that presidents make use of their substantive discretion when putting their own executive house in order.

The literature on executive branch management bears this out. Presidents use their institutional unilateral authority, especially authority that allows greater use of discretion, to protect their executive "turf." Presidents are often saddled with a bureaucracy that they must attempt to control (Moe 1985, 1998). As presidential responsibility grew over time, presidents attempt to control the executive branch more furtively (Dickinson 1996). As a result, presidents have turned to formal and informal powers to navigate the "administrative presidency" (Nathan 1983). Modern presidents use their unilateral tool kit to design agencies that are responsive to their needs (Howell and Lewis 2002). As a means to encourage (or demand) unity with executive goals, presidents may attempt to overcome vertical coordination problems by using unilateral directives to induce compliance to presidential goals. Specific rules will create coherent directives, which allow for less interpretation and fewer vague calls for action (see Aberbach and Rockman 2000). The clarity of the coordination and communication from the president to the executive branch is important in facilitating program success (Krause and Dupay 2009), making unilateral action an important element of how presidents manage their programs and attain policy success through internal changes to the executive branch.

The results in Table 5.2 show how the extent of conflict between the branches may influence the president's decision to issue a command order. The four models in Table 5.2 consider the effect of *interbranch* variables—ideological distance and majority party size—on the expectations of the use of command orders.[32] In the first two models, the results are contrary to expectations. The coefficients for the ideological distance between the president and the median member of the House and Senate are negative but not statistically significant.[33] In the third model, the coefficient for the size of the majority party is negative and statistically significant, but the marginal effect (−.5 percent) is very small.[34] The effects are very modest, with a less than 1 percent change in probability of issuing a command order.

TABLE 5.2.

Issuing routine and command orders: Interbranch measures.

	Distance between president and Senate	Distance between president and House	Majority party size (Senate and House)	Senate filibuster pivot
Second term	0.218	0.186	0.089	−.0.097
	(0.242)	(0.236)	(0.237)	(0.243)
Second half	0.789 ***	0.773 ***	0.724 ***	0.692 ***
	(0.200)	(0.196)	(0.195)	(0.195)
	[19.4%]	[19.0%]	[17.8%]	[17.0%]
Election year	−0.507 **	−0.505 ***	−0.452 **	−621 ***
	(0.212)	(0.212)	(0.212)	(0.215)
	[−12.3%]	[−12.3%]	[−11.0%]	[−15.0%]
Second half, second term	−0.248	−150	−0.311	−0.216
	(0.323)	(0.329)	(0.322)	(0.324)
Congressional hearings	2.92 ***	2.91 ***	2.89 ***	2.93 ***
	(0.166)	(0.166)	(0.166)	(0.167)
	[61.5%]	[61.4%]	[61.1%]	[61.7%]
Constitutional authority	2.04 ***	2.05 ***	1.96 ***	1.94 ***
	(0.266)	(0.267)	(0.272)	(0.272)
	[41.3%]	[41.4%]	[40.1%]	[39.8%]
Substantive discretion	0.866 ***	0.868 ***	0.854 ***	0.909 ***
	(0.178)	(0.178)	(0.187)	(0.180)
	[21.5%]	[231.6%]	[21.2%]	[22.6%]
Prior congressional agenda	1.37 ***	1.38 ***	1.33 ***	1.40 ***
	(0.173)	(0.174)	(0.173)	(0.175)
	[32.8%]	[33.0%]	[31.9%]	[33.3%]
Distance between president and Senate median member	−0.574 (0.435)	—	—	—
Distance between president and House median member	—	−0.870 (0.474)	—	—
Majority party size (Senate and House)	—	—	−0.021 * (0.014) [−0.5%]	—
Distance between president and Senate filibuster	—	—	—	3.25 *** (0.764) [81.0%]
N	1,468	1,468	1,468	1,468
Pseudo R^2	0.389	0.390	0.389	0.397
Log-likelihood	−619.0	−618.2	−618.8	−610.7
Likelihood ratio χ^2	789.0 ***	790.6 ***	789.4 ***	805.6 ***
Reduction in error	60.8%	59.2%	60.2%	60.8%

Note: Dependent variable: Presidents issue a "command" order (dichotomous).

*** Indicates statistical significance at $p < 0.01$.

** $p < 0.05$.

* $p < 0.10$.

Standard errors are in parentheses. The percentage of expected change is in brackets (holding all other variables at their mean). Tests are two-tailed tests.

Although the ideological distance between the president and majority party medians in the House or Senate does not have a significant effect on the number of command orders issued, the ideological distance between the president and the Senate filibuster pivot is consistent with our expectations. The coefficient is positive and statistically significant, and the marginal effect is substantively large, with the president 81 percent more likely to issue a command order as the ideological distance between the Senate filibuster pivot and the president increases. When the two are ideologically closer, this may allow the president to legislate more effectively and persuade the sixtieth member of the Senate (and thus almost a supermajority of the Senate) to join the president's policy initiative. Greater distance implies less of a chance to convince an ideologically disparate senator to join the president's coalition and thus cement some form of legislation acceptable to both.

Table 5.3 investigates the *intrabranch* conflict when Congress is internally divided. The results indicate that presidents are *more* likely to issue a command order as party heterogeneity increases in the House and Senate but *less* likely when polarization increases between the parties in the House. The first two models in Table 5.3 show, interestingly, that presidents are less likely to issue a command order as polarization *between* the parties in the House increases but not in the Senate. The coefficient for polarization between the parties in the House is negative and statistically significant. The marginal effect shows that presidents are 17 percent less likely to issue a command order as polarization increases. Presidents do not want to step on the toes of a dysfunctional party, which could still be capable of making law or challenging the president. This contradicts the expectation that presidents would issue more command orders taking advantage of Congress's presumed inability to act.

Examining a related but distinct environment in the third and fourth models, presidents are more likely to issue a command order when the ideological distance increases *within the parties* in both the House and Senate. The coefficients for *Party Heterogeneity* are positive and statistically significant. The marginal effect shows that presidents are 104 percent more likely to issue a command as party heterogeneity increases in the House and 61 percent more likely in the Senate. Greater ideological

TABLE 5.3.
Issuing routine and command orders: Intrabranch measures.

	Party polarization (Senate)	Party polarization (House)	Party heterogeneity (House)	Party heterogeneity (Senate)
Second term	0.161 (0.235)	0.060 (0.237)	−0.038 (0.251)	−0.032 (0.246)
Second half	0.677 *** (0.202) [16.7%]	0.747 *** (0.195) [18.3 %]	0.690 *** (0.195) [17.0%]	0.744 *** (0.195) [18.3%]
Election year	−0.459 *** (0.212) [−11.2%]	−0.488 *** (0.211) [−11.9%]	−0.458 *** (0.211) [−11.2%]	−0.449 *** (0.212) [−11.0%]
Second half, second term	−0.325 (0.326)	−0.474 (0.330)	−0.257 (0.322)	−0.312 (0.323)
Congressional hearings	2.90 *** (0.166) [61.2%]	2.93 *** (0.167) [61.7%]	2.89 *** (0.166) [61.2%]	2.89 *** (0.166) [61.2%]
Constitutional authority	1.99 *** (0.271) [40.6%]	1.80 *** (0.280) [37.7%]	1.89 *** (0.276) [39.1%]	1.85 *** (0.277) [38.6%]
Substantive discretion	0.879 *** (0.178) [21.8%]	0.912 *** (0.179) [22.7%]	0.857 *** (0.178) [21.3%]	0.852 *** (0.178) [21.2%]
Prior congressional agenda	1.35 *** (0.173) [32.2%]	1.34 *** (0.173) [32.1%]	1.34 *** (0.173) [32.1%]	1.34 *** (0.173) [32.2%]
Party polarization	−0.175 (.203)	−0.715 *** (0.263) [−17.8%]	—	—
Party heterogeneity	—	—	4.18 ** (2.04) [104.0%]	2.47 *** (1.02) [61.5%]
N	1,468	1,468	1,468	1,468
Pseudo R^2	0.388	0.392	0.390	0.391
Log-likelihood	−619.5	−616.0	−617.8	−617.0
Likelihood ratio χ^2	787.9 ***	795.1 ***	791.4 ***	793.0 ***
Reduction in error	61.3%	62.7%	61.9%	62.0%

Note: Dependent variable: Presidents issue a "command" order (dichotomous).

*** Indicates statistical significance at $p < 0.01$.

** $p < 0.05$.

* $p < 0.10$.

Standard errors are in parentheses. The percentage expected change is in brackets (holding all other variables at their mean). Tests are two-tailed tests.

disparity within the parties signals a greater inability to reach an agreement within the chamber and, therefore, more likelihood that the president will issue a command order to take advantage of the confusion.

CONCLUSION

The range of unilateral orders, even seemingly routine orders, demonstrates the scope of presidential power in a shared system. Philip Cooper (2014), writing in the *Washington Post*, echoed these distinctions in the utility of unilateral orders:

Some presidential directives are mundane—orders managing civil-service employees or military personnel, for example—but many others, such as the stack of orders and memoranda issued by Bush in the months after the attacks of Sept. 11, 2001, have had broad and lasting effects. They can be used to create or reorganize executive branch offices or agencies, such as John F. Kennedy's order creating the Peace Corps and Bush's creation of the Office of Homeland Security. And, of course, the Bush administration used executive orders to establish its Guantanamo detention policies.

Command orders are more consequential and controversial than those that are routine. Command orders are fodder for distrust and potential erosion of the separation of powers and provoke partisan skirmishes. Routine orders, even if they do not evoke interbranch friction, can tell us much about the separation of powers and how the branches jointly manage the workings of government.

As Moe and Wilson argue, the president is not "Congress' agent" (1994). Indeed, "part of his responsibility as the chief executive is to enforce the law, so he will necessarily be cognizant of the legislative will and seek to advance it in many of his activities" (Whittington and Carpenter 2003). Even so, the Constitution imbued each institution with a different set of responsibilities, together possessing, overlapping, and interconnecting authority. By separating power as it does, the Constitution allows for the president to either implement policy as designed by the other branches or to engage in autonomous action for the good of the institution or the country. Command orders are directly connected to the president's agenda and make use of his or her ability to act with dispatch, whereas routine orders are generally consensually used to monitor and manage the business of government. The variation in the issuance of these orders shows that they are unique from one another and are fundamentally distinct from unilateral orders used at other points in the policy process.

Independent presidents act strategically when issuing command orders, especially because they have a short window to initiate policy. They enter office with a massive bureaucracy not of their own making that they have to manage and make function for them. They must maximize several advantages they have as chief executive. *Independent* presidents take advantage of greater substantive discretion and rely on constitutional (either real or argued) warrants to act, especially in matters that involve the executive branch. They issue more command orders when they are in the second half of their terms. Presidents, to broach an institutional divide left by partisan electoral politics or to leave a lasting policy legacy, issue more unilateral orders at the end of their terms. Political brinksmanship may be present as *independent* presidents are more likely to act with a command order when Congress is considering the issue publicly through hearings, in an attempt to use these orders to stem actions Congress might take on the issue. *Independent* presidents act using command orders when the parties in Congress are more ideologically heterogeneous and less likely to come to consensus. At least in terms of the president's viewpoint, a disorganized party is a more opportune time to issue a command order than greater prospective ideological or partisan conflict within each chamber. *Independent* presidents, too, take advantage of a distant filibuster pivot by issuing more command orders in these instances, allowing them to pursue their own agenda when Congress is less able to stop them.

These two types of orders demonstrate interplay between institutional demands and political incentives, shaped by the necessity of frequent and repeated interactions between the branches. There is an institutional restriction at play where presidents are reluctant to challenge larger and stronger majorities in Congress. Although the effect is modest, presidents are less likely to act independently by issuing a command order as the majority party in Congress increases in size. Presidents tread lightly in issuing command orders when the parties are polarized, perhaps aware of the tenuous nature of their use of executive authority via unilateral order. Presidents do not bait Congress into a fight knowing that they may lose. They respect the institutional responsibility to work with Congress rather than to act alone. Even so, the president is willing to use command orders when the parties in Congress are internally fragmented, often leading to legislative paralysis. Presidents pounce on these opportunities to push their agenda.

CHAPTER SIX

An Independent President or Administrator?

Orders to Preempt and Support Congress

AT THE CENTER OF THE DEBATE about presidential power are questions of how presidents use unilateral action in reaction to legislation being considered. Presidents are able to issue unilateral orders as a substitute for legislation or to work with Congress on legislative outcomes; yet these processes may be intertwined. Within the legislative process, the president's actions are influenced by the power-sharing arrangements that are part of the Constitution (Bond and Fleisher 1990). Congress has the control in the legislative arena, and presidents may participate, but they may also strategically undertake unilateral action. The dual nature of the executive influences how presidents use unilateral orders in relation to legislation. As *administrators*, presidents use unilateral action as a bargaining tool as part of their efforts to work with Congress toward mutual goals. In Neustadt's (1990) view, presidents are a bargaining agent in the system, and they must use their interpersonal skills to persuade, cajole, or pressure members of Congress to act. As *independents*, presidents use unilateral orders to both circumvent and to streamline legislation. Unilateral orders often subvert the legislative process and facilitate the president's ability to make policy by fiat (Cooper 1986; Shull 1993; Mayer 2001). In this way, the president's unilateral orders allow him to "do what Congress could not or would not do" (Neighbors 1964).

The tension concerning when presidents use their unilateral power to cajole or usurp the legislative process is at the heart of a separate and shared power system. A president who acts in the role of an *administrator* chooses to pursue unilateral policy making conversant with the legislative process. From the president's perspective, this is a tenuous choice because the process of passing legislation is afflicted by collective action problems, an outlay of political capital, lengthy debates, and large transaction costs, but this path does provide certainty in achieving a lasting policy outcome.

Through hearings on legislation, Congress signals the policy preference of committee members. The president may decide to show support by initiating part of the proposed policy. This provides assurance to members of Congress of the president's ability and commitment to execute the policy. In this way, unilateral action could be considered an efficiency tool, rather than an obstructionist tool, to help Congress overcome collective action problems and where both branches get something they want.

PRESIDENT OBAMA AND UNILATERAL ORDERS IN THE LEGISLATIVE ARENA

President Obama's unilateral orders illustrate how a president acts as both independent and administrator in relation to achieving his goals in the legislative arena. In his first State of the Union address to Congress, President Obama spoke about the importance of clean energy, noting that "to truly transform our economy, to protect our security, and save our planet from the ravages of climate change, we need to ultimately make clean, renewable energy the profitable kind of energy." But to accomplish this goal he turned to the legislative branch and said, "So I ask this Congress to send me legislation that places a market-based cap on carbon pollution and drives the production of more renewable energy in America. That's what we need. And to support that innovation, we will invest $15 billion a year to develop technologies like wind power and solar power, advanced biofuels, clean coal, and more efficient cars and trucks built right here in America." Congress did respond. Rep. Waxman (D-CA) introduced H.R. 2454, the American Clean Energy and Security Act of 2009. On the same day the bill passed the House, President Obama issued a Statement of Administrative Policy (SAP) supporting the bill, noting:

The President has called on Congress to enact forward-looking energy legislation that would spur U.S. development of advanced, clean energy technologies to reduce our dependence on oil, strengthen our energy and national security, create millions of new jobs all across America, and restore America's position as a global leader in efforts to mitigate climate change and address its worst consequences. The administration commends the House Energy and Commerce Committee for its extraordinary efforts in developing historic bipartisan comprehensive energy and climate legislation that creates the framework to accomplish these goals. The administration strongly supports House passage of H.R. 2454.

In further support of the bill and the goal of clean energy, before the legislation passed, President Obama issued Executive Order 13514, synergistically promoting federal leadership in clean energy through environmental, energy, and economic performance. In short, not all intervention by the president has the nefarious purpose of relegating Congress to a bit player.

On the other hand, presidents may decide to bypass negotiations with Congress and, instead, act as an *independent* by adopting policy unilaterally with a "stroke of a pen." This approach enables the executive to "act quickly and with flexibility in responding to problems and changing political, economic and social circumstances as they arise" (Moe and Howell 1999). Presidents may disapprove of the tone or content of proposed legislation and issue an order that contradicts congressional will by unilaterally altering a proposed change to the status quo. President Obama faced this dilemma in 2011, when members in the House, frustrated with a lack of transparency, public participation, and clear guidance requirements for major rules in the rule-making process, introduced legislation proposing regulatory reform. Three bills had a significant number of co-sponsors and, after being reported out of committee, were headed to the floor for debate. In a statement of administrative policy (SAP), Obama stated, "The Administration is committed to ensuring that regulations are smart and effective, that they are tailored to advance statutory goals in the most cost-effective and efficient manner, and that they minimize uncertainty." President Obama responded to H.R. 527, Regulatory Flexibility Improvements Act of 2011, and H.R. 3010, Regulatory Accountability Act of 2011, with SAPs explaining how the bills "would impose unnecessary procedures on agencies and invite frivolous litigation."[1] His SAP in response to H.R. 10, "Regulations from the Executive in Need of Scrutiny Act of 2011," was particularly critical of "the requirement imposing a joint resolution of approval be enacted by the Congress before any major rule of Executive Branch agencies could have force or effect." Obama argued:

This radical departure from the separation of powers between the Executive and Legislative branches would delay, and in many cases, thwart implementation of statutory mandates and execution of duly enacted laws, increase business scrutiny, undermine much-needed protections of the American public and create unnecessary confusion.[2]

President Obama issued his SAPs on the same day each of the bills was reported to the House by the Rules Committee, which was to establish the conditions for floor debate. Preferring an administrative rather than a legislative solution, President Obama issued Executive Order 13610, his alternative to legislation. In his order, Obama referred to Executive Order 13563, "Improving Regulation and Regulatory Review," noting that it was designed to improve ongoing and retrospective regulatory review, but agreed that "further steps should be taken, consistent with law, agency resources, and regulatory priorities, to promote public participation in retrospective review, to modernize our regulatory system, and to institutionalize regular assessment of significant regulations." His new order clearly preserved the intent of Executive Order 13563 and maintained control over any changes by specifying that the decision to invite public suggestion is "to be determined by the agency head in consultation with OIRA" and that agencies shall continue to report to OIRA on the retrospective review efforts.[3] Importantly, his order preempted efforts by the House, but his actions were far from the reform that the members sought. Instead, Obama did little more than pay lip service to the legislation intended to thwart his control over the regulatory process.

This divergent use of unilateral power in the legislative process during the Obama Administration demonstrates the paths a president might take. If unilateral orders can be used functionally as alternatives to legislation, when and how does a president choose to "substitute prerogative for statutory authority" (Pious 2009)? Presidents have a choice to issue unilateral orders to support the legislative process or "in lieu" of legislation (Belco and Rottinghaus 2014). This suggests flexibility in a president's use of unilateral orders in the legislative arena: sometimes to halt the legislative process, sometimes to foster it. Both of these actions are consistent with the dual nature of the executive. There is an integrated nature to unilateral orders, which can be observed when they are considered in the context of the legislative process rather than as completely divorced from it. This opens the door to explanatory notions of shared political power via unilateral order pinpointing where and when an *independent* president issues unilateral orders to work against Congress by preempting legislation and an *administrator* president issues unilateral orders to work with Congress by supporting legislation. Within the framework of the legislative process, shared powers, rather than separate powers, prevail as evidence of the frequency or infrequency of the (im)balance of power.

PRESIDENTS AND UNILATERAL ACTION
IN THE LEGISLATIVE ARENA

In an effort to improve their chances for success, presidents may choose to enter the legislative arena using two primary means sanctioned by the Constitution: by suggesting an agenda item to Congress, as outlined by Article II, Section 1 of the Constitution (Fisher 1998; Rudalevige 2002; Cameron and Park 2008) and the veto (Cameron 2000). Moving outside of their constitutionally prescribed role, presidents can use direct or unilateral action as a means of improving their success in implementing their policy agenda (Mayer 2001; Cooper 2002; Warber 2006). Unilateral action is strategically useful for presidents when faced with a legislative process that forces them to share political powers (Mayer 2001; Howell 2005). The process of issuing unilateral orders is generally described as an alternative to bargaining with Congress (Moe and Howell 1999; Howell 2003), although Jones (2005) argues, "Efforts to comprehend presidential power in lawmaking require study of Congressional power even if the president acts 'with the stroke of a pen' as when issuing executive orders. Those who are separated must agree or acquiesce if there is to be law."

When considering whether to issue a unilateral order, presidents face an integrated cost–benefit trade-off, especially with respect to the legislative makeup of Congress and the possible intervention of the judiciary. The executive must weigh the long-term cost of the permanence of legislation with the short-term benefit of the expediency of a unilateral order that may be undone by Congress or overturned by the courts. Invoking unilateral powers to circumvent legislation specifically involves weighing the cost of angering a recalcitrant Congress with the benefits of acting with dispatch (Sala 1998). As Mayer (2009) suggests, presidents prefer legislation as a means to achieve policy goals but opt for unilateral action as their "second-best" option when they face strong congressional opposition. Deering and Maltzman (1999) argue that "a president's willingness to issue an executive order depends upon both his positive power to get legislation enacted by Congress and his negative power to stop legislation overturning such an order." The president's unilateral action is not strictly combative nor is it totally cooperative—there is variation depending on his or her authority to act, the political environment, and the institutional arrangements.

Invoking a unilateral order is one way a president, acting as an *administrator*, has of showing support when topics are already on the legislative agenda, especially when the two branches are seeking to cooperate on the issue. When the president and Congress work together toward mutually satisfactory goals, the president may help legislation to pass by issuing a unilateral order that supports part of Congress's policy. Unilateral action in relation to legislation could then be considered an efficiency tool to help Congress overcome collective action problems it may face. Presidents may desire to work with Congress toward a mutually agreeable solution and issue an order to further the process. When President Obama announced in his 2014 State of the Union Address his goal to raise the minimum wage, he acknowledged that "Congress does need to get on board." He recognized the legislative efforts of Sen. Tom Harkin (R-IA) and Rep. George Miller (D-CA) and acknowledged that through an executive order he was able to lead by example but "to reach millions more" would require legislation (Lowery 2014).[4]

In another case, President Obama had to choose whether to work with Congress when he faced opposition to the drilling moratorium he instituted after the Gulf Oil Spill disaster.[5] Critics of the ban argued that the action would only cause additional harm to those who had already been damaged by the spill. Federal District Court Judge Martha Feldman agreed, overturning the moratorium as being "overly broad."[6] Even after the Court's ruling, the award of drilling permits remained at a standstill, and the House pursued legislation to reverse President Obama's moratorium.[7]

The day before the bill was scheduled for a vote, President Obama voiced his opposition to the bill in a SAP noting that the legislation would limit executive branch discretion over development in the Outer Continental Shelf (OCS), opening up areas in the North and Central Atlantic Coasts, the Southern California Coast, and offshore Alaska.[8] Despite President Obama's objections, the bill passed the House. Shortly afterward, President Obama then took actions to support Congress's position and "ordered the Interior Department to conduct annual lease sales in Alaska's National Petroleum Reserve and speed up seismic work that is a precursor to drilling off the south and mid-Atlantic coasts."[9] Then, he issued an executive order establishing an interagency working group to coordinate domestic energy development and permitting in Alaska.[10] The president began working with Congress toward a mutually agreeable goal.

As *independents*, however, presidents may use unilateral orders as an obstructionist tool. When they disagree with the ideological or political direction of legislation, presidents may issue a preemptive order as an alternative to congressional action. This should depend on the nature of legislation, the issue, and the partisan makeup of Congress. As Mayer (2009) suggests, presidents prefer legislation as a means to achieve policy goals but opt for unilateral action as their "second-best" option when they face strong congressional opposition. President Obama disapproved of the changes to infrastructure and transportation development proposed in H.R. 7, the American Energy and Infrastructure Jobs Act of 2012. The bill would significantly reduce the planning, environmental review, and permitting requirements of infrastructure and transportation projects. The bill, as enrolled in the House, authorized the Department of Transportation, the federal lead agency, at the request of the project sponsor to adopt and use a decision-making process that integrates the planning and environmental review process of a rail project in National Environmental Policy Act (NEPA) proceedings. The bill directed the Secretary of Transportation to establish a program to eliminate duplicative state and federal environmental reviews and approvals of rail projects. It directed the Secretary of Transportation to treat a rail project as a class of action categorically excluded from environmental review requirements promulgated by the Council on Environmental Quality, if specified circumstances applied.[11] The day after the bill was reported out of committee, President Obama issued a SAP opposing the bill because it would "significantly weaken environmental protections for transportation projects and undermine civic engagement in the decision making process."[12] A few weeks later, he preempted the review process to short-circuit administrative and environmental reviews by issuing an executive order designed to further enhance and strengthen the process involving federal permitting and review of infrastructure projects.[13] In this disagreement between the branches, President Obama decided to circumvent Congress.

INDEPENDENCE AND PREEMPT OR ADMINISTRATOR AND SUPPORT

As in Chapter 5, we assign each order into one of two categories. Depending on the president's strategy, unilateral orders can be preemptive orders or supportive orders. Acting as *independents*, presidents can use preemptive politics when Congress is poised to act (Moe and Howell 1999; Mayer 2001; Howell 2003). For example, President Ford used preemptive politics to thwart Congress's participation in intelligence oversight. Following on the heels of investigations into intelligence abuses by the Central Intelligence Agency during the Nixon administration, Congress sought to establish a formal role for itself (Mayer 2001; Best 2004). On January 29, 1976, Senator Frank Church introduced the Intelligence Oversight Act in order to establish a standing Senate Committee on Oversight and to prohibit covert and clandestine activity unless the committee was first informed.[14] The Senate Committee on Governmental Affairs held daily hearings on the bill.[15] But President Ford wanted to maintain greater internal oversight of clandestine activities and acted first, by issuing an executive order on foreign intelligence activities. Ford's executive order was part of a "concerted effort to preempt legislation that would have established tighter Congressional control and more specific restrictions on the conduct of intelligence agencies" (Mayer 2001).[16] In the order, President Ford sought to "establish policies to improve the quality of intelligence needed for national security, to clarify the authority and responsibilities of the intelligence departments and agencies, and to establish effective oversight to assure compliance with law in the management and direction of intelligence agencies and departments of the national government." Consistent with his effort to preserve the president's dominance in intelligence affairs, President Ford transmitted to Congress proposed legislation to reform the U.S. foreign intelligence community to insure that future legislative efforts conformed to his preferences.[17]

President Reagan used unilateral action to preempt legislation when he issued Executive Order 12532, "Prohibiting Trade and Certain Other Transactions Involving South Africa."[18] Although President Reagan was willing to impose some of the economic sanctions that Congress wanted, his objective was to maintain economic relations with South Africa through constructive engagement. The House bill imposed more stringent economic sanctions than the Senate version, but the two chambers were willing to reconcile their differences because both agreed to severely restrict trade relations between the two countries.[19] Unless President Reagan took some decided action, he would be faced with the need to exercise his veto, which risked a veto override from a determined Congress. A few days before the Senate was scheduled to take up the House conference report reconciling the two bills, Senator Richard Lugar (R-IN), the bill's sponsor and Chairman of the Senate Foreign Relation Committee, was shown a draft executive order that effectively included some, but not all, of the content of the bill approved in the House Conference Report (Howell 2003; Lugar 1988; Treverton and Varley 1992).[20] The order successfully preempted the legislation Congress was considering.[21]

President Clinton issued two executive orders to preempt Congress during a contentious battle over the Omnibus Budget Reconciliation Act of 1993.[22] Both Executive Order 12857 on budget control and Executive Order 12858 on the deficit reduction fund were issued to replace language that had been removed from the legislation before he signed the bill into law.[23] In his remarks on signing the executive orders, President Clinton spoke against those whose procedural maneuvering "blocked action for these needed reforms." But he reassured members of Congress:

These orders are almost completely identical to the provisions adopted by the House and approved by a majority in the Senate. The deficit reduction order creates a deficit reduction trust fund, an account in the Treasury that guarantees that the savings from the reconciliation bill are dedicated exclusively to reducing the deficit. This locks in deficit reduction and mandates all members of the executive branch to follow these procedures.[24]

In an effort to work together with Congress, presidents in the role of *administrators* may invoke unilateral orders to support legislation. To initiate supportive congressional actions, a president may establish a commission for fact finding or policy development to centralize policy development in the executive branch (Warber 2006). If Congress is considering major policy changes, the president can shift the new policy to a more moderate version (Howell 2003). President Reagan's Executive Order 12348 established an advisory committee on federal real property in support of a Senate resolution, declaring that the United States needed to improve on managing its assets.[25] The committee set forth some recommendations for the president and executive branch to follow. Similarly, the president may direct the federal government to take specific action that supports proposed legislation. In 1979, Congress was considering the Paperwork Reduction Act, which the president had publicly endorsed. On the same day he signed an executive order, President Carter transmitted a federal paperwork reduction message to Congress outlining the content of the order and articulating the specific benefits of the legislation Congress was considering with the hope that Congress would make the proposed legislation and his order permanent.[26]

SUPPORT AND PREEMPT ORDERS OVER TIME

Figure 6.1 charts the use of unilateral orders to support and preempt legislation from Presidents Gerald Ford to George W. Bush. Interestingly, presidents issue more orders to support legislation, which suggests they may generally be reluctant to intervene by using executive power against Congress in the legislative arena. There is, however, significant variation across presidents. At one extreme is President Clinton, who issued 101 total orders, and at the other is President George W. Bush, who issued only twenty total orders. President Clinton, undeterred from letting Congress move first, more often stepped in with a supportive or preemptive unilateral order during the legislative policy-making phase. In contrast,

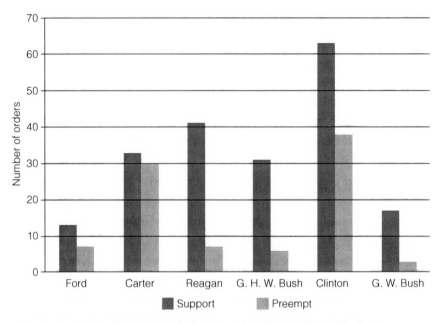

FIGURE 6.1. Use of support and preempt orders by president. The figures represent the total orders that support and preempt legislation by each president.

Bush was more prone to issue a veto threat or to veto legislation. Generally, however, presidents issued very few preemptive orders. Clinton issued the most with thirty-eight preemptive orders and George W. Bush the fewest with only three. Presidents appear to prefer using supportive orders. The frequency of supportive orders increases over time but falls significantly with the administration of George W. Bush.

Presidents Ford and George W. Bush are outliers in the number of orders issued during the legislative process. They also represent two extremes in the prevailing political conditions and the president's exercise of power. President Ford had to contend with a resurgent Congress and a divided government, whereas President George W. Bush enjoyed Republican majorities in both houses of Congress for most of his administration. President Ford was committed to working with Congress, whereas President George W. Bush may not have needed this strategy, preferring instead to emphasize his constitutional authority, unitary control over the executive branch, and supremacy over the legislative branch in times of crisis (Bush 2010).

When presidents do use unilateral orders in the legislative process, as Presidents Ford and George W. Bush illustrate, they appear to be willing to act whether government is unified or divided. A divided government may produce more interbranch friction, and this institutional tension can be handled through unilateral action when other ways like negotiation with legislative party leaders may be more difficult. In a unified government, intraparty diversity or heterogeneity can significantly slow the legislative process and limit the ability of Congress to organize to act on legislation at all. This phenomenon tends to hurt presidents who attempt to manage ideologically diverse parties most frequently. Specifically, Democratic Presidents Carter and Clinton both governed with Democratic majorities but during times when ideological preferences within the party were more diverse. In Figure 6.1, Carter and Clinton made the most frequent use of both supportive and preemptive orders, despite the differences in the number of years in office and the time period in which they served. It is interesting to note that President Reagan, who served for two terms in office under a divided government, and George H. W. Bush, who served one term in office under a divided government, issued comparatively more supportive orders and significantly fewer preemptive orders than Carter and Clinton.

EXPECTATIONS OF INDEPENDENT ACTION
IN THE LEGISLATIVE PROCESS

Restating the expectations from Chapter Two, *independent* presidents should be more likely to preempt legislation when the issue is on their agenda. Likewise, when political circumstances present the need to expediently enact the president's agenda into law, a president in the later stages of the administration and in election years should be more likely to preempt legislation. *Independent* presidents are expected to issue more orders preempting legislation under increasing gridlock within Congress caused by greater polarization between the parties or ideological differences within parties. Independent presidents are more likely to issue an order preempting legislation when there is a greater ideological distance between the president and the median member in the House and Senate or between the president and the Senate filibuster pivot.

The sponsorship of legislation may also have an effect on the president's decision to preempt legislation. Because of the unique nature of this phase of the policy process, we include variables to capture the origin of the legislation with which the president is concerned. When bill sponsors are less closely aligned with the president's preferences, the sponsorship of legislation may have an effect on the president's decision to preempt or support the legislation. Specifically, presidents should be more likely to preempt legislation when the bill sponsor's ideology is distant from them or the bill sponsor is of the opposite party. Cosponsorship signals to agenda setters and party loyalists about the preferences of the individual cosponsor (Krehbiel 1995; Krehbiel and Kessler 1996; Kroger 2003). When the president and the cosponsors are farther apart ideologically, the president will be more likely to intervene with a preemptive order.

DATA AND METHODS

A dichotomous dependent variable, *Preempt*, was constructed to operationalize when presidents issued a unilateral order preempting a bill on Congress's agenda. Coding the dichotomous dependent variable consisted of a two-stage process. First, an analysis of the content of the order was conducted to determine whether the subject, issue, or topic related to a bill on the congressional agenda.[27] Second, the content of the order was analyzed in comparison to the bill to determine whether the order could be categorized to support or preempt the bill. The threshold for a bill being on the congressional agenda was based on whether it had been enrolled in one of the two chambers and had received a hearing before a subcommittee, committee, or the full chamber (Edwards, Barrett, and Peake 1997; Edwards and Barrett 2000). The hearing had to have been held within the same session and prior to or on the same date the order was issued. This criterion establishes a higher standard than bill introduction, which requires no commitment from committee and party leaders. Scheduling and holding a hearing on a bill signifies participation by party and committee leaders.

The content of each order was analyzed in relation to the content of the bill(s) on Congress's agenda to determine whether it was used in support, or to preempt, the relevant bill. The dependent variable, *Preempt*, was coded 1 if the order preempted legislation and 0 otherwise, which includes orders that support legislation. The analysis of the bill and order yielded a total of 289 orders—198 in support and 91 that preempt. Intercoder verification reveals substantial agreement between the coders with respect to the coding for preempt and support classifications.[28] A unilateral order was considered to preempt a bill when the president: (1) took action contrary to Congress's intent on the legislation, (2) implemented executive action not included in the bill, (3) vetoed a bill and issued a unilateral order in lieu of the bill, or (4) issued an order in lieu of expired authority. President George H. W. Bush's Executive Order 12711 implementing policy related to the Nationals of the People's Republic of China was coded as *preempt* because he vetoed H.R. 2712 and issued a unilateral order in lieu of the legislation (see discussion in Chapter 2). President Reagan's Executive Order 12532 that prohibited trade with South Africa was coded as *preempt* because President Reagan substituted his policy through a unilateral order, after H.R. 1430 and S. 635 were being considered in conference.

Unilateral orders that support legislation require that the order (1) created or extended a federal advisory task force or commission, (2) implemented a portion of a bill, (3) ordered the executive branch to take specific action Congress expressed in the legislation, (4) offered some endorsement of the bill, or (5) clarified the position of the president or the executive branch on all or specific provisions of the bill. From the preceding examples, President Clinton's three executive orders creating federal advisory committees were coded to *support* legislation because the president ordered the executive branch to take action addressed in the bill.[29] President Carter's Executive Order 12174 was coded as *support* because he directed the federal government to take specific action in support of the Paperwork and Redtape Reduction Act.

Several variables used in previous chapters are included to test the expectations pertaining to whether presidents were working with or against Congress in the legislative process.[30] The variables used to measure *intrabranch* gridlock include the extent of polarization between the parties in the House and Senate (*Party Polarization House/Senate*) and the distance in ideology between members within the parties in the House and Senate (*Party Heterogeneity House/Senate*). The variables used to measure *interbranch* gridlock include the ideological distance between the president and key members of Congress including the median member for the House and Senate (*President and House/Senate*) and between the president and the Senate filibuster pivot (*President and Filibuster*). The presidency-centered variables related to the president's agenda (*Presidential Agenda*) and committee hearings unrelated to legislation but on the general subject of the unilateral order (*Congressional Hearings*) and temporal political variables, which might affect the president's strategy (*Second Term, Second Half of Term, Election Year*).

Five primary variables are used to test the expectations about bill sponsorship and cosponsorship. First, the ideological distance between the president and the bill's sponsor (*Sponsor Distance*) is calculated by taking the absolute value of the difference of the CS-NOMINATE scores for the president and the individual bill sponsor. Second, a dummy variable is used to measure whether the president and the sponsor were of the same party (*Bill Sponsor Opposite Party*). Third, a dummy variable is included for the chamber in which the bill originated (*Senate Sponsor*). Fourth, a continuous variable is included for the number of cosponsors (*Number of Cosponsors*). Fifth, a categorical variable is included to identify whether the bill's cosponsors were all members of the president's party (*Cosponsor Partisanship*). The variable was coded 0 for all members of the president's party, 1 for a mix of bipartisan members, and 2 for all cosponsors of the opposite party of the president.[31] Because there is a dichotomous dependent variable, a series of logistic regression models is used to analyze the data, and the marginal effects of the coefficients are used to explain the results.

WHEN PRESIDENTS SUPPORT OR PREEMPT LEGISLATION

Table 6.1 identifies the frequency with which presidents issue a unilateral order to preempt or support a bill at different stages in the legislative

TABLE 6.1.
Cross tabulations of the type of order and stage in the
legislative process.

	Support	Preempt
Subcommittee hearing	28.7% (56)	8.8% (8)
Committee hearing	30.1% (59)	15.5% (14)
Vote by one chamber	33.6% (66)	51.1% (46)
Vote by both chambers	4.5% (9)	5.5% (5)
Conference committee	1.5% (3)	4.4% (4)
Cleared for the White House	1.5% (3)	2.2% (2)
Signed by the president	0.0% (0)	2.2% (2)
Vetoed by the president	0.0% (0)	10.0 (9)

Note: Data were compiled by the authors. N = 286. Percentages are column percentages. N is shown in parentheses. The stages signify advancement in the legislative process.

process. This table shows that the White House is attentive to congressional action and strategic in taking unilateral action in relation to the
legislative process. The president issues an order to support a bill more
often after a subcommittee hearing, committee hearing, or a vote by one
chamber. He or she issues an order to preempt a bill most often after a
vote by one chamber. Presidents veto legislation, then issue an executive
order in lieu of legislation, about 10 percent of the time. In 1976, President
Ford vetoed Senate Joint Resolution 121, which provided for quarterly
adjustments in the support price for milk. In disapproving a similar bill
the prior month, the president said: "To further reduce the demand for
milk and dairy products by the increased prices provided in this legislation would be detrimental to the dairy industry. A dairy farmer cannot
be well served by government action that prices his product out of the
market."[32] In lieu of legislation, President Ford issued Proclamation 4423,
establishing import limits on dried milk in an effort to help curb the supply and increase demand.[33]

The key question in this chapter is, which conditions lead presidents
to use unilateral action to preempt or support legislation? In the following tables, a positive coefficient indicates that a president preempts
legislation, whereas a negative coefficient indicates that the president is

less likely to preempt legislation and to instead work with Congress to support their legislative approach.[34] One primary expectation was that presidents should issue more orders to preempt during an election year or later in their term when their political fortunes are lessened or their ability to bargain is diminished. In Tables 6.2 and 6.3, the coefficients for the election year are positive but not significant. The coefficients for second-term presidents and presidents in the second half of either their first or second term are negative but never statistically significant. However, the coefficients for the second half of the second term (*Second half, second terms*) in the third model in Table 6.2 and the fourth model in Table 6.3 are positive and statistically significant. This suggests that when presidents are at the end of their terms, under certain conditions they are willing use unilateral action to preempt legislation. The effect is more sporadic than the use of unilateral orders generally discovered in other contexts.

In Tables 6.2 and 6.3, the coefficients for *Presidential Agenda* in each of the models are positive and statistically significant, suggesting that presidents are more willing to preempt Congress using a unilateral order, when the issue is of stated importance to them.[35] *Independent* presidents seek to preserve their policy commitments on their agendas even when it means having to act *against* Congress to further the White House's agenda. Across all of the models in Tables 6.2 and 6.3, presidents were between 22 and 27 percent more likely to preempt legislation when the issue was on their agenda. One prominent example is President Clinton's Executive Order 12857 on budget control and Executive Order 12858 on the deficit reduction fund, which preserved the commitments he fought for in the Omnibus Budget Reconciliation Act of 1993. President Clinton spoke of these two fiscal tools in his first address before a Joint Session of Congress on his goals to create "a higher rate of economic growth, improved productivity, more high-quality jobs, and an improved economic competitive position in the world." He further noted, "In order to accomplish both increased investment and deficit reduction, something no American Government has ever been called upon to do at the same time before, spending must be cut and taxes must be raised."[36]

Tempering the likelihood of a preemptive action by an *independent* president are congressional hearings held on a topic *before* legislation is

TABLE 6.2.
Issuing support and preempt orders: Interbranch measures.

	Sponsorship cosponsorship	Distance between president and Senate	Distance between president and House	President and Senate filibuster
Second term	−0.258 (0.595)	−0.399 (0.530)	−0.632 (0.514)	−0.582 (0.547)
Second half	−539 0(.548)	−0.151 (0.442)	−0.384 (0.422)	−0.452 (0.424)
Election year	0.326 (0.470)	0.175 (0.392)	0.116 (0.392)	0.348 (0.406)
Second half, second term	0.818 (.740)	0.743 (.643)	1.07 * (0.638) [24.1%]	0.850 (0.642)
Congressional hearings	−1.88*** (0.370) [−38.6%]	−1.30 *** (0.304) [−28.7%]	−1.37 *** (0.301) [−30.4%]	−1.48 *** (0.296) [−30.4%]
Presidential agenda	1.84 ** (0.821) [22.5%]	1.96 *** (0.655) [26.2%]	1.93 *** (0.655) [26.2%]	2.00 *** (0.658) [26.2%]
Senator sponsor	−0.387 (0.384)	—	—	—
Number of cosponsors	0.007 (0.004)	—	—	—
Cosponsor partisanship	0.915 *** (0.346) [17.0%]	—	—	—
Bill sponsor in opposite party	1.56 ** (0.803) [20.8%]	—	—	—
Distance between president and bill sponsor	−0.024 (0.458)	—	—	—
Distance between president and House/ Senate	—	−2.45 ** (0.917) [−49.8%]	−1.94 ** (0.950) [−39.7%]	—
Distance between president and Senate filibuster	—	—	—	−1.64 ** (1.51) [−28.5%]
N	242	288	288	288
Pseudo R^2	0.228	0.136	0.128	0.119
Log likelihood	−115.5	−155.0	−156.6	−158.2
Likelihood ratio χ^2	68.56 ***	49.11 ***	45.97 ***	42.86 ***
Reduction in error	30.6%	27.4%	23.0%	21.9%

Note: Dependent variable: presidents issue an order "preempting" legislation.

*** Indicates statistical significance at $p < 0.01$.

** $p < 0.05$.

* $p < 0.10$.

Percentage of expected change is shown in brackets (holding all other variables at their mean). Tests are two-tailed tests.

TABLE 6.3.
Issuing support and preempt orders: Intrabranch measures.

	Party heterogeneity (Senate)	Party heterogeneity (House)	Party polarization (Senate)	Party polarization (House)
Second term	−0.931 (0.639)	−0.641 (0.585)	−0.763 (0.504)	−0.574 (0.516)
Second half	−0.446 (0.424)	−0.469 (0.422)	−0.214 (0.447)	−0.574 (0.516)
Election year	0.221 (0.390)	0.247 (0.388)	0.184 (0.388)	0.272 (0.389)
Second half, second term	0.931 (0.639)	0.919 (0.639)	0.945 (0.635)	1.19 ** (0.645) [26.8%]
Congressional hearings	−1.50 *** (0.296) [−33.2%]	−1.49 *** (0.296) [−33.0%]	−1.29 *** (0.307) [−28.5%]	−1.35 *** (0.302) [−29.9%]
Presidential agenda	1.90 *** (0.654) [26.1%]	1.98 *** (0.661) [26.7%]	2.14 *** (0.671) [27.6%]	2.11 *** (0.667) [27.4%]
Party heterogeneity (Senate)	1.87 (2.57)	—	—	—
Party heterogeneity (House)	—	−3.02 (4.69)	—	—
Party polarization (Senate)	—	—	3.82 ** (1.55) [77.7%]	—
Party polarization (House)	—	—	—	1.18 ** (0.506) [27.3%]
N	288	288	288	288
Pseudo R^2	0.117	0.117	0.133	0.131
Log likelihood	−158.5	−158.6	−155.6	−155.9
Likelihood ratio χ^2	42.22 ***	42.11 ***	48.05 ***	47.31 ***
Reduction in error	21.9%	21.9%	24.1%	27.4%

Note: Dependent variable: presidents issue an order "preempting" legislation.

*** indicates statistical significance at $p < 0.01$.

** $p < 0.05$.

* $p < 10$.

Percentage of expected change is shown in brackets (holding all other variables at their mean). Tests are two-tailed tests.

discussed in committee. Presidents are about 30 percent less likely to issue orders that preempt legislation (or more likely to support) when Congress is holding hearings on topics that relate to the topic of the president's unilateral order. This finding implies that the president listens to Congress before and after the creation of legislation and uses their unilateral powers to support congressional efforts. For instance, during the first half of Clinton's first term in office, Congress held committee hearings on policy concerning the hostile actions by Cuba to the United States. Relations with Cuba reached crisis proportions during the second half of Clinton's first term in office. Legislation responding to the Cuban crisis was introduced and proceeded quickly through the House and Senate. On the day the Cuban Liberty and Democratic Solidarity Act of 1996 was reported out of conference, President Clinton issued Proclamation 6867 announcing his policy declaring a National Emergency with Respect to Cuba, in support of the direction of congressional hearings and legislation.[37]

Table 6.2 also shows the results of the effects of *interbranch* gridlock on the president's decision to issue an order preempting legislation. The expectation was that differences in ideology and partisanship between the president, bill sponsors, and cosponsors should increase the likelihood of orders preempting legislation.[38] The results support part of the expectation. In the first model, the coefficient for the ideological distance between the president and the sponsor of the legislation is negative, which would suggest that presidents are less likely to preempt legislation as the ideological distance increases, but it is small and not statistically significant. The results in the first model show that presidents are more likely to preempt legislation that does not have political support from their party. The president is more likely to preempt legislation when the bill sponsor is of the opposite party as the president (21 percent) or when the partisanship of cosponsors is bipartisan or of the opposite party (17 percent).

The results for the presence of probable conflict between the branches do not suggest that an *independent* president is more likely to use unilateral action to preempt legislation. The results in the second, third, and fourth models in Table 6.2 show that presidents are *less likely* to issue unilateral orders preempting legislation as the ideological distances between the president and the median members of the House (−40 percent) and Senate

(−50 percent), and the Senate filibuster (−29 percent) increases.[39] This contradicts the expectations, but it suggests that presidents act strategically when issuing preemptive orders that key members of Congress may oppose. The executive–legislative dynamic clearly shapes the president's willingness to unilaterally move with or against Congress. An example of this is the White House's consideration of an executive order during the Carter administration outlining the standards for merit selection of judges, which urged the Senate to consider underrepresented groups as judicial candidates. Despite the fact that it was a Carter campaign promise, there was internal White House dissent about whether to issue the order. One staff member wrote that the administration would "face a rebellion" in the Senate if they issued an executive order on the issue. Better to avoid a confrontation and meet with the senators themselves ("Democrats particularly," it was suggested) because there were other ways to achieve policy goals and "there is at least one other way to kill the cat besides shooting it: we can stuff it with butter."[40] Yet President Carter did subsequently issue an executive order; however, the timing of the president's unilateral order ensured that his executive action then supported H.R. 7843, a bill that had widely passed both chambers in Congress, which the White House worked with Congress to pass. The bill advised the president "in selecting nominees to the Federal judgeships created by this Act give due consideration to qualified individuals regardless of race, color, sex, religion, or national origin."[41] As a result, instead of advising the Senate, the president's executive order advised the nominating commission "to make special efforts to seek out and identify well qualified women and members of minority groups as potential nominees."[42]

The prediction concerning the influence of increasing gridlock within Congress was that the president should be more likely to issue a unilateral order that preempts legislation, but the results only partially support this. A lack of party unity, as signaled by greater heterogeneity within the parties, has little effect, but the polarization between the parties prompts presidents to issue a preemptive order. Specifically, in the first and second models in Table 6.3, the coefficients for heterogeneity are negative for the House and positive for the Senate, but neither is statistically significant. However, in the third and fourth models, the coefficients for polarization between the parties are both positive and statistically significant. Presidents are more likely to issue more orders that preempt legislation when there is greater polarization between the parties in the Senate (77 percent) and the House (27 percent).

Presidents take advantage of the paralysis of institutional polarization to issue orders preempting proposed legislation. President Clinton's Proclamation 6920, establishing the Grand Staircase–Escalante National Monument, preempted legislation that was years in the making. The land that makes up the national monument had been at the center of controversy as early as 1936, when the Department of the Interior proposed setting aside nearly eleven acres of land in southeast Utah as the Escalante National Monument (Poll, Alexander, Campbell, and Miller 1989; Durrant 2007). Controversy erupted over the proposed classification of wilderness lands during Clinton's administration.[43] The Republican Party had majority control in both the House and Senate, but the chambers had differing views. They were mired in competing proposals over how to classify the lands. Because he was facing an election battle, President Clinton mounted a silent campaign to proclaim much of the land a national monument. In a theatrical moment, President Clinton issued Proclamation 6920 standing atop the Grand Canyon while onlookers watched the release of a bald eagle (Belco and Rottinghaus 2009).

On what policy issues are presidents more likely to preempt? Table 6.4 displays a cross tabulation of the types of preemption by the policy area. In general, presidents are most likely to issue preemptive orders in the area of natural resources and lands. Historically, Congress has delegated considerable authority to presidents to act in such matters, and presidents have taken full advantage. Specifically, Congress granted the president broad discretionary power to proclaim national monuments under the Antiquities Act of 1906 (16 U.S.C. § 431–433). The Act provides for unilateral action because the president is not required to consult with Congress, the state in which the monument is located, or the public prior to proclaiming a national monument. In many cases, Congress has actively disapproved of the president's action. President Clinton's proclamation establishing the Grand Staircase–Escalante National Monument was a source of congressional debate for over twenty years. The order

TABLE 6.4.
Unilateral preemption by type and issue.

	Foreign trade/aid	National defense/ emergencies	Social welfare/ justice	Governmental relations	Public lands/ resources
Direct executive branch	19% (4)	19% (4)	10% (2)	24% (5)	29% (6)
Executive action not in legislation or while resolution disapproving is before Congress	4% (2)	4% (2)	4% (2)	6% (3)	82% (41)
President vetoes bill and issues order instead	27% (3)	18% (2)	18% (2)	18% (2)	18% (2)
President issues order in lieu of expired authority	0%	88% (7)	0%	0%	12% (1)

Note: Percentages are row percentage totals, and total for each category is in parentheses below the percentage. Pearson χ^2 = 60.18, p < 0.001.

was considered by some to be an act of stealth policy making, in which President Clinton decided the fate of the controversial lands, surprising both Congress and the state of Utah. An outraged Congress duly explored the implications of executive power under the Act but decided ultimately not to curtail presidential authority to proclaim national monuments (Belco and Rottinghaus 2009).

Although presidents do not issue many preemptive orders in lieu of expired authority, where the authority to act has lapsed, presidents are more likely to issue such an order when it relates to national defense. Virtually all of the cases where presidents issued a preemptive order were national defense or security issues (88 percent). In several instances, presidents invoked authority of the Export Administration Act of 1979. President Reagan cited national security concerns in finding

. . . that the unrestricted access of foreign parties to United States commercial goods, technology, and technical data and the existence of certain boycott practices of foreign nations constitute in light of the expiration of the Export Administration Act of 1979, an unusual and extraordinary threat to the national security, foreign policy and economy of the United States and hereby declare a national economic emergency to deal with that threat.

However, "notwithstanding the expiration of the Export Administration Act of 1979," President Reagan issued the order, stating,

To the extent permitted by law, this Order also shall constitute authority for the issuance and continuation in full force and effect of rules and regulations by the President or his delegate, and all orders, licenses, and other forms of administrative action issued, taken or continued in effect pursuant thereto, relating to the administration of section 38(e) of the Arms Export Control Act.[44]

CONCLUSION

When and how *administrator* presidents choose to bargain with Congress or *independent* presidents act to unilaterally set policy in the legislative process is critical to understanding the nature of the presidency. The president's legislative and unilateral strategy varies depending on institutional and political circumstances. Presidents may short-circuit the bargaining process by intervening with a preemptive action. At other times, the president may satisfy congressional interests by issuing a supporting order. The former suggests a potentially problematic constitutional mishap where executive power dominates legislative power. The latter implies that the branches are separate but share governing power. Presidents obstruct this shared process when they issue unilateral orders preempting legislation and reinforce it when they issue orders that support proposed legislation. Unilateral orders are, therefore, more integrated into the legislative process than presumed.

Unilateral orders are issued in lieu of legislation as a means for resolving inter- and intrabranch conflict. The president's willingness to issue a unilateral order that circumvents legislation is greater when Congress is unable to successfully make policy. Specifically, this occurs when intrabranch polarization is higher or when the president is less likely to be overturned by a unified Congress. In 2014, President Obama issued two unilateral orders related to issues concerning equal pay for women. Congress had considered legislation in the past and was doing so when the president issued the orders. According to Laura Bassett, both orders mirrored:

provisions of the Paycheck Fairness Act, which Congress has twice failed to pass. One would prohibit federal contractors from retaliating against employees who share their salary information with each other. The provision is inspired by Lilly Ledbetter, the namesake of the first bill Obama signed on equal pay in 2009, who worked for nearly 20 years at Goodyear Tire and Rubber Co. before discovering that men in her same job with equal or lesser experience were earning significantly more money than she was. The second executive order will instruct the Department of Labor to create new regulations requiring federal contractors to report wage-related data to the government, in the hope that it will hold them more accountable for salary differences based on sex or race.[45]

In 2014, Congress reconsidered legislation to codify the president's two orders, but it ultimately failed to pass in the Republican-controlled House, during a volatile midterm election year. The president's order jump-started the legislative process, receiving support in the Democratic-led Senate, but the final effect of the two unilateral orders (without legislative backing) was of somewhat limited reach because the orders affected government entities only.

Presidents are clearly interested in using unilateral orders to their advantage. They issue unilateral orders to facilitate legislative progress even when they may have incentives to advance their policies independently by preempting Congress, such as when the branches are further apart ideologically or when the issue is on the president's agenda. Presidents are willing to support proposed legislation to help Congress overcome their collective action problem, especially if Congress has signaled that the issue is of concern to them. In doing so, they retain some control over the legislative process and signal to an opposition Congress the direction they prefer. Congress may continue to act, but at least the president has moved the wheels of government closer to him or her when change might otherwise not occur. Presidents take advantage of institutional incapacity but are equally reluctant to pursue an independent policy course, which suggests that unilateral orders are integrated into the shared power arrangement that governs the constitutional system.

CHAPTER SEVEN

An Independent President or Administrator?

Orders That Adapt and Implement Law

THE NEED TO MAINTAIN A SEPARATION of institutional powers is central to the political system. Under the U.S. Constitution, Congress is the source of "all legislative powers" with the authority "to make all Laws," whereas the president is expected to "take care that the Laws be faithfully executed." The transition from the creation of law to the execution of law, in theory, appears seamless as one branch respectfully hands power to another. But the transition of power is not always straightforward because the presumptive *last word* rests in the execution of law giving presidents significant power to unilaterally create policy. And efforts to restrain the president's exercise of discretion are difficult, even with Congress casting a watchful eye over the president after law is enacted. For example, in an effort to hold President Obama accountable for his exercise of discretion in implementing the Patient Protection and Affordable Care Act (PPACA), Speaker John Boehner (R-OH) asked members of the House, "Are you willing to let any president choose what laws to execute and what laws to change?"[1] The purpose of his question was to gain a "no" vote from members of the House to agree to sue the president for violating his constitutional duty to execute the law.

Unilateral orders give presidents the ability to exercise discretion choosing when and how to execute law. As the head of a unitary branch of government, presidents can unilaterally direct the actions of the executive branch and private citizens through the use of executive orders and policy proclamations. Institutional and political factors may motivate presidents to exercise discretion when implementing law. And, after law is enacted, presidents may chafe at the constraints placed on their authority or policy and decide to adapt rather than implement law. That there is no perfect solution and the president's constitutional duty to faithfully execute law remain sources of controversy between the branches. The puzzle is, how do presidents use unilateral orders to execute law within

a system of separate and shared power? As in the other stages of the legislative policy process, presidents use unilateral orders to execute law
consistent with their dual roles.

As *administrators*, presidents use unilateral orders to implement law
by faithfully adhering to the intent and design of legislation. As *independents*, presidents adapt law exercising their discretion to achieve their
own policy goals. The difficulty, though, is determining when presidents
are faithfully executing law and when they are adapting law to meet
their own policy goals. President Obama used unilateral orders both as
a faithful *administrator* and an *independent* president in executing the
PPACA of 2010. In the act, Congress called for the president to "establish, within the Department of Health and Human Services, a council
to be known as the 'National Prevention, Health Promotion and Public
Health Council'" to "provide coordination and leadership at the Federal
level, and among all Federal departments and agencies, with respect to
prevention, wellness and health promotion practices, the public health
system, and integrative health care in the United States."[2] In the role of
a faithful *administrator*, President Obama issued Executive Order 13544
establishing the Council, specifying the membership, and citing the purpose consistent with the language of the law.[3]

A few months before, however, President Obama acted as an *independent* president when he issued Executive Order 13535 to honor his
commitment to implement the language of the Stupak-Pitts Amendment
that had been omitted from the PPACA:

It is necessary to establish an adequate enforcement mechanism to ensure that
Federal funds are not used for abortion services (except in cases of rape or
incest, or when the life of the woman would be endangered), consistent with
a longstanding Federal statutory restriction that is commonly known as the
Hyde Amendment. The purpose of this order is to establish a comprehensive,
Government-wide set of policies and procedures to achieve this goal and to
make certain that all relevant actors—Federal officials, State officials (including
insurance regulators) and health care providers—are aware of their responsibilities, new and old.

By agreeing to adapt the provisions of the law, President Obama secured the votes he needed to meet his goal.

As illustrated throughout this book, this is familiar ground for the dual executive with respect to unilateral action. Before legislation has been introduced, the president acts as an independent by using unilateral orders to act first to influence the formulation of policy in Congress and, as an administrator, by exercising routine functions. After bills are on Congress's agenda, the president acts as an independent, by issuing unilateral orders to preempt legislation, and as an administrator, to support the legislative process. In executing law, presidents as *administrators* use unilateral orders to carry out their duty as part of a combined effort with Congress. As *independents*, presidents use them exercising greater discretion as they pursue their own agenda by adapting law. These distinctions echo the differences concerning the dual role of the executive. Presidents can issue unilateral orders to faithfully execute law by drawing on authority delegated by Congress, allowing both branches to achieve their policy goals. The need to exercise discretion to respond to ambiguity in law, changing circumstances, and their own policy goals can motivate presidents to adapt law.

THE DUAL EXECUTIVE AND EXECUTING LAW

The framers of the Constitution intended Congress to be the "first branch" by enumerating powers to the legislature that it had not to other branches (Spitzer 1993). The Constitution, though, did not neglect the president. The document ensured that the branches share power but placed Congress first among the equals. A narrow reading of the executive, as offered by some at the Constitutional Convention, was that presidents should be considered clerks whose primary function is to execute the laws of the legislature (Madison 1911). In this context, the president's role seems fairly straightforward. Congress enacts a law, and the president's responsibility is to direct the executive branch to implement the will of the legislative branch through a series of formal and informal rules (Kerwin 1994).

Is the president a faithful executor as the Constitution requires or strategic in the decision about whether to implement law? Neustadt (1990) conceives his "president-clerk" as one who must both follow and lead in his relationship with Congress. By this standard, the president is the *motor* that runs government, and Congress functions as the *brakes* (Dahl 1967). He or she is tasked with fulfilling the expectations of an enacting Congress that places the brakes on the president in legislation by delegating authority and even instructions sufficient only to carry out its goals. Meanwhile, when implementation is complicated by divergent political goals, the president may decide instead to adapt law to suit his or her policy objectives. The decision the president must make is to adhere to the role of administrator and faithfully execute law or to take independent action by adapting law.

With the implementation of law, the two branches share power. Through delegation, the independence of the legislative and executive branches is preserved, but, in reality, the lines begin to blur. That is, law may reflect the goals of Congress by establishing policy objectives, although the discretion over how to implement them is delegated to the president (Fisher 1997). Congress is required only to establish an "intelligible principle" with sufficient direction for the president to follow in executing the law.[4] And, generally, deference is given to the executive branch on the interpretation and application of the law in question.[5] Therefore, the execution of law through faithful adherence is more likely when Congress specifically prescribes the president's role. With that role prescribed in law, the president is more of an *administrator* implementing law, consistent with his or her role envisioned in the Constitution.

When legislation passed by Congress does not capture their policy vision, or Congress attempts to curtail their constitutional powers, presidents may decide not to acquiesce to congressional control. Rather than faithfully implementing a law, presidents may consider using their unilateral order to adapt the policy. For authority, presidents can draw on their express powers, as well as those that are implied and inherent in the Constitution and in their role as chief executives. President may rely on a plausible assertion of Article II authority, combined with a showing of congressional silence or acquiescence. The extent of their authority under implied and inherent power is generally dependent on whether the action and interpretation are based on a narrow or interpretative reading of the Constitution and whether it touches on domestic or foreign affairs.[6] Importantly, by adapting law, presidents are able to exercise independence in policy making and to retain control over the executive branch (Nather 2014).

FAITHFUL IMPLEMENTATION

Faithful implementation is straightforward. Both chambers of Congress pass the same version of a bill, present it to the president for signature, he or she signs it and then issues a unilateral order citing the law and directing the executive branch to carry out the necessary action. Implementing policy generally requires the president and Congress to work together, where Congress powers the ship of state with the president at the helm. To satisfy the need for an intelligible principle, Congress may define only the policy goal, giving the president sufficient discretion to carry out the legislative intent. On July 1, 2010, President Obama signed the Comprehensive Iran Sanctions, Accountability, and Divestment Act of 2010 (CISADA) into law. CISADA amended the Iran Sanctions Act of 1996 (ISA), strengthening existing U.S. sanctions with respect to the Iranian energy industry, adding the potential for the imposition of serious limits on foreign financial institutions' access to the U.S. financial system if they engage in certain transactions involving Iran.[7] To implement his authority to impose or waive these new sanctions, President Obama issued Executive Order 13574 delegating decision-making authority to the secretaries of state and the treasury related to these newly created sanctions.[8]

Following Congress's lead, President George W. Bush also engaged in faithful implementation. Under the Magnuson-Stevens Fishery Conservation and Management Act (2007), Congress established a broad policy goal to end overfishing in America by replenishing fish stocks and enforcing fishing laws. Citing his intention to assist in ensuring faithful execution of the law, President Bush issued an executive order requiring the establishment of regulations and management measures for the protection of the striped bass and red drum fish population in federal waters.[9] The president's authority was very broad in scope in the Clean Diamond Trade Act (2003), where Congress established a policy goal as an intelligible principle for him to follow.[10] In the findings, Congress stated that the United States had an obligation to help sever the link between diamonds and conflict and press for implementation of the Kimberly Process Certification Scheme. Congress gave the president discretion regarding an effective date, the decision to delegate his authority, and the means for gaining international acceptance, all of which were incorporated into the executive order implementing the law.[11]

The president and Congress are more likely to share power when unilateral orders are used to implement a triggering event such as a national emergency, trade agreement, or treaty. In negotiating trade agreements, the president may have broad discretion to enter into negotiations with foreign nations, but they are not effective unless Congress adopts implementing legislation (Krutz and Peake 2009). The process is lengthy, and sometimes one administration handles the negotiations and a later administration works with Congress to develop the legislation. The North America Free Trade Agreement was negotiated by President George H. W. Bush but was signed and implemented by President Clinton.[12]

Another way the two branches share power is when the president needs Congress to authorize administrative changes *within* the executive branch to create new employment opportunities, to alter and create job descriptions, and to make changes in duties and salaries. Facing rising inflation and the need for budget reductions, President Ford sought authorization to set ceilings on federal salary increases. He appealed to Congress for authorization in his annual State of the Union Address in 1975, his proposed budget, and a legislative initiative. Congress was unwilling to set a federal salary ceiling, but it did enact the Executive Salary Cost of Living Adjustment Act of 1975, which President Ford implemented through executive order.[13] The president and Congress may work together in the design of legislation affecting the executive branch. In 1985, President Reagan was concerned over retaining and enhancing the well-being of those serving in the military. Cooperation between the branches resulted in the Military Family Act of 1985, which provided hiring preferences for military spouses.[14] President Reagan issued an executive order directing the Secretary of Defense to implement the Act.[15]

Although presidents seek Congress's support to authorize actions within the executive branch, they may prefer flexibility for managing personnel, arbitrating interagency disputes, the transfer and disposition of federal property, and the creation of commissions (Cooper 2002). President Reagan, during his first term in office, investigated a variety of methods for reducing personnel costs and increasing efficiency in executive agencies. Through the creation of the Committee on Cost Control, Reagan developed the concept of an employee exchange between the public and private sector as one effort toward achieving these goals. Congress provided legislative support for the program by enacting the Executive Exchange Program Voluntary Services Act of 1986, enabling President Reagan to implement through executive order an experimental program on executive exchange.[16] Similarly, the president may request authorization from Congress to accomplish a major reorganization. The authorization of reorganization authority was one of President Carter's earliest legislative requests. Congress enacted the Reorganization Act of 1977, prohibiting Congress from amending plans once they had been approved.[17] President Carter embarked on a major reorganization of the executive branch early in his administration in an effort to improve government efficiency during 1977 and 1978 and issued a number of executive orders that eliminated, redesigned, and created agencies.

The creation of agencies within the executive branch also gives presidents another opportunity to share power with Congress. According to Lewis (2003), "Presidents would prefer to create agencies by statute as long as they have had influence in the agency's crafting." President Ford signed the Energy Reorganization Act, which provided for the establishment of the Energy Research and Development Administration (ERDA) and the president's Energy Resource Council.[18] In his remarks before signing the law, he paid tribute to the combined efforts of Congress and the administration in saying:

I just want to thank all the Members of Congress who are here. I can recall rather vividly when this recommendation came to the Congress, and I am especially pleased that I have an opportunity to sign the legislation which establishes ERDA. I think it is a tremendous step forward. It is really the result of hard work by the Congress and, I think, good recommendations by the Administration.[19]

Presidents may begin by creating an agency through unilateral action and later ask Congress to establish the agency through legislation even when that places Congress in the president's national intelligence arena. Following the terrorist attacks of 2001, President Bush created the Office of Homeland Security through executive order.[20] In a message to Congress, he initially "rebuffed" most proposed legislation on the subject (Rudalevige 2002).[21] Recognizing the benefits of a cabinet agency created by statute, President Bush returned to Congress with a legislative proposal to create the Department of Homeland Security (Perrow 2007).[22] Congress responded by enacting the Homeland Security Act of 2002, which President Bush implemented through executive order.[23]

The redesign of an agency may serve to give the president greater control within the executive branch and satisfy a congressional objective at the same time. In conjunction with the Department of Homeland Security, President Bush sought to centralize national intelligence. In response to the president's legislative initiative, Congress established the Director of National Intelligence (DNI) under the Intelligence Reform and Terrorism Prevention Act of 2004.[24] In his remarks on signing the act, President Bush acknowledged that "a key lesson of September the 11th, 2001, is that America's intelligence agencies must work together as a single, unified enterprise." The Intelligence Reform and Terrorism Prevention Act of 2004 created the position of director of national intelligence to be appointed by the president with the consent of the Senate. After the Senate had approved the appointment, President George W. Bush issued an executive order and effectively fulfilled a long-term congressional objective to curb the independence of the director of the CIA, who henceforth would report to the DNI.[25] The president was able to satisfy a goal of Congress and maintain control over the executive branch.

ADAPTING LAW

Although the president's role as an administrator in implementing legislation seems to dominate, there is still the opportunity to adapt laws enacted by Congress. The president may choose not to follow the direction in the law or adhere to Congress's recommendations or suggestions. Instead, presidents may decide to strike out on their own by issuing a unilateral order that states their own position related to the recently enacted law. The content of the unilateral order may relate to a law recently passed, but the president chooses not to rely on that particular statute. Instead, he or she may cite the Constitution and laws *generally* indicating the president is guided by his or her own policy objectives. This is the *independent* president exercising his or her prerogative. That president may, at the time he or she signs a bill into law, issue a signing statement that indicates his or her satisfaction or dissatisfaction with the new law. According to Ainsworth, Harward, and Moffett (2012), "The specific comments may raise, among other issues, policy concerns, exhortations for future legislative activity, guidelines for the implementation of the law by bureaucratic agents, or constitutional objections to provisions within the legislation." But signing statements are effective only if the president takes some type of supplemental policy action. Unilateral orders are one tool presidents can use to adapt legislation by directing the executive branch to guide their own policy action.

The president's unilateral order may adapt a law by expanding or enhancing the intent or meaning, incorporating specific elements from the law. On May 20, 2009, President Obama signed the Fraud Enforcement and Recovery Act (FERA) of 2009 into law. In his signing statement he remarked that it "provides Federal investigators and prosecutors with significant new criminal and civil tools to assist in holding accountable those who have committed financial fraud" and "these legislative enhancements will help the Department of Justice to combat" different types of fraud. He objected to only one provision in the law, which was the requirement that "every department, agency, bureau, board, commission, office, independent establishment, or instrumentality of the United States to furnish to the Financial Crisis Inquiry Commission, a legislative entity, any information related to any Commission inquiry."[26] A few months later, President Obama issued Executive Order 13519 establishing the Financial Fraud Enforcement Task Force chaired by the attorney general and comprised of the heads of departments and agencies with the Department of Justice first on the list.[27] In issuing the order, the president cited his constitutional authority and the laws of the United States of America but not the recently enacted law. In a subcommittee hearing on the Oversight of the Financial Fraud Enforcement Task Force, the question rose over the relationship of the law to the president's newly created task force. Senator Grassley (R-IA) remarked:

This task force was created in November of 2009. Senator Leahy and I wrote the Fraud Enforcement Recovery Act [FERA] of 2009, signed into law May of 2009. The legislation increased the resources available to the Justice Department to combat criminal and civil fraud. It also provided additional resources to the FBI and the SEC. Combating fraud was on Congress's radar before the creation of the task force. Given that, regardless of the existence of the task force, fraud-related crime was being investigated and prosecuted.

The additional resources and provisions may have spurred the president to create the task force but, importantly, he established a reporting system consistent with the objection he voiced in his signing statement. Acting as an *independent*, President Obama adapted the provisions of FERA by channeling inquiries through the attorney general, rather than furnishing information directly to Congress's Financial Crisis Inquiry Commission, as required by the law Congress passed.

In another example, when Congress enacted the Government Performance and Results Act of 1993 (GPRA), President Clinton remarked when signing the bill into law that he and Vice President Gore agreed that it was "an important first step in the efforts to reform the way the Federal Government operates and relates to the American people."[28] The GRPA had an incremental, long-term program that required federal agencies to launch pilot projects and to develop strategic plans and measure outcomes (Moynihan 2003). President Clinton and the vice president previously had embarked on White House–led National Performance Review (NPR) designed to streamline government, initiate ways of increasing the public's trust in government, and to press on agencies the means of using customer service to accomplish this goal.[29] President Clinton's executive order, which he issued one month after signing the GPRA, borrowed from both sources. Citing his constitutional authority and the laws of the United States, Clinton established customer service standards from the executive branch, created NPR, and adopted two of the expressed purposes in the GPRA to improve federal program effectiveness and public accountability by focusing on outputs and service quality.[30]

The president may decide to use unilateral action when Congress attempts to direct, recommend, or offer its sense regarding presidential action. In 2011, President Obama signed the Budget Control Act of 2011 into law. This was legislation that he had earlier supported with an SAP wholeheartedly endorsing the Budget Control Act.[31] The law directed presidential action when it imposed caps on discretionary programs to reduce funding by more than $1 trillion over a ten-year period. After the bill was signed into law, President Obama issued Executive Order 13589 citing authority "vested in me as President by the Constitution and the laws of the United States of America, and in order to further promote efficient spending in the Federal Government." The order sought to preserve the president's authority over the executive branch, requiring only that the federal government adopt "measures promoting efficient government spending that reflected the goals of the newly enacted law.[32] Given an opening, the president took it to shape the outcome to his preferences.

When Congress enacted the Special Foreign Assistance Act of 1986, Congress required the president to assist the government of Haiti in recovering stolen assets, and specifically in doing so "the president shall exercise the authorities granted by Section 203 of the International Emergency Economic Powers Act."[33] President Reagan issued an executive order prohibiting transactions involving property related to Haitian nationals but chose not to rely on his emergency powers, citing instead the Foreign Assistance Act.[34] His unilateral order fulfilled Congress's request and, at the same time, reinforced the position he articulated in his signing statement that a congressional mandate specifying actions to be taken by the government would unreasonably detract from the flexibility necessary to formulate and conduct a sound foreign policy.[35]

Presidents may also decide to adapt law when they are pursuing one policy direction and Congress another. President Carter and Congress faced this problem regarding the management and destruction of nuclear waste. Having established an Interagency Review Group on Nuclear Waste Management to assist in planning, the president was committed to researching all possible alternative sites. Congress, on the other hand, was

committed to one location. When President Carter signed the appropriations bill that provided funding for construction of the Waste Isolation
Pilot Plant project in New Mexico, he stated in his signing statement that
he did not endorse the project.[36] A few months later, he issued an executive order cancelling the project and created a state planning council to
participate in determining the future location.[37] In this way, the president
has the final say, even after legislation has been passed by Congress and
signed into law.

EXPECTATIONS FOR ORDERS THAT ADAPT LAW

We restate the expectations from Chapter 2 in this section. Under the
separation of powers, presidents are ultimately faced with the decision
to implement legislation as Congress intended or exercise discretion by
adapting law. The president's institutional response should be influenced
by both political conditions and the delegation of authority. During the
legislative process, an integral component is the decision to establish the
extent and controls on the president's actions. The delegation of authority
succeeds not only in expressing Congress's intent; it also gives the president's unilateral orders the weight of law. The delegation of authority is a
significant source of power that allows the president to unilaterally direct
the actions of others. Therefore presidents should be more likely to adapt
law when Congress has delegated broad discretion and presidents cite that
power as a source of authority. Presidents who lack sufficient discretion
can still shift policy in their direction relying on their own authority. As
independents, presidents are more likely to adapt law citing their broad
constitutional authority.

Presidents who adapt law are more concerned with their agenda, which
they seek to adopt, using both the legislative and administrative processes.
The president's agenda provides a master list from which the president's
future administrative and legislative accomplishments are drawn. Focused
on getting their legislative priorities on Congress's agenda, presidents
may work with Congress transmitting a legislative package or program.
When there is dissension between the branches, a recently enacted law
the president is required to execute may not fully reflect the president's
position. Presidents who have a particular policy outcome in mind, or one

they have promised to the public, may find themselves using unilateral orders to achieve their policy agenda as it relates to recently enacted law.

Presidents should therefore issue more orders that adapt law when they are reaching the end of a term in office. This includes the second half of their first term in office and at the very end of their terms in the second half of their second term. *Independent* presidents should also be more likely to issue orders that adapt law when they are politically more powerful in relation to Congress. When government is unified, the expectations of policy between the branches are generally compatible and presidents are more likely to implement law. When government is divided, presidents may choose to adapt law, conceivably shifting it closer to their preference or filling in gaps in the law to their own liking. As the parties in Congress become more heterogeneous or polarized, presidents will seize their opportunity to adapt law. Difference in ideology between the president and the pivotal voters in the House and Senate may mean that the two branches are less able to agree on legislation, and law may not reflect the president's policy preference. However, presidents have a chance to pursue their policy goal after law is enacted. The expectation is that presidents are more likely to adapt law to ultimately achieve their policy goals as the ideological distance between them and the pivotal members of Congress increase.

DATA AND METHODS

The data include only unilateral orders that were used to implement or adapt a recently enacted law. This *includes* all unilateral orders that execute law but *excludes*, by necessity, laws that are self-executing or those where there is simply no recent law to enact. To determine whether an order relates to a recently enacted law, the content of each order was analyzed to identify laws cited in the order and its relationship to recently enacted laws even when no law was specifically cited. Several electronic databases were searched to identify whether a law relating to the order had been enacted during the president's administration.[38] The next step was to determine whether the president's unilateral order was used to faithfully implement or adapt a law. An order faithfully implemented law when the *specific statute* was cited in the order, and the law was enacted within one of the two legislative sessions that make up the four years of the president's administration. An order met the criteria for adapting law when it related to a law enacted within one of the two legislative sessions that make up the four years of the president's administration, and the president *did not cite the law exclusively* as a source of authority in the order. A binary dependent variable (*Adapt*) was created and coded 1 if the unilateral order was used to adapt law and 0 otherwise, which included orders used to implement law as the base case. The total number of orders that relate to the execution of recently enacted law includes a total of 476, of which 386 were issued to implement law and ninety to adapt law.

Political factors influence the type and extent of authority delegated to the president and the executive branch through instructions, guidelines, and statutory limits. A variable to represent the president's term in office specifically whether the president is in his second term (*Second Term*), the second half of his first term (*Second Half*) or both (*Second Half, Second Term*). Presidents are influenced by the type and extent of authority Congress delegates through the inclusion of instructions, guidelines, and statutory limits in law. The variables that measure the president's source of authority and discretion include when they cite their constitutional authority (*Constitutional Authority*) and the extent of discretion granted by Congress (*Substantive Discretion*). One institutional factor is the president's agenda, which he develops together with the executive branch and Congress. The president formulates a comprehensive agenda from which the legislative program is presented to Congress. Two variables operationalize the president's agenda, including whether the issue was on the president's agenda (*Presidential Agenda*) and whether the issue was one of the White House's legislative initiatives (*Legislative Initiative*).

Political conditions should also influence the president's decision to execute law. Variables measuring of *interbranch* and *intrabranch* gridlock are included as in the past chapters. Interbranch gridlock is operationalized by the difference in ideology between the president and the key member of each chamber, including the ideological distance between the president and the median member of each chamber (*President and Senate/ House*) and the ideological distance between the president and the Senate filibuster pivot (*President and Filibuster*). Intrabranch gridlock is operationalized using the ideological distance between the median members of the parties in each chamber (*Polarization House/Senate*). Because the dependent variable is binary, a series of logistic regression models are used to show the difference in likelihood that a president will issue an order that adapts law over one that implements law.[39]

ORDERS THAT ADAPT AND IMPLEMENT LAW OVER TIME

Figure 7.1 charts the dual roles of the *administrator* and *independent* president at work by presidential administrations. The presumption outlined in the Constitution is that presidents are more likely to be faithful *administrators*, and presidents over time seem to generally comply. Of the 476 orders issued to execute law, 386 were issued to implement law and ninety were used to adapt law.[40] Presidents use the leverage they have to pursue their agenda using their unilateral orders to occasionally adapt law, but the numbers show they use it infrequently. There is, though, a

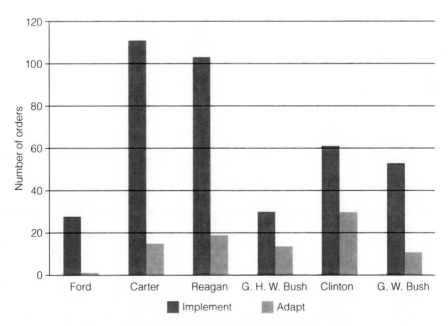

FIGURE 7.1. Presidents and the execution of law. The bar total represents the total orders in each category (implement and adapt) by president.

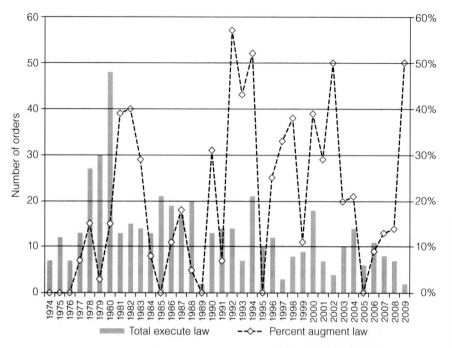

FIGURE 7.2. Presidents and the execution of law. The bar total represents the total orders in the execution category. Percentages on the right represent the percentage of times an order is used to adapt law out of all orders in the execution category.

steady rise in the number of instances of orders being used to adapt laws beginning with the Ford administration and rising to a peak during the Clinton administration. Presidents Reagan and Clinton, who were both two-term presidents, issued more orders to adapt legislation than Presidents Carter and George H. W. Bush, who were only one-term presidents.

The ratio of augment orders out of the total orders in this phase of policy process is also of interest. Figure 7.2 graphs the number of orders that are used to execute law in total in relation to the percentage of times an order is used to adapt (augment) law. Presidents seem to issue a higher percentage of orders to adapt law soon after arriving in office, which may reflect the honeymoon effect as presidents enjoy favorable support and may be able to get away with more. The percentage of orders that are used to adapt law rises consistently in 1978, 1981–1982, 1991, and 2002. By the middle of a president's term, the rate of adaptive orders issued slows. It could be that the Congress has gotten wise to the president's strategy and has required specific guidelines for implementation that do not allow the president to deviate from them or specifies a self-executing process. It could also be that Congress has decided to write legislation more favorable to the president's position that acts as a disincentive to adapt law. The amount of legislation enacted may also decrease, giving the president fewer opportunities to implement or adapt legislation.

WHEN PRESIDENTS IMPLEMENT
OR ADAPT LEGISLATION

Tables 7.1 and 7.2 show the results for the measures of interbranch and intrabranch conflict. Positive coefficients signal coefficients that presidents are more likely to adapt legislation, whereas negative coefficients signal coefficients less likely to adapt (more likely to implement). In Table 7.1, because of the high correlation between the ideological distance between the president and the House median member and the ideological distance between the president and the Senate filibuster pivot, the latter was estimated in a separate model. As expected, the results from the three models in Table 7.1 and the two in Table 7.2 support the contention that presidents who issue a unilateral order to *adapt* legislation are the picture of a more independent executive. First, such an executive is more likely to cite constitutional authority (9 to 10 percent more likely) when issuing an adaptive order. Second, presidents are more likely to adapt legislation when the issue is on their agenda (21 to 22 percent more likely). This happens when Congress is pursuing one policy direction and the president another, as President Carter did when he issued an executive order adapting the law funding the Waste Isolation Pilot Plant project in New Mexico.

Presidents are less likely (5 to 6 percent less likely) to issue an order that adapts law when it is one of their legislative initiatives. This is not surprising because presidents are able to get more of what they want in the legislation when they initiate the process. This suggests that, when presidents have greater input into the legislative process, it lessens their need to adapt law to meet their policy goals. At times, the president's order serves as a legislative initiative that Congress will use to adopt executive

TABLE 7.1.
Issuing implement and adapt orders: Interbranch measures.

	Distance between president and Senate	Distance between president and House	Distance between president and filibuster
Second term	-1.94 *** (0.515) [-18.0%]	-1.66 *** (0.483) [-16.4%]	-1.59 *** (0.478) [-15.7%]
Second half	-1.08 *** (0.389) [-13.7%]	-0.924 *** (0.374) [-11.7%]	-0.837 *** (0.363) [-10.4%]
Election year	0.726 (0.345)	0.649 (0.339)	0.543 (0.337)
Second half, second term	1.71 *** (0.605) [28.3%]	1.51 ** (0.602) [24.3%]	1.46 *** (0.603) [23.3%]
Constitutional authority	0.983 * (0.479) [9.0%]	1.05 * (0.478) [9.7%]	1.08 * (0.475) [9.9%]
Substantive discretion	0.399 (0.291)	0.359 (0.288)	0.362 (0.286)
Presidential agenda	2.22 *** (0.397) [22.7%]	2.11 *** (0.387) [22.0%]	2.04 *** (0.382) [21.1%]
Legislative initiative	-0.561 ** (0.306) [-5.8%]	-0.582 ** (0.303) [-6.1%]	-638 *** (0.305) [-6.6%]
Distance between president and House or Senate	1.75 ** (0.800) [20.2%]	1.21 (0.852)	—
Distance between president and filibuster	—	—	2.45 ** (1.43) [28.6%]
N	476	476	476
Pseudo R^2	0.155	0.149	0.151
Log likelihood	-194.6	-196.0	-195.6
Likelihood ratio χ^2	71.8 ***	69.0 ***	69.8 ***
Reduction in error	2.22%	3.33%	4.44%

Note: Dependent variable: Coded 1 for orders that adapt law and 0 for orders that implement law.

*** Indicates statistical significance at $p < 0.01$.

** Indicates statistical significance at $p < 0.05$.

* Indicates statistical significance at $p < 0.10$.

The percentage of expected change is shown in brackets (holding all other variables at their mean). Tests are two-tailed tests.

TABLE 7.2.
Issuing implement and adapt orders: Intrabranch measures.

	Party polarization in the Senate	Party polarization in the House
Second term	−1.78 *** (0.496) [−17.2%]	−1.84 *** 0(.511) [−17.8%]
Second half	−0.813 ** (0.364) [−10.1%]	−0.941 *** (0.372) [−11.8%]
Election year	0.636 ** (0.337) [8.1%]	0.635 ** (0.337) [8.1%]
Second half, second term	1.56 *** (0.603) [25.3%]	1.70 *** (0.607) [28.3%]
Constitutional source of authority	0.928 (0.487) [8.7%]	0.971 ** (0.484) [9.0%]
Substantive discretion	0.377 (0.287)	0.377 (0.286)
Presidential agenda	2.00 *** (0.383) [20.7%]	2.00 *** (0.382) [20.8%]
Legislative initiative	−0.621 ** (0.303) [−6.4%]	−0.612 ** (0.302) [−6.4%]
Party polarization House/Senate	4.01 ** (1.92) [46.6%]	7.50 ** (3.83) [87.2%]
N	476	476
Pseudo R^2	0.154	0.153
Log likelihood	−194.9	−195.1
Likelihood ratio χ^2	71.3 ***	70.8 ***
Reduction in error	3.33%	4.44%

Note: Dependent variable: Coded 1 for orders that adapt law and 0 for orders that implement law.
*** Indicates statistical significance at $p < 0.01$.
** Indicates statistical significance at $p < 0.05$.
* Indicates statistical significance at $p < 0.10$.
The percentage of expected change is shown in brackets (holding all other variables at their mean). Tests are two-tailed tests.

policy. President Carter's Executive Order 12036 explicitly identified allowable and prohibited actions regarding foreign surveillance by agencies (Barilleaux and Zellers 2010); Congress incorporated this into the Foreign

Intelligence Surveillance Act (FISA).[41] The act represented a significant effort in Congress's efforts to formalize intelligence policy through legislation instead of executive order or administrative directives. FISA permitted the president, acting through the attorney general, to authorize electronic surveillances for foreign intelligence purposes without a court order in certain circumstances. In his statement on signing FISA, Carter acknowledged this legislation as being "the first step toward the goal of establishing statutory charters for our intelligence agencies."[42] He issued an executive order implementing the actions set forth in the act, authorizing electronic surveillance for foreign intelligence purposes.[43] When the law was amended to include foreign intelligence physical searches, President Clinton issued a revised executive order implementing the changes to the law necessitating organizational and administrative changes within the executive branch.[44]

Some of the results, however, contradict the expectations. Presidents appear less likely to use unilateral orders to adapt law when legislative sessions are coming to a close. In Tables 7.1 and 7.2, the coefficients for the term in office indicate that presidents are less likely to issue an order to adapt law in their second terms (15 to 18 percent less likely) or in the second half of their term in office (10 to 13 percent less likely). This suggests that the president is not the lame duck he or she is often accused of being and that the two branches may be effectively able to work together even as their collective time in office dwindles. However, at the very end of their tenure in office—the true definition of last minutes action—they are much more likely (23 to 28 percent more likely) to use their orders to facilitate their own policy as a means to leave a legacy. The implication is that, when they are truly with one foot out of the Oval Office, presidents work diligently to ensure that their policy is adopted. The effects of an election year on the president's unilateral action show mixed results. In Table 7.1, the effect of an election year is considered with interbranch measures, and the coefficient is positive but is not statistically significant. In Table 7.2, the coefficients are both positive and statistically significant; they indicate that the president is more likely (8 percent more likely) to issue a unilateral order that adapts law.

Interbranch and interbranch relations play a role in the president's decision to act with independence in the executing law. The ideological differences between the president and key members of the Senate influence the president's unilateral action. In Table 7.1, it is more likely that the president will issue an order to adapt legislation as the ideological distance increases between the president and the median member of the Senate (20 percent more likely) and the Senate filibuster (28 percent more likely). The coefficient for the ideological distance between the president and the House median member is positive but not statistically significant. In Table 7.2, polarization between the parties in the two chambers is an important predictor. The president is significantly more likely to issue an adaptive order when the polarization in the House increases (87 percent more likely) and the Senate (46 percent more likely). These actions taken together demonstrate a panoply of interests when presidents take advantage of their first *and* last mover advantage. Congress is demonstrably unable to stop the president at this stage, giving the president a greater hand in executing his or her preferences. When executing law, *independent* presidents have their last opportunity to bend the outcome to their preferred policy direction. This does not mean that presidents rewrite law, but it can alter the effect of a law. As a result, presidents retain a significant advantage over Congress.

SIGNING STATEMENTS AND UNILATERAL ORDERS THAT EXECUTE LAW

A look at the relationship between signing statements and the use of unilateral orders to execute law completes the picture of the president. Signing statements can provide valuable insight into the president's position on the law. As Cooper (2005) explains, presidential signing statements "identify provisions of the legislation with which the president has concerns and (1) provide the president's interpretation of the language of the law (2) announce constitutional limits on the implementation of some of its provisions, or (3) indicate directions to executive branch officials as to how to administer the new law in an acceptable manner." Conley (2011) notes that signing statements are related to interbranch relationships, where Congress and the president adapt to their political circumstances. Signing statements can be rhetorical, with presidents thanking members of Congress for their participation and acknowledging the progress made by cooperation between the branches (Kennedy 2014).

To distinguish between these two very different uses of signing statements we use the rhetorical/constitutional coding scheme adopted by Kelley and Marshall (2008; see Kelley 2007). Consistent with their approach, in a *rhetorical* statement, the president conveyed support for members of Congress and endorsement of the legislation. In a *constitutional* statement, the president raised one or more constitutional objections to the language and the duties required in the law. The measure differentiates between those signing statements in favor of the legislation in a signing statement (*rhetorical statement*) and those opposed (*constitutional objection*). The data consist of signing statements issued by the president related to a law he executed with unilateral action. Each signing statement was read and analyzed to determine when the president expressed his discontent and constitutional objections or conveyed some type of support for Congress and/or the law.

Figure 7.3 shows that presidents issue more rhetorical signing statements related to laws they implement through unilateral action.[45] This is understandable because presidents who endorse the legislation are more likely to ensure it is implemented consistent with the law. By the time the legislation has passed, presidents and Congress have often agreed on the specifics (Marlow 2011). However, presidents implement law even after expressing their specific objections to the legislation in a constitutional signing statement. Apparently objections, even constitutional ones, do not prevent them from implementing law. Nor does expressing their specific objections to the legislation in a constitutional signing statement prevent presidents from adapting law, although this occurs very infrequently in general and less frequently in relation to those orders the president uses to implement law. Surprisingly, presidents issue more signing statements affirming the legislation even when they adapt the execution of the law through unilateral action, although the differences are minor.

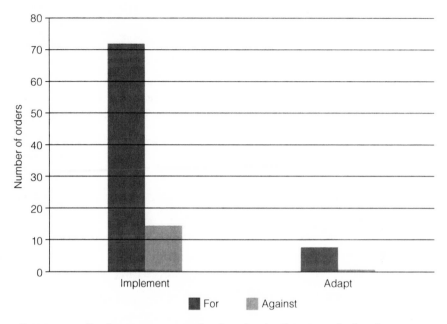

FIGURE 7.3. Signing statements and orders that implement and adapt law. The figures show the relationship between the use of signing statements for (rhetorical) or against (constitutional) law and when an order was issued to implement or adapt the same law.

CONCLUSION

The creation of law connects the president to Congress from the agenda-setting stage, through the legislative process, and finally, in the execution of law. The dual functions of the president means presidents must decide between faithfully executing law consistent with congressional expectations or acting more independently by adapting law to suit their policy goals. The decision to implement or adapt law reveals much about executive–legislative action and the transition of power. Based on the number of unilateral orders issued that execute law, presidents act more often in the role of *administrators*. A president is charged with executing law because "part of his responsibility as the chief executive is to enforce the law, so he will necessarily be cognizant of the legislative will and seek to advance it in many of his activities" (Whittington and Carpenter 2003).

Indeed, presidents are less likely to act as independents, and more as *administrators*, in several scenarios. Presidents are less likely to adapt law when the legislation was of their initiative. This is not surprising because presidents are able to get more of what they want when they initiate the process. They are less likely to adapt law generally in their second half of terms and second terms. However, extending their first and last mover advantage, presidents are more likely to act as *independents* in moments when the issue is on their agenda. Their desire to achieve their policy goals by adapting law is greater with ideological differences between the branches and within the chambers suggest that Congress may not be willing, or able, to support them. When time is running out in the second half of their second term, presidents are more likely to issue adaptive orders to cement their policy legacy before leaving office. These actions taken together demonstrate the panoply of interests that explain when presidents act first, or last, to their advantage.

CHAPTER EIGHT

Conclusion

Unilateral Orders in a Separated and Shared Power System

WIDESPREAD MISTRUST OF A MUSCULAR EXECUTIVE originally limited the power of the president in the Constitution. One result of this was the absence of an express provision for executive lawmaking through a unilateral process. But, over time, presidents have adapted, transformed, and expanded their powers (often with the help of Congress) to allow them to act unilaterally using executive prerogative and independent authority. The advantage of unilateral action is that presidents do not need to cooperate with the other branches. According to Howell (2005), "When unilateral powers are exercised, legislators, judges and executive [sic] do not work collectively to effect meaningful policy change, and opportunities for change do not depend upon the willingness and capacity of different branches of government to cooperate with one another." He concludes that a president's strategy is to "figure out when legislators and judges are likely to dismantle a unilateral action taken, when they are not, and then to seize upon those latter occasions to issue public policies that look quite different from those that would emerge in a purely legislative setting." This may, however, be only part of the role and function of unilateral orders. Viewing unilateral orders through the lens of the president's political and institutional responsibilities provides clarity to a system that requires strong leadership and shared policy making with Congress.

THE DUAL EXECUTIVE AND THE
USE OF UNILATERAL ORDERS

Considering the president as a dual executive helps to uncover the types of unilateral orders he or she issues. Presidents engage both their *independent* executive role in exercising their unilateral discretion and their *administrator* role by working with their lawmaking partners to facilitate government function. Take administrator orders first. Although presidents appear to act "first and alone," the reality is often much different. As administrators, presidents rely on congressionally delegated powers when issuing unilateral orders, demonstrating that the building blocks of these orders are fundamentally connected as the Constitution designed. Importantly, presidents act differently when they cite Congress as the authority for an order than when they cite their own authority. Presidents issue more statute-based orders and routine orders (versus command orders) when Congress is stronger, yielding to concerns about executive overreach. Presidential support of legislation via unilateral orders is enhanced when Congress signals the importance of the legislation through hearings. In these cases, and others, presidents appear to respect the lawmaking power of Congress. When the branches agree, presidents implement legislation so as not to go against a unified Congress. Specifically, presidents near the end of legislative sessions are more likely to implement legislation (as long as it is not the final end of a president's tenure in office).

The executive and legislative branches are linked in almost every capacity, frequently making the issuance of unilateral orders a *joint* effort. Presidents and Congress often agree on the delegation of power, the appropriate balance of the use of this power, and the duration of the authority to act. The nature and type of the delegation possessed by presidents matters in terms of how they act, although presidents typically have more broad authority than narrow authority. Congress often has a specific policy outcome in mind and chooses to limit executive discretion (Epstein and O'Halloran 1999). Presidents are more likely to issue routine orders when citing Congress, an indication that government activity can be accomplished to a degree by unilateral authority. This linked fate does not always mean that the president's ability to act is restrained. Congress could restrain the president, but generally does not, and instead grants him or her broad authority to act. As a consequence, when presidents have broad authority to act as dictated by statue, they are more likely to act as *independents* and issue command orders.

In other instances, however, the politics of the policy process does not always lend itself to accommodation; the branches will often disagree over matters of policy, and presidents do not hesitate to act on their own in specific circumstances. These are instances where presidents act as *independents* and pursue their policy goals with unilateral orders. Presidents issue more orders citing only the Constitution's commander in chief clause and presidency-based executive orders (instead of a statute) when Congress is less strong, allowing for fewer chances for the president to be overturned. Presidents issue more commander in chief orders during wartime. This hints at the tactics of a president during times of national crisis. Presidential prerogative power (especially during times of emergency) allows presidents to rely on their own judgment and authority to act (Mansfield 2003). Presidents are more likely to act on their own authority in moments where the two branches are politically at odds.

INITIATING UNILATERAL ACTION
EARLY IN THE POLICY PROCESS

Presidents act unilaterally in pursuit of their objectives both early and late in the policy process. The use of command orders—where presidents issue a unilateral order before the legislative process has begun, but when the issue is on their political agenda—demonstrates moments where they are able to effectively set the policy stage in line with their preferences. Presidents are more likely to issue command orders when they are politically weaker (in the second half of their terms), when they have greater substantive discretion, when they rely on constitutional authority, when Congress is internally polarized, and when the Senate filibuster pivot is more ideologically distant from the president. The most important element of a command order is that it is directly connected to the president's agenda. Presidents can use these orders to set an agenda or to initiate a policy, making them powerful first movers. The results clearly demonstrate a president willing to act on his or her own behalf using unilateral orders. These events are most likely to occur when presidents are less able to legislate or when the outcome, left to the bargaining process, would yield a legislative outcome unfavorable to the president.

UNILATERAL ACTION IN THE LEGISLATIVE ARENA

The *independent* model of the president's unilateral orders extends to the legislative arena. In the ongoing debate over legislation, presidents can use their unilateral authority to subvert the legislative process because they can act as first movers. A president preempts proposed legislation when

Congress is less capable of making policy, when the president is less likely to get overturned, when the president is less capable of bargaining, and when the president has an acute interest in the issue. Specifically, presidents are more likely to act against Congress when they have identified the issue as part of their agenda, when the polarization between the parties in Congress is greater for both the House and the Senate, and (occasionally) when presidents are in the latter stages of their terms. This view of the institutions hints that presidents act in ways that are in fact "threatening" or "troublesome" to Congress when they use their authority to act unilaterally (Moe and Wilson 1994). The implication is that presidents do use their unilateral powers to further their own interests, even over the possible political objections of Congress. This research supports the theory of the unilateral executive willing and able to move swiftly in the face of prospective legislation, even if this means appropriating the legislative process.

Presidents do not always act against Congress when they issue an order related to legislation; in some cases they act in support, presumably to facilitate passage or further congressional aims. Presidents are more likely to support legislation when Congress has held hearings on the subject, when the president is of the same party as the sponsor of the legislation, or when the ideological difference between the president and chamber median is smaller. This is a somewhat counterintuitive finding because most scholarship on the subject presumes that presidents, when acting unilaterally, do so in ways that are incompatible with congressional preferences (see Martin 1999; Fine and Warber 2012). This highlights how the process of creating policy is shared between the executive and legislative branches. Presidents are cognizant of possible congressional intervention to overturn their orders and chart a cautious course in using their unilateral actions to interject their policy preferences.

Although perhaps this is unintended, issuing a unilateral order may spur Congress to act. An internal memorandum during the Clinton administration detailed "a list of outstanding and suggested executive orders from the children and families team" and discussed Congress's reaction to two of the potential executive orders. The first would prohibit discrimination against parents in the federal workplace, an issue announced in the

State of the Union address in 1999 but not pursued. The memorandum notes that "Senators Dodd and Kennedy introduced the 'Ending Discrimination Against Parents Act of 1999' in November 1999 and President Clinton released a statement of support at the time of the introduction."[1] An executive order was recommended to "roll out" at the White House Conference on Teenagers to "allow us to highlight the Dodd-Kennedy bill once again." The second order would expand the definition of "family" in the Family Medical Leave Act (FMLA) to include domestic partners. The memorandum noted that in June 1999, Congresswoman Maloney introduced a bill to expand the definition of "family member" to "include domestic partner, grandparent, parent in law, adult child or sibling." Issuing the order would "persuade Congress with an impetus to provide legislative 'fixes.'"[2]

UNILATERAL ACTION AND EXECUTING LAW

Perhaps the most shared decision presidents make is whether to implement legislation Congress has passed and they have signed. Presidents sign and implement legislation for political and institutional reasons. These are occasions where the president self-monitors. Presidents either understand that the legislation may be closely tied to the public will or are unwilling to disrupt Congress's reified place in the constitutional order. Yet, in their roles as *independents*, presidents issue unilateral orders that adapt law, giving the president flexibility and suggesting—once again—the willingness to share power with Congress but to act separately when it suits his or her purpose. This is especially true when there is an agenda dispute, during election years, when the president believes the Constitution gives him or her authority, late in a president's second term, when Congress and the president are at loggerheads, and when the parties in Congress are more internally polarized. As has been consistent throughout history, presidents strive to protect their office so as to maintain the powers accrued to the institution.

Presidents do run the risk of angering Congress by not implementing legislation as faithfully as Congress presumes they should. A resurgent Republican Congress and a weakened White House battled in 2013 and 2014 over implementation of the president's signature health care policy.

President Obama used his authority to delay implementation of specific features that would have burdened specific groups (such as small businesses). Responding to this general theme but citing executive actions by the Obama administration that have changed or delayed the carrying out of the president's health care law, Speaker Boehner indicated that "House Republicans are not prepared to move forward in partnership with a Democratic administration that they believe will not fairly and impartially carry out the laws they pass" (Weisman 2014). He continued: "The American people, including many of my members, don't trust that the reform that we're talking about will be implemented as it was intended to be." The president's use of unilateral power in an environment with mutual distrust can create long-term dysfunction. In this scenario, both parties are to blame in a recurring cycle of policy gridlock, suggesting serious implications to the content and function of the president's unilateral action.

THE (UNILATERAL) IMPERIAL PRESIDENT?

There has been a great deal of debate surrounding the expansion of presidential power, culminating in questions about the nature of presidential authority and the acceptability of presidential prerogative. As an institution, the presidency is designed to be of limited power, primarily subject to the other branches of government; a robust institution, yes, but indisputably interconnected to the other branches by a constitutional backstop. Despite this intentional design, presidential power and authority have been accumulated, centralized, and expanded over time. Rossiter (1956) blissfully claimed the president has powers "that would have made Caesar or Genghis Kahn or Napoleon bite his nails with envy." Healy (2008) warned of the expansion of presidential power and argues that the "imperial Presidency is the price of making the office the focus of our national hopes and dreams." Legal scholars embracing a strong president (and presidency) model suggest that presidents are bound by Congress only with respect to funding—and little else (see Yoo 2005). They claim presidents have "sole power to execute the laws and remove subordinate officials" under the "unitary executive" (Calabresi and Yoo 2008). These powers are especially pronounced when considering a state of emergency.

Yoo (2009) further suggests that presidents are celebrated for "boldness" and expanding the arc of presidential power.

Similarly, commentators and scholars have argued that the post-9/11 president exemplifies executive power run amuck. Many argue that the aftermath of terrorist attacks pushed the presidency off the constitutional foundation by imbuing it with greater powers. Taking this a step further, Posner and Vermeule (2010) suggest that, in a post-9/11 state of affairs, neither Congress nor the judiciary is realistically capable of setting or enforcing national security policy. The executive (especially headed by a strong president) is the only institution in government with the centralized strength the system requires to manage complex and interconnected national security policy. The Bush administration embraced this notion, and many justified the expansion of presidential authority with the argument that "the President had to do what he had to do to protect the country" (Goldsmith 2007). Although often limited to international (but perhaps extending to domestic) conflict, John Yoo—arguing from his position as head of the OLC—suggested that President Bush had broad powers to act offensively or defensively:

In light of the text, plan, and history of the Constitution, its interpretation by both past Administrations and the courts, the longstanding practice of the executive branch, and the express affirmation of the President's constitutional authorities by Congress, we think it beyond question that the President has the plenary constitutional power to take such military actions as he deems necessary and appropriate to respond to the terrorist attacks upon the United States on September 11, 2001.[3]

Why is this happening? First, the reverence and expectations of the president create constitutionally perverse incentives to expand authority and power to meet institutional demand (Healy 2008). The Bush administration, "acting on public demand," initiated several aggressive unilateral counterterrorism programs (Goldsmith 2012). Second, lack of political engagement with the issues of importance and/or the appropriate scope of presidential power contributes to presidential aggrandizement (Crenson and Ginsberg 2007). A president without enough public pressure to share power continues to grab power. Third, Congress has been less than attentive in policing the president and the executive branch. Rudalevige (2005) argues that a "new imperial presidency" has returned and that a lax Congress is to blame in part for executive resurgence. He notes, "The fact is that we have had an invisible Congress as much as an imperial president," and both presidential assertiveness and legislative deference are at "unprecedented levels." Delegation of power by Congress inhibits the ability of liberal legalism to constrain the executive (Posner and Vermeule 2010). No story about assertive presidential unilateral power can be complete without a passage about congressional assent (Marshall and Haney 2010).

Congress has pushed back against executive power. Opposition politicians have chastised President Obama for aggressive assertions of executive discretion and accuse him of "arrogance and sidestepping the political process" after he issued directives on gun control, health care, and immigration (Mason 2014). For instance, in 2014 when the Supreme Court took the case of whether President Obama's unilaterally issued regulations on greenhouse gas emissions exceeded his authority, a frustrated Congress pounced. In a brief filed with the Supreme Court, Republican lawmakers challenged the president's specific and general use of unilateral orders and "pressed that theme, one that hewed closely to criticism of the administration's delays in carrying out the Affordable Care Act, its decision not to defend the Defense of Marriage Act in court, and its tolerance of state marijuana laws in Colorado and Washington" (Liptak 2014a). A brief from Representative Michele Bachmann (R-MN) and other House Republicans argued:

The regulations under challenge were "an intolerable invasion of Congress's domain that threatens to obliterate the line dividing executive from legislative power." The brief added that the regulations were "perhaps the most audacious seizure of pure legislative power over domestic economic matters attempted by the executive branch" since President Harry S. Truman tried to take control of the nation's steel mills during the Korean War. (Liptak 2014a)

In response to executive action to defer deportation for young immigrants who entered the United States illegally, Representative Steve King (R-IA) noted: "Americans should be outraged that President Obama is planning to usurp the Constitutional authority of the United States Congress and grant amnesty by edict to 1 million illegal aliens," and "President Obama, an ex-constitutional law professor, whose favorite word is audacity, is prepared to violate the principles of Constitutional Law that he taught" (quoted in James 2012).

Despite these warnings and protests by members of Congress, the situation may not point universally toward a powerful and unaccountable president. Fatovic (2009) suggests that the constitutional design that separates power is more critical to the function of the system than the notion of an inherent presidential power to act. Presidents can restrain themselves (with "virtue"), but, if they do not, the separation and sharing of powers allows for appropriate checks on abuses of executive authority. Although he documents the resurrection of the "imperial president," Savage (2007) argues that "Congress sometimes willingly cedes extraordinary new authority to the White House," which hardens with time and lack of Congressional response. Jack Goldsmith argues that, without question, the presidency as an institution is more powerful than it was before 9/11; despite "unfathomable" powers of the modern president, "We have witnessed the rise and operation of purposeful forms of democratic (and judicial) control over the Commander in Chief, and have indeed established strong legal and constitutional constraints on the presidency." Presidential "syncopation" with the other institutions in government creates a "harmonious system of mutual frustration" that would make James Madison proud.

This latter conclusion is closer to the truth than the apocryphal warnings about the danger of centralized presidential power, at least with respect to the pattern of the use of unilateral powers as described in this book. Presidential unilateral power to issue executive orders and proclamations is tethered to congressional warrant and constitutional boundaries. In short, because the powers of the branches are linked, Congress has some control over presidential actions before the president acts. This is pronounced even in the president's use of orders that cite Congress—these orders are limited by congressional statute (sometimes decades old), which allows the president to act in ways that Congress might not have originally intended. Similarly, presidents are more likely to implement legislation relating to the executive branch when they are given greater substantive discretion over the process. In both cases, Congress could restrict this authority. Although Congress cannot force the president's hand in terms of what they cite, Congress can significantly restrict what presidents use to carry their policy into law, involving duration and effect. Presidents are most primed to act unilaterally when they have the authority to do so and the political need to succeed. Congress has the capacity to restrict one type of action (through delegation) and monitor the other (the president's agenda).

CONGRESSIONAL OVERSIGHT COUNTS

Presidents cannot always be counted on to self-check their behavior, follow the predetermined parameters of action by Congress, or respect their position in the constitutional order. Congress, the courts, and the public have a role in monitoring and restraining presidential power (Kleinerman 2009). Congress, by not acting to negate or mute the president's unilateral action, may tacitly endorse the action (Howell 2003). Vigilant oversight from Congress is therefore a critical component of presidential power, both in the present and for the future. Representative Robert Barr (R-GA), in a committee hearing related to his proposed legislation to place a thirty-day "review" period for executive orders by Congress, admitted that Congress as a whole needs to be more willing to check the president on matters of unilateral power. He noted:

I think perhaps, Mr. Nadler, that this piece of legislation that I have proposed here, which is, I think, the minimal that we address, at least to some extent this problem is borne out of a sense perhaps of frustration with looking at the unwillingness perhaps of Congress over the years to stand up and address this problem and reassert its proper role.

He concluded by suggesting:

This legislation does not cure the problem, but it does legislatively require Congress, I think, as a practical matter, perhaps not as a legal matter, but as a practical matter, to address these issues, and it also forces the executive branch to send to Congress its proposed order so Congress has an opportunity, full opportunity perhaps, which they simply haven't exercised up to this point, but they still have technically that opportunity now, to do it in a way that focuses legislative and executive branch attention on the importance of making sure that these have some sort of review, so that we can avoid crises later on.

Even a conservative voice, Representative Ron Paul (R-TX), testified in the same hearing, "We also must recognize that much of this has happened because of the negligence of Congress. It isn't just the President who takes over. The administration of the various parties takes over because of our negligence, and we have to recognize that."[4]

Congressional intent, oversight, and consensus play a major role in providing a platform for presidential action. If the legislation is more strongly tied to the perceived will of a more unified Congress, presidents are more likely to act in accord with congressional preferences. Orders preempting legislation are less likely when Congress has early hearings on a subject. By holding hearings to signal their intent, the branches can communicate more effectively and coordinate more efficiently. Presidents are less likely to issue orders based on their own inherent political authority to challenge a Congress with larger and more unified majorities, and presidents are more encouraged to work with Congress in these cases by citing congressional statute in their orders.

Congressional goals may match executive goals on policy issues, allowing the branches to work together. Early in the morning in the final week of the 1960 campaign, presidential candidate Senator John F. Kennedy first spoke of the idea for an international service organization. Less than a year later, the newly elected President Kennedy established the Peace Corps in March 1961 by an executive order relying on congressional authority.[5] The Peace Corps was the cornerstone of Senator Kennedy's new covenant with America and the world. Additionally, it offered a more robust sense of international community service for a generation of young volunteers. The idea was set in serious motion as early as January 1960 by the "pioneering legislative work of Congressman Henry S. Reuss and Senator Hubert Humphrey" (Ashabranner 1971). In establishing the institutional apparatus of the Peace Corps, Kennedy explicitly relied on congressional authorization in the Mutual Security Act (Sullivan 1964) and legislative efforts going back to 1957 as the basis for his order (Rice 1985). The president took a risk in establishing the Peace Corps by executive order, but "Kennedy did not act without assurances that his program would have Congressional blessing" because he "conferred with members of Congress in advance and was promised support" (Carey 1970).

Twenty years later, citing his constitutional authority, President Carter issued Proclamation 4771, requiring draft registration for American citizens aged eighteen to twenty-six who were born after January 1, 1980.[6] Although Carter was credited with establishing the program, Congress played a significant role in its development, having first ordered the president to "prepare and transmit to the Congress a plan for a fair and equitable reform of the existing law providing for registration and induction of persons for training and service in the Armed Forces."[7] Carter acknowledged congressional authorization for the program by noting within the proclamation that "Congress had made available the funds under House Joint Resolution 521 signed by me on June 27, 1980."[8] Carter acknowledged the part played by Congress in his signing remarks, stating that the proclamation implemented the joint resolution.[9]

The balancing and blending of powers frames the debate about the president's use of unilateral powers. Cronin (1989) argued:

The enduring challenge for us today is to encourage the appropriate presidential leadership we need and simultaneously to strengthen the constitutional checks and balances necessary to ensure that our presidential form of government always remains accountable. We need to affirm our desire for a government by rule of law and not by a self-proclaimed indispensable individual.

Reformers argue that the institutions of government need to be more aggressive in checking and balancing each other with proper oversight, diminished partisanship, and a sense of the common good (Shane 2009). It may be that this is already happening. Greater disagreement within Congress engenders more independent orders, but greater disagreement between Congress and the president—which was presumed to be a condition creating more independent presidential orders—often leads to fewer such orders (especially in the legislative process). Presidents issue command and preemptive orders only when Congress is less capable of acting (due to party polarization or intrachamber polarization) rather than when the ideological distance between the president and Congress is greater. Presidents act to move the policy process along—although not always antagonistically—when they are more likely to disagree with Congress.

A PRESIDENTIAL SELF-CHECK?

These findings substantiate the idea that there is a self-check at work. The question is, *Why*? Why would a president foster the legislative process by issuing more statute-based or supportive orders when the size of the majority party is stronger in a Congress ideologically opposed to him or her? This action suggests that presidents balance the political incentives to act with dispatch and the institutional needs for cooperation. Although partisanship clearly exists, and interbranch skirmishes periodically dot the political landscape, the balance of political power remains intact. This balance of power is apparent when presidents, in their second terms, are more likely to implement rather than adapt law. Despite a political incentive to steadfastly pursue their agenda solo at this stage, presidents act more as *administrators* and push law into policy. Presidents issue orders to support legislation when the issue has been discussed, as in a congressional hearing, which is when they might be expected to pursue independent action. But, in these moments, presidents, especially when they are front and center in the lawmaking process, respect the balance of power.

One cause of this self-restraint is public opinion. Presidents may sense that public preferences run against the use of unilateral actions and reduce their reliance on such tools. The public's beliefs about the proper course of the rule of law may cause them to react negatively to the president acting alone (Reeves and Rogowski 2016). There is a political cost to presidents who act unilaterally, and these costs shape both the timing and the scope of the action (Christenson and Kriner 2015). Presidents may also prefer a legislative route when the opportunity presents itself. As Mayer (2009) suggests, presidents prefer legislation as a means to achieve policy goals but opt for unilateral action as their "second-best" option (439). Rather than pursue a unilateral strategy that may be undone by future presidents or by Congress, presidents may attempt to make policy the old-fashioned way and bargain with the legislature. The trade-offs between unilateral orders and legislative activity demonstrate that presidents are strategic about how and when they push one lever of power or the other (Dickinson and Gubb 2016; Ouyang and Waterman 2015; Rottinghaus 2015). This book demonstrates that unilateral action remains a viable option in the right circumstances.

These results challenge the notion of a rampant *presidentialism* that marauds over a weak Congress that is too feeble to stop it. Shane (2009) suggests that the "gravest implication for day-to-day governance" in partisan politics arises "from the conjoining of partisanship with the attempted aggrandizement of presidential authority." In some instances, presidents employ their prerogative powers when they are institutionally strongest (such as with greater discretion), but at other times they restrict their actions so as to not upset the balance of power with Congress (such as the presence of greater majority size or greater putative ideological disputes with Congress). Although presidents clearly pursue their own political agenda with these orders, it is obvious that there is a balance at work, either because of purposive restraint on the part of the president or an adequate check from an imposing legislature ready to act. The interaction between the exogenous political incentives to act and the endogenous institutional structure generates institutional responsibility, which may restrain presidential action (Spiliotes 2000). This outcome is not solely dictated by the president's political environment, such as whether or not government is unified or not, but rather a combination of linked interbranch agendas, powers, and responsibilities.

SEPARATED AND SHARED (UNILATERAL) POWERS

The theme of separate and shared powers prominently addresses the debate between Neustadt's version of bargaining on one hand and studies of unilateral action on the other. The resolution is really a compromise between these two positions, with presidents strategically altering their behavior in light of legal, institutional, and political limitations. In a way, Neustadt has it wrong. His view of why presidential commands are not followed is that they are not self-executing and can be achieved only through bargaining with Congress or other power sharers. This view overlooks the reality that unilateral orders are often the result of bargains with Congress and that they are integrated into the legislative framework. Presidential power for Neustadt is an "outgrowth of the personal ability of individual officeholders rather than as an attribute of institutional capacity" (Jacobs and Shapiro 2000). Unilateral powers are both institutional *and* personal. The institutional capacity and desire to act with or against Congress frames the president's choices. Presidents employ their personal prerogative to act unilaterally when they have greater authority to do so and when Congress is less able to act.

In another way, Neustadt has it right. The Constitution does not provide for "separated" powers, but, rather, "separated institutions sharing powers" (1990). Considering unilateral actions as only a presidential decision misses a critical element of the way that these orders are routinely used, especially in the legislative arena or through implementation. Presidents may simultaneously be using their unilateral orders (which are a formal, institutional power) to negotiate and share power with Congress (a "personal" power) (Dickinson 2008). Presidents rely on congressional authority, which may need to be bargained, and use unilateral orders as a threat to guarantee some executive control over the process (Marshall 2011). Depending on when and how these orders are used, they may trend toward the formal instead of the bargained-for, especially in instances where presidents are keen to make a quasi-policy decision on their own using their formal powers. On the other hand, these powers may lean more toward the bargained-for than the formal when presidents use their orders to support legislation or to assist in the implementation of law. Making sure decisions are made and the policy process is active is often more important to a president than pursuing a particular agenda.

President Obama, often chastened for acting on his own, has used both his bargaining leverage and his unilateral authority in the same instance. The Obama administration's pronouncement that the administration planned to use either the "pen" (unilateral powers) or the "phone" (persuasion) underscores the idea that the president might either sign "executive orders or use[s] the bully pulpit of the White House as convening power to make progress on issues ranging from the economy to the environment" (Rucker 2013).[10] In early 2013, the White House issued twenty-three new unilateral rules on gun control in the wake of a school shooting tragedy in

Connecticut, including steps to strengthen background checks, promote research on gun violence, and provide additional training. By pursuing an overhaul of the nation's gun laws, the president "is wagering that public opinion has evolved enough after a string of mass shootings to force passage of politically contentious measures that Congress has long stymied" (Rucker and O'Keefe 2013). Simultaneously with these unilateral actions, the president "hosted groups of Republican senators for dinner, and his Chief of Staff, Denis McDonough, tried to repair relations with several key senators." This meeting achieved no specific significant legislative breakthroughs, although both parties, led by Senator Patty Murray (D-WA) and Representative Paul Ryan (R-WI), arrived at a budget deal later in the year (Rucker 2013). Although presidents possess multiple tools to make policy, both internal and external factors (including mutual influence) affect unilateral action.

Ultimately, there is support for both the model of an *independent* president who uses unilateral orders to push an agenda, head off possible congressional legislation, and selectively implement legislation, and for an *administrator* president who is willing to share management of government action, support legislative efforts, and faithfully implement legislation. Through unilateral orders, presidents execute the dual responsibilities of the executive. Presidents have a great deal of prerogative concerning when to act and the political circumstances under which they do so, but, at the same time, presidents self-check their actions based on the ability of Congress to overturn their orders, through a shared sense of the need to keep government moving, and out of respect for constitutional balance. Congress can constrain presidents to a degree, by limiting their actions through delegation, or they can force presidents to follow certain statutory procedural actions. Shared unilateral powers imply that presidential authority and action are linked to Congress, both through the possibility of political battles that presidents want to avoid and the ability of Congress to structure the president's choices prior to taking unilateral action. The shared nature of unilateral orders does not preclude an active president. Presidents remain strong actors in the political system.

APPENDIX A

Coding Methodology for the
President's Agenda, Congress's
Agenda, and Committee Hearings

COMPILING THE PRESIDENT'S AGENDA

We created a *presidential agenda* variable by identifying the priorities of the administration for each congressional session. The objective was to identify whether the content of a unilateral order was on the president's policy agenda *prior* to the date the order was issued. We compared the content of an order with the content of public speeches, addresses to Congress, letters to Congress, statements, remarks, comments, and the president's legislative initiatives for each congressional session to determine whether it was included on the president's agenda. The sources we used to develop this variable were *Public Papers of the Presidents, American Presidency Project, Congressional Quarterly Weekly,* and *Congressional Quarterly Annual.*

We did not limit ourselves to only the president's legislative initiatives as a measure of whether the order was on the presidential agenda because we are interested in presidents' public agendas as they relate to their ability to keep campaign and governing promises. As an example, pertaining to President Carter's proclaiming of national monuments in Alaska as previously described, President Carter specifically discussed the necessity for protecting lands in Alaska at several points to Congress and the public.[1] In his State of the Union address on January 19, 1978, President Carter remarked as to his intentions:

Last year, I sent Congress a proposal for use of Federal lands in Alaska. This proposal will protect 92 million acres for the public, will create or expand 13 national parks and reserves, 13 national wildlife refuges, and will confer wild and scenic river status on 33 waterways. I hope Congress will adopt these measures, which are needed this year to preserve the unique natural treasures of Alaska and, at the same time, permit the orderly development of Alaskan resources.

COMPILING COMMITTEE HEARINGS AND
BILLS ON CONGRESS'S AGENDA

Key words from a content analysis of each unilateral order were used as a starting point in identifying whether a unilateral order related to a committee hearing or bill on Congress's agenda. We used the key words to search electronic and bound volumes to identify whether the topic or subject of a unilateral order had been discussed by Congress in committee hearings or had been addressed in the subject or content of a bill. The electronic and bound data sources we searched include *ProQuest Congressional, Library of Congress (THOMAS), Congressional Bills Project, Congressional Record, Congressional Quarterly Weekly,* and *Congressional Quarterly Almanac.*[2] From the search we were able to generate a legislative history of the topic or subject of each unilateral order before it was issued by the president. Table A.1 provides an example of an executive order and the key words that were used to search for committee hearings and legislation.

Table A.2 shows some example of hearings that related to the topic or subject of an executive order. The first column lists the number of the

TABLE A.1.
Executive orders and key words used to search for committee hearings and legislation before the order was issued.

Order	Title	Key words
EO-12834	Ethics Commitments by Executive Branch Appointees	Ethics, executive agency, revolving door, lobbying
EO-12835	Establishment of the National Economic Council	National Economic Council, council, economic advisors, President's Council
EO-12836	Revocation of Certain Executive Orders Concerning Federal Contracting	Federal contracting, federal construction contracts, construction contracts, project agreements, workplace
EO-12837	Deficit Control and Productivity Improvement in the Administration of the Federal Government	Deficit control, administrative expenses, federal agencies, administration expenses federal agencies, federal agency budgets
EO-12838	Termination and Limitation of Federal Advisory Committees	Federal advisory committees, committee termination, reduction of advisory committees, advisory committees, Federal Advisory Committee Act

TABLE A.2.

Examples of committee hearings that relate to the topic or subject of an executive order before it was issued.

EO-12844	House Committee on Energy and Commerce Subcommittee on Energy and Power to Review DOE FY 1994 budget proposal 4/21/1993 CIS No. 94-H361-7
EO-12845	
EO-12846	Senate Committee on Foreign Relations Subcommittee on European Affairs on American Policy in Bosnia 2/18/1993 CIS No. 93-S381-15; House Committee on Armed Forces on Use of Force in the Post–Cold War Era 3/3/1993 and 3/4/1993 CIS No. 93-H201-31
EO-12847	
EO-12848	Senate Committee on Banking, Housing and Urban Affairs on HUD Components of President Clinton's Economic Stimulus Plan 2/23/1993 CIS No. 93-S241-20; House Committee on Banking, Finance and Urban Affairs Subcommittee on Housing and Community Development on Need for Permanent Housing for the Homeless 3/24/1993 CIS No. 93-H241-60; House Committee on Banking, Finance and Urban Affairs Subcommittee on Housing and Community Development on Homelessness in America 4/23/1993 CIS No. 94-H241-72

TABLE A.3.

Examples of proposed legislation related to the topic or subject of a unilateral order before it was issued.

Order	Legislation
EO-11803	S 2832 Earned Immunity Act of 1974 House Committee on the Judiciary Subcommittee on Courts, Civil Liberties and the Administration of Justice Amnesty 3/8, 3/11, 3/13/1974 CIS No 74-H521-59
EO-11804	S 2832 Earned Immunity Act of 1974 House Committee on the Judiciary Subcommittee on Courts, Civil Liberties and the Administration of Justice Amnesty 3/8, 3/11, 3/13/1974 CIS No 74-H521-59
EO-11810	S 3792 Export Administration Amendments approved by both houses and sent to conference
PR-4313	S 2832 Earned Immunity Act of 1974 House Committee on the Judiciary Subcommittee on Courts, Civil Liberties and the Administration of Justice Amnesty 3/8, 3/11, 3/13/1974 CIS No 74-H521-59

executive order, and the second column lists the committee hearings during which a similar (or identical) topic was discussed that the president later addressed in his executive order.

Table A.3 provides some examples of proposed legislation that related to the topic or subject of a unilateral order before it was issued. For a topic to be placed on the congressional agenda requires a bill to be introduced and at least one hearing held on the bill after it has been introduced (Edwards, Barrett, and Peake 1997). The first column lists the number of the executive order, and the second column lists the bill that the president later addressed in his executive order.

Congressional Action and Presidential Response

UNILATERAL ORDERS AND
LEGISLATIVE PRODUCTIVITY

As shown throughout the book, presidents are not just solo actors—they are a representative part of an institutional system in which Congress plays a major part by passing legislation (or not) and providing opportunities for the president to act. Considering this interaction, presidential legislative success or failure may largely determine the degree and volume of unilateral presidential action. For instance, in 2013, in the aftermath of a mass shooting at an elementary school in Connecticut, President Obama sought to separately "embrace a comprehensive plan to reduce gun violence that will call for major legislation to expand background checks for gun purchases and lay out 19 separate actions the president could take by invoking the power of his office" (Shear and Steinhauer 2013). A complete examination of the role of unilateral orders in the policy-making system must examine both the cause and effects of unilateral power. Specifically, more frequent legislative action may require presidential implementation (necessitating more unilateral actions). For example, Gleiber and Shull (1992) argue that unilateral orders are used as a way for presidents to reinforce congressional legislative outcomes, allowing presidents to ensure proper implementation of the laws (see Krause and Cohen 1997). As Congress legislates more, the opportunities and necessity for presidents to act unilaterally will correspondingly increase. The larger volume of legislation may increase the president's options to act, either because the executive can choose how to implement these orders or can make progress on policy issues by implementing legislation passed by Congress.

To complement our measures of executive policy making, we model the impact of greater legislative output as a component of more frequent use of orders to implement policy. We include a summary measure of legislative output in a single scale by using the method employed by Grant and Kelly (2008) who use Stimson's (1999) algorithm (as calculated by W-CALC) to create a macro index of legislative activity over time ("Legislative Production Index [LPI]"). Specifically included in the index is the number of statutes enacted, innovative legislation, multiple measures of important legislation passed, and key votes taken. The method combines these individual variables and estimates a single measure of a latent concept using multiple indicators and can overcome problems of "scaling and coverage" to generate an index of multiple time series (Grant and Kelly 2008). To start, they created an index for each series, expressing each point as a ratio of an arbitrary fixed reference point, so that the scale is common and there is a central tendency. This "backwards recursion" is repeated until "all issues have contributed to the estimation and information about all time points has been exhausted" followed by the same process moving from the beginning to the end (Stimson 1999). After the summary indexes were created, through the process of eliminating those individual series that were negatively correlated with the final index, the final measure was refined to produce a dyadic algorithm that measured the underlying concept of legislative action. This is done to "avoid inclusion of completely irrelevant information" (Grant and Kelly 2008).

We include the number of requests in the annual State of the Union Message (*SOTU Requests*), taken from Light (1999) and Ragsdale (2009). Several scholars use this variable to measure the president's agenda (Eshbaugh-Soha 2005; Cohen 2012) since the State of the Union message serves as a public record from which presidents publicize their legislative preferences and begin to persuade Congress of the importance of the policies promoted. This measure captures the size of the president's legislative agenda and can be shorthand for their legislative requests for that year. Presidents leverage their first-mover advantage in these instances and engage in "front-end" legislative agenda activity (Ponder 2005). The advantage to using the State of the Union requests is that these measures are fixed at a consistent margin over time encompassing an annual agenda and are comparable across presidents. This is a relatively "pure" measure of presidential initiatives because it is largely exogenous to the production or agenda formation of Congress.

TABLE B.I.
Count models for legislative influence on implementation.

	Divided government	Distance: Senate	Distance: House	Distance: Senate	Distance: House
Second term	0.074 (0.134)	−0.090 (0.122)	−0.021 (0.128)	−0.007 (0.127)	−0.005 (0.128)
Second half	0.543 *** (0.107)	0.476 *** (0.106)	0.476 *** (0.105)	0.484 *** (0.106)	0.464 *** (0.106)
Election year	0.174 * (0.104)	0.225 ** (0.106)	0.207 ** (0.104)	0.255 ** (0.106)	0.201 ** (0.104)
War	−0.601 *** (0.123)	−0.475 *** (0.124)	−0.583 *** (0.121)	−0.410 *** (0.129)	−0.531 *** (0.128)
SOTU policy requests	−0.029 *** (0.007)	−0.021 *** (0.008)	−0.030 *** (0.007)	−0.016 ** (0.008)	−0.030 *** (0.007)
Legislative policy production	0.015 *** (0.003)	0.015 *** (0.003)	0.014 *** (0.003)	0.035 *** (0.010)	0.028 *** (0.009)
Divided government	−0.566 *** (0.124)	—	—	—	—
Distance between chamber and president	—	−0.642 *** (0.211)	−0.666 *** (0.189)	—	—
Distance between chamber and president * legislative policy production	—	—	—	−0.026 *** (0.013)	−0.015 *(0.012)
N (years)	35	35	35	35	35
Pseudo R^2	0.423	00.385	.394	0.398	0.400
Log likelihood	−86.9	−92.6	−91.2	−90.7	−90.4
Likelihood ratio χ^2	127.7 ***	116.2 ***	119.0 ***	120.0 ***	120.6 ***

Note: Dependent variable: Total count by year of orders that implemented a law passed by Congress. Models are Poisson models.

*** Indicates statistical significance at $p < 0.01$.

** Indicates statistical significance at $p < 0.05$.

* Indicates statistical significance at $p < 0.10$.

Does greater legislative output produce more presidential implementation unilateral orders? Table B.1 displays several models that use Poisson count models to explain the factors that predict more orders. Generally, controlling for several variables that might lead to more unilateral orders, greater legislative output (indexed) produces more presidential implementation orders (both faithful and adaptive). The results are consistent across each of the models. As Congress's legislative production increases from a standard deviation below the mean to one standard deviation above the mean, the number of unilateral implementation orders rises from nine to about fourteen. These findings suggest that presidents do respond to Congress by implementing legislation passed by the legislature. Although there is political abrasion between the branches, the shared responsibility to act to matriculate legislation into law is communally acted on.

Interestingly, when there is more potential friction between Congress and the White House, presidents are less likely to issue unilateral orders to implement law, consistent with the expectations. For each of the three measures of interbranch friction—divided government, the ideological distance between the president and the median member of the House, and the ideological distance between the president and the median member in the Senate—an increase in disagreement between the branches of government produces fewer orders that implement law. When government is divided, the number of implementation unilateral order reduces from sixteen to nine. Table B.1 includes a dummy variable that interacts the distance from the median member in the Senate and House and the amount of legislative production. The idea is that greater legislative production from a Congress who is less likely to agree with the White House should lead the president to reduce the number of orders implementing what may be odious legislation to the executive. In the models that include the interaction between the House and Senate median ideological distance and legislative production, presidents reduce the number of orders implementing legislation. As the interacted legislative output and greater Senate ideological distance measure rises from a standard deviation below the mean to one standard deviation above the variable's mean, the number of implementation orders falls from about thirty to about six. The political leverage presidents employ to implement less when there is a greater chance of political disagreements again shows that presidents are both responsible partners and illusive adversaries of Congress.

Notes

CHAPTER ONE

1. Savage 2012.

2. Executive Order No. 13658, "Establishing a Minimum Wage for Contractors," 79 *Federal Register* 9851 (February 20, 2014).

3. Kim 2014.

4. Department of Homeland Security, "Memorandum on Exercising Prosecutorial Discretion with Respect to Individuals Who Came to the United States as Children and with Respect to Certain Individuals Who Are the Parents of U.S. Citizens or Permanent Residents, by Secretary Jeh Charles Johnson." 2014; available at www.dhs.gov/sites/default/files/publications/14_1120_memo_deferred_action.pdf.

5. John Boehner, "Speaker Boehner to President Obama: This is Not How American Democracy Works," Press Release, November 20, 2014. Available at www.speaker.gov/press-release/speaker-boehner-president-obama-not-how-american-democracy-works.

6. Bob Goodlatte, "Statement on President Obama's Unilateral, Unconstitutional Immigration Actions," press release, November 20, 2014. Available at http://judiciary.house.gov/index.cfm/press-releases?ID=2496A9DC-E3FC-4595-9C8F-3A8DB0C7EA75

7. Sessions 2014.

8. Barack Obama, "Remarks on the No Child Left Behind Act, September 23, 2011," Public Papers of the President, American Presidency Project; available at www.presidency.ucsb.edu/ws/index.php?pid=96798&st=&st1.

9. U.S. Department of Education, "Letters from the Education Secretary or Deputy Secretary," by Arne Duncan (2011). Available at www2.ed.gov/policy/gen/guid/secletter/110923.html.

10. Executive Order No. 13535, "Ensuring Enforcement and Implementation of Abortion Restrictions in the Patient Protection and Affordable Care Act," 75 *Federal Register* 15599 (March 29, 2010); and Patient Protection and Affordable Care Act (PPACA) of 2010, Public Law 111–148, *U.S. Statutes at Large* 124 (2010): 119.

11. Rep. Virginia Foxx (R-NC), speaking on H.R. 3590, 111th Cong., 1st sess., *Congressional Record* 155 (November 5, 2009): H 12434.

12. Preservation of Access to Care for Medicare Beneficiaries and Pension Relief Act of 2010, H.R. 3962, 111th Congress. The Nelson amendment (No. 2962) was included in the Senate version of the bill, but on December 8, 2009, the Senate voted to table the motion.

13. Farley 2010 and PolitiFact.com 2012.

14. Barack Obama, "Remarks on Signing the Patient Protection and Affordable Care Act, March 23, 2010," Public Papers of the President, American Presidency Project; available at www.presidency.ucsb.edu/ws/index.php?pid=87660&st=&st1.

15. Executive Order No. 13535, "Ensuring Enforcement and Implementation of Abortion Restrictions in the Patient Protection and Affordable Care Act," 75 *Federal Register*

15599 (March 29, 2010), "By the authority vested in me as President by the Constitution and the Laws of the United States of America, including the 'Patient Protection and Affordable Care Act,'" Public Law 111–148, *U.S. Statutes at Large* 124 (2010): 119.

16. Executive Order No. 13626, "Gulf Coast Ecosystem Restoration," 77 *Federal Register* 56749 (September 13, 2012); and The Resources and Ecosystems Sustainability, Tourist Opportunities, and Revived Economies of the Gulf Coast States Act of 2012, Public Law 112-141, *U.S. Statutes at Large* 126 (2012): 405.

17. Barack Obama, "Statement of Administrative Policy: H.R. 4348, Surface Transportation Extension Act of 2012, Part II, April 17, 2012," Statements of Administration Policy, American Presidency Project; available at www.presidency.ucsb.edu/ws/index.php?pid=100532.

18. The order revoked Executive Order No. 13554, "Establishing the Gulf Coast Ecosystem Restoration Task Force," 75 *Federal Register* 62313 (October 8, 2010).

19. *Marbury v. Madison*, 5 U.S. 158 (1803); *Kendall v. United States*, 37 U.S. 522 (1838); and *National Treasury Employees Union v. Nixon*, 492 F.2d 587 (1974), quoting *Nixon v. Sirica* (p. 712 of 487 F.2d [1973]). See *Panama Canal Co. v. Grace Lines, Inc.*, 356 U.S. 309 (1958); *Wilbur v. United States ex rel. Kadrie*, 281 U.S. 206, 218–222 (1930); *Work v. United States ex rel. Rives*, 267 U.S. 175, 177–178 (1925); *Ballinger v. Frost*, 216 U.S. 240, 249 (1910); *Garfield v. United States ex rel. Goldsby*, 211 U.S. 249 (1908); *Roberts v. United States ex rel. Valentine*, 176 U.S. 219, 229–231 (1900); *United States v. Schurz*, 102 U.S. 378 (1880); *McGaw v. Farrow*, 472 F.2d 952, 955–957 (1973); and David Schwartz and Sydney Jacoby, "Litigation with the Federal Government," Philadelphia, Joint Committee on Continuing Legal Education of the American Law Institute and the American Bar Association (1970).

20. Office of Management and Budget, "Quality of Life Review #1: Memorandum to Heads of Department and Agencies from George P. Schultz, Director, OMB, Agency Regulations, Standards and Guidelines Pertaining to Environmental Quality, Consumer Protection, Occupational and Public Health and Safety," by George P. Schultz (1971); available at www.thecre.com/ombpapers/QualityofLife1.htm.

21. Executive Order No. 12044, "Improving Government Regulations," 43 *Federal Register* 12661 (March 24, 1978).

22. Established by the Paperwork Reduction Act of 1980, Public Law 96-511, *U.S. Statutes at Large* 94 (1980): 2812; available at www.whitehouse.gov/omb/organization.

23. Executive Order No. 12291, "Federal Regulation," 46 *Federal Register* 13193 (February 17, 1981).

24. Shabecoff 1981.

25. Executive Order No. 12866, "Adjustments of Rates of Pay and Allowances for the Uniformed Services," 58 *Federal Register* 51735 (October 4, 1993), restricted OMB to major rule review but maintained, substantively, cost–benefit analysis. Major rules are defined in 5 U.S.C. § 804(2).

CHAPTER TWO

1. Executive Order No. 13657, "Changing the Name of the National Security Staff to the National Security Council Staff," 79 *Federal Register* 8823 (February 14, 2014).

2. Executive Order 13658 Establishing a Minimum Wage for Contractors 79 *Federal Register* 9851(February 20, 2014).

3. The president's authority is discretionary under Section 9A and mandatory under Section 10 of the Railway Labor Act of 1926, Public Law 69-257, *U.S. Statutes at Large* 44 (1926): 577.

4. Executive Order No. 13241, "Providing an Order of Succession within the Department of Agriculture," 66 *Federal Register* 246 (December 21, 2001); Executive Order No. 13242, "Providing an Order of Succession within the Department of Commerce," 66 *Federal Register* 246 (December 21, 2001); Executive Order No. 13243, "Providing an Order of Succession within the Department of Housing and Urban Development," 66 *Federal Register* 246 (December 21, 2001); Executive Order No. 13244, "Providing an Order of Succession within the Department of the Interior," 66 *Federal Register* 246 (December 21, 2001); Executive Order No. 13245, "Providing an Order of Succession within the Department of Labor," 66 *Federal Register* 246 (December 21, 2001); Executive Order No. 13246, "Providing an Order of Succession within the Department of the Treasury," 66 *Federal Register* 246 (December 21, 2001); Executive Order No. 13247, "Providing an Order of Succession within the Department of Veterans Affairs," 66 *Federal Register* 246 (December 21, 2001); Executive Order No. 13250, "Providing an Order of Succession within the Department of Health and Human Services," 67 *Federal Register* 8 (January 11, 2002); and Executive Order No. 13251, "Providing an Order of Succession within the Department of State," 67 *Federal Register* 8 (January 11, 2002).

5. The president's agenda constitutes a high bar because the president has publically prioritized the issue. We utilized electronic and bound copies of the Public Papers of the President to identify issues on the president's agenda. The electronic sources were www.presidency.ucsb.edu/ws/ and www.archives.gov/federal-register/publications/presidential-papers.html.

6. Executive Order 12307, "President's Commission on Hostage Compensation," 46 *Federal Register* 30483 (June 9, 1981), authorized the commission to conduct public hearings and gave the commission additional time to prepare the report, and Executive Order 12317, "President's Commission on Hostage Compensation," 46 *Federal Register* 42241 (August 20, 1981), gave the commission additional time to prepare the report.

7. Emergency Chinese Immigration Relief Act of 1989, H.R. 2712 101st Congress; George H. W. Bush, "Memorandum of Disapproval for the Bill Providing Emergency Chinese Immigration Relief, November 30, 1989," Public Papers of the President, American Presidency Project, available at www.presidency.ucsb.edu/ws/?pid=17883; and Executive Order No. 12711, "Policy Implementation with Respect to Nationals of the People's Republic of China," 55 *Federal Register* 13897 (April 13, 1990).

8. Omnibus Export Amendments Act of 1990, H.R. 4653 101st Congress; and George H. W. Bush, "Memorandum of Disapproval for the Omnibus Export Amendments Act of 1990, November 16, 1990," Public Papers of the President, American Presidency Project, available at www.presidency.ucsb.edu/ws/?pid=19059.

9. Executive Order No. 12735, "Chemical and Biological Weapons Proliferation," 55 *Federal Register* 48587 (November 20, 1990).

10. The Alaska Native Claims Settlement Act of 1971, Public Law 92-203, *U.S. Statutes at Large* 85 (1971): 688, contained a key provision that gave Congress a five-year period to act on the secretary of the interior's withdrawal of nearly 80 million acres from unreserved lands in Alaska. Section 2 of the Antiquities Act of 1906, Public Law 59-209, *U.S Statutes at Large* 34 (1906): 225.

11. The Alaska National Interest Lands Conservation Act of 1978, H.R. 12625 95th Congress, passed the house on May 19, 1978.

12. Proclamation Nos. 4611–4617 and 4620–4627, 43 *Federal Register* 57,009–57,052 and 57,067–57,131 (December 5, 1978).

13. *Congressional Quarterly 1993*, 241–246.

14. Executive Order No. 12864, "United States Advisory Council on the National Information Infrastructure," 58 *Federal Register* 48773 (September 17, 1993); Executive Order 12881, "Establishment of the National Science and Technology Council," 58 *Federal Register* 62491 (November 26, 1993); and Executive Order No. 12882, "President's Committee of Advisors on Science and Technology," 58 *Federal Register* 62493 (November 26, 1993).

15. Executive Order No. 11969, "Administration of the Emergency Natural Gas Act of 1977," 42 *Federal Register* 6791 (February 4, 1977); and Emergency Natural Gas Act of 1977, Public Law 95-2, *U.S. Statutes at Large* 91 (1977): 4.

16. For a debate on the unitary executive and whether the president has discretionary authority over executive branch agencies receiving delegated statutory authority directly, see Lessig and Sunstein (1994) and Calabresi and Prakash (1994).

17. Executive Order No. 12642, "Designation of the Secretary of Defense as the Presidential Designee under Title I of the Uniformed and Overseas Citizens Absentee Voting Act," 53 *Federal Register* 21975 (June 8, 1988); and Uniformed and Overseas Citizens Absentee Voting Act of 1986, Public Law 99-410, *U.S. Statutes at Large* 100 (1986): 924.

18. Executive Order 12101, "Privileges, Immunities and Liability Insurance for Diplomatic Missions and Personnel," 43 *Federal Register* 54195 (November 17, 1978); and Diplomatic Relations Act of 1978, Public Law 95-393, *U.S. Statutes at Large* 92 (1978): 808.

19. Ethics in Government Act Amendments of 1985, Public Law 99-190, *U.S. Statutes at Large* 99 (1985): 1185.

20. Executive Order No. 12549, "Debarment and Suspension," 51 *Federal Register* 6370 (February 18, 1986).

21. Meacham 2012, quoting from Cunningham 1963: 90.

CHAPTER THREE

1. Memoranda are not included because they do not have the same formal characteristics of executive orders and policy proclamations: (1) They are not traditionally published in the *Federal Register*; (2) there is no formal process for their creation as there is for executive orders and policy proclamations; (3) they are used to direct the actions of the executive branch, often in conjunction with executive orders and proclamation; and (4) presidents rarely cite a source of authority or discuss memoranda in speeches.

2. U.S. Congress, House Committee on Government Operations, "Executive Orders and Proclamations: A Study of a Use of Presidential Powers," 85th Congress, 1st session, 1957.

3. Emancipation Proclamation, January 1, 1863; Presidential Proclamations, 1791-1991; Record Group 11; General Records of the United States Government; National Archives.

4. At Jefferson's urging in a letter dated July 18, 1793, James Madison produced five articles under the name Helvidius arguing against the expansive reading of the president's constitutional power (Madison 1906).

5. Proclamation No. 26, "Respecting the Nullifying Laws of South Carolina," December 10, 1832.

6. Proclamation 4031, "Proclaiming the Suspension of the Davis-Bacon Act of March 3, 1931," 53 *Federal Register* 3457 (February 25, 1971).

7. Proclamation 4074, "Imposition of Supplemental Duty for Balance of Payments Purposes," 53 *Federal Register* 15724 (August 17, 1971).

8. Proclamation No. 5887, "Suspension of Entry as Nonimmigrants of Officers and Employees of the Nicaraguan Government," 53 *Federal Register* 43185 (October 26, 1988).

9. Proclamation 80, "Calling Forth the Militia and Convening an Extra Session of Congress," April 15, 1861; Proclamation 81, "Declaring a Blockade of Ports in Rebellious States," April 19, 1861; Proclamation 82, "Extension of Blockade to Ports of Additional States," April 27, 1861; Proclamation 83, "Increasing the Size of the Army and Navy," May 3, 1861; Proclamation 84, "Declaring Martial Law, and Suspending the Writ of Habeas Corpus in the Islands of Key West," May 10, 1861; and Proclamation 86, "Prohibiting Commercial Trade with States in Rebellion," August 16, 1861.

10. Proclamation 1364, "Declaring that a State of War Exists between the United States and Germany," April 6, 1917; Proclamation 1370, "Conscription," May 19, 1917; and Proclamation 1419, "Government Assumption of Control of Transportation Systems," December 26, 1917.

11. Proclamation 2487, "Unlimited National Emergency Confronts the Country," May 27, 1941; Proclamation 2497, "Blacklisting 1,800 Latin American Firms for Aiding Germany or Italy," July 17, 1941; and Proclamation 2537, "Alien Internment," January 14, 1942.

12. *Grisar v. McDowell* 73 U.S. 363 (1869); and *United States v. Midwest Oil Co.* 236 U.S. 459 (1915).

13. Forest Reserve Act (March 3, 1891; 26 Stat. §1103).

14. The Fulton Amendment to the Agricultural Bill of 1907 (34 Stat. §1269-1271).

15. Using implied power President Taft issued a proclamation entitled "Temporary Petroleum Withdrawal No. 5" on September 27, 1909, withdrawing 3 million acres in California and Wyoming from oil excavation. Taft 1916: 136; and *United States v. Midwest Oil Co.*, 236 U.S. 459 (1915).

16. On August 9, 1974, at 12:03 pm, Chief Justice Warren E. Burger administered the oath of office to Gerald R. Ford, who then spoke briefly from the East Room of the White House, broadcast live on radio and television to a nation who had just seen Nixon depart in disgrace as the first president ever to resign.

17. Proclamation No. 4311, "Granting Pardon to Richard Nixon," 39 *Federal Register* 32601, (September 10, 1974).

18. Jack Wehle, "Reserve and Guard Units Called up for Gulf Standby," *Army Times*, March 9, 1998: 26.

19. Executive Order No. 13076, "Ordering the Selected Reserve of the Armed Forces to Active Duty," 63 *Federal Register* 9719 (February 26, 1998).

20. Department of State, U.S. Export Controls, A Resource on Strategic Trade Management and Export Controls; available at www.state.gov/strategictrade/resources/c43182.htm.

21. The methodology used for compiling the president's agenda, Congress's agenda, and committee hearings is presented in Appendix A.

22. "Karen Tramontano and Thomas Freedman to Chief of Staff," April 10, 2000, Papers of Bruce Reed, Domestic Policy Council, William Clinton Presidential Library, Box 109.

23. "Bruce N. Reed to Elena Kagan," Domestic Policy Council, October 20, 1998, Papers of Bruce Reed, William Clinton Presidential Library, Box 109.

24. See Chapter Two, note 2.

25. U.S Congress, House, Committee on Science, Space and Technology's Technology Policy Task Force, "Review of Previous Studies," 100th Congress, 1st session; U.S. Congress, House, Committee on Science, Space and Technology's Subcommittee on Energy Research and Development, "Technology Transfer," 100th Congress, 1st session; and Steel and Aluminum Energy Conservation and Technology Competitiveness Act of 1988, Public Law 100-680, *U.S. Statutes at Large* 102 (1988): 4073.

26. Steel and Aluminum Energy Conservation and Technology Competitiveness Act of 1988, Public Law 100-680, *U.S. Statutes at Large* 102 (1988): 4073.

27. Ronald Reagan, "Statement on Signing the Steel and Aluminum Energy Conservation and Technology Competitiveness Act of 1988, November 17, 1988," Public Papers of the President, American Presidency Project; available at www.presidency.ucsb.edu/ws/index.php?pid=35176.

CHAPTER FOUR

1. Barack Obama, "Remarks at the Betty Ann Ong Chinese Recreation Center in San Francisco, California," November 25, 2013.

2. Barack Obama, "Remarks by the President in Address to the Nation on Immigration," November 20, 2014. Beginning in 2012, Department of Homeland Security Secretary Janet Napolitano issued guidance for case-by-case deferred action with respect to those who came to the United States as children, commonly referred to as Deferred Action for Childhood Arrivals, or DACA. In citing the past actions of presidents, President Obama may be referring to "indefinite voluntary departure" actions known as the "Family Fairness" program, implemented by the Immigration and Naturalization Service (INS) in the Reagan and Bush administrations to promote the humane enforcement of the law and ensure family unity who did not qualify for legalization under the Immigration Reform and Control Act (IRCA) of 1986. For a chronological overview of these citations, see American Immigration Council Reagan-Bush Family Fairness: A Chronological History, available at www.immigrationpolicy.org/just-facts/reagan-bush-family-fairness-chronological-history.

3. Department of Justice, "The Department of Homeland Security's Authority to Prioritize Removal of Certain Aliens Unlawfully Present in the United States and to Defer Removal of Others," November 20, 2014, available at www.justice.gov/sites/default/files/olc/opinions/attachments/2014/11/20/2014-11-19-auth-prioritize-removal.pdf.

4. Memorandum from Lynn R. Coleman to Suart Eizenstat and Robert Lipshutz, "re: Draft Executive Order on Environmental Effects Abroad of Major Federal Actions." No date. Executive Order 12114, 6/78–7/8/78, CF, O/A/ 420, Staff Offices Counsel McKenna, Box 126, Jimmy Carter Presidential Library.

5. U.S. Congress, Staff of House Committee on Government Operations, "Executive Orders and Proclamations: A Study of a Use of Presidential Powers," 85th Congress, 1st session, 1957, Committee Print.

6. Executive Order No.11030, "Preparation, Presentation, Filing, and Publication of Executive Orders and Proclamations," 27 Fede*ral Register* 5847 (June 21, 1962), amended by Executive Order No. 11354, "Amending Executive Order No. 11030 of June 19, 1962, with Respect to the Preparation of Presidential Proclamations," 32 *Federal Register* 7695 (May 26, 1967); and Executive Order No. 12608, "Elimination of Unnecessary Executive Orders and Technical Amendments to Others," 52 *Federal Register* 34617 (September 9, 1987).

7. U.S. Congress, House Committee on Rules Subcommittee on Legislative and Budget Process, "Statement of Robert Bedell, Former Administrator with OMB: The Impact

of Executive Orders on the Legislative Process: Executive Lawmaking?," 106th Congress, 1st session, 1999, 3.

8. Gibson 2006; interview with John Harmon, former Assistant Attorney General in the Office of Legal Counsel, Carter administration, August 30, 2005.

9. Memorandum from David A. Stockman to the president, "re: Proposed Executive Order Entitled 'Exercise of Authority under Section 218 of Title 18 of the United States Code,'" October 27, 1983. Record Group 51, Stack 650, Row 51, Compartment 31, Shelf 5, National Archives, College Park, Maryland.

10. Memorandum from Ronald A. Kienlen, OMB Associate General Counsel, for William M. Nichols, OMB General Counsel, to Robert J. Lipshutz, Counsel to the President, "re: Proclamation Waiving Import Fees and Duties," April 6, 1979. Record Group 51, Stack 130, Row 49, Compartment 32, Shelf 4, National Archives, College Park, Maryland.

11. See note 3.

12. *Youngstown Sheet and Tube Co. et al. v. Sawyer*, 343 U.S. 579 (1952).

13. Executive Order No. 13489, "Presidential Records," 74 *Federal Register* 4669 (January 26, 2009). Executive Order No. 13489 revoked EO 13233, "Further Implementation of the Presidential Records Act," 66 *Federal Register* 56025 (November 5, 2001).

14. "Jennifer O'Connor to Erskine Bowles, et al.," August 30, 1995, Paper of Roscoe Conkling, Domestic Policy Council, William Clinton Presidential Library, Box 21.

15. Executive Order 13658 Establishing a Minimum Wage for Contractors 79 *Federal Register* 9851(February 20, 2014).

16. Department of Labor, Final Rule, "Establishing a Minimum Wage for Contractors," 79 *Federal Register* 194 (October 7, 2014): 60634; available at www.gpo.gov/fdsys/pkg/FR-2014-10-07/pdf/FR-2014-10-07.pdf.

17. Congressional authority is signaled by the president citing a joint resolution of Congress, a specific public law, a specific statute or the U.S. Code or "laws of the United States." For example, President Wilson in Proclamation 1364 declared, "by joint resolution of the Senate and House of Representatives . . . it is provided by Section 4067 of the Revised Statutes." A president's authority is signaled by a president invoking his or her powers as president generally or his or her powers under the Constitution. For example, in Proclamation 233 President Grant declared, "By reason of all these considerations, I, Ulysses S. Grant, President of the United States . . ."

18. Executive Order No. 10925, "Establishing the President's Committee on Equal Employment Opportunity," 26 *Federal Register* 1977 (March 8, 1961).

19. Executive Order No. 10980, "Establishing the President's Commission on the Status of Women," 26 *Federal Register* 12059 (December 16, 1961).

20. Table 4.3, later in the chapter, shows the results from a regression analysis of the data for these joint sources of authority.

21. Although other variables are often included in other models evaluating the ways that presidents use unilateral tools, such as presidential approval, we chose a reductive and parsimonious approach and one that was specific to the relations between the branches. We did, however, estimate alternative models including these (and other) variables. Most of the additional variables did not reach standard levels of statistical significance when included with the variables in the original model specification, but the key variables for us remained consistent.

22. The majority party may be the president's party or the opposite party and is used to measure the effectiveness of the party in power to legislate. The variable of divided

government is used to measure the effect of when the president's party is in control of one or both chambers.

23. "Unity" is coded as the percentage of time that the majority party voted together on legislation. Keith T. Poole, May 2010. DW NOMINATE Data; available at http://voteview.ucsd.edu/dwnl.htm. The website notes by way of explanation, "The files below contain the party unity scores by Congress for every Democrat and Republican voting on at least 10 party unity votes in the Congress. A party unity vote is defined as one where at least 50 percent of Democrats, vote against at least 50 percent of Republicans" (see Poole and Rosenthal 1997).

24. A Poisson model models the probability of observing any observed count using the Poisson distribution. The Poisson model is specified: $u_i = E(y_i \mid x_i) = \exp(x_i\beta_1 + \ldots + x_i\beta_n)$; where each observation has a value of u and the observed count for observation i is drawn from a Poisson distribution with mean u_i (Long and Freese 2006) and n is the total number of independent variables. A negative binomial model (which accounts for observed heterogeneity, or "overdispersion") is any series where tests of the log likelihood ratio = α reveal positive and significant tests for overdispersion. Because overdispersion can artificially deflate standard errors, tests for such overdispersion are utilized to determine the appropriate model (tests use a log likelihood-ratio test that $\alpha = 0$). The negative binominal: $u_i = \exp(\beta_0 + \beta_1 x_{i1} + \ldots + \beta_n x_{in})$; where n is the total number of independent variables. This captures the rate of overdispersion, where the variance is larger than the mean. Depending on the nature of the overdispersion (if any), the appropriate model is used in the following discussion.

25. The percentage change in the expected counts from the following models is for a δ unit change in x_k, holding all the other variables constant. Percentage change calculated by $100 \times (\exp[\beta_k \times \delta] - 1)$; where β_k is a favor change in x_k.

26. No collinearity with respect to time was present in these data series, negating the need to use a model to account for collinearity in the series such as a Poisson Exponentially Weighted Moving Average model or a Poisson Autoregressive model (see Brandt and Williams 2001). Alternative models that aggregate proclamation totals in each category by year (instead of by Congress) reveal similar results.

27. For an in-depth look at the constitutional and statutory sources of president's unilateral orders see Fisher (2007).

28. *INS v. Chadha*, 462 U.S. 919 (1983).

29. Just as delegation may appear to be broad until discretionary constraints are factored in (Epstein and O'Halloran 1999), the same is true if a statutory provision contains more than one type of discretion. An example of this is the authority delegated to the president under the Trade Act of 1974 (U.S.C. 19 § 2461–2467) to designate and provide duty-free treatment from any beneficiary developing country subject to a specific process and is required to seek advice from the International Trade Commission on eligible articles. The president is subject then to two types of discretion, substantive and procedural, substantiating the need to code both.

30. Intercoder checks on the amount of discretion reveal substantial agreement. After the initial coding, a second coder was given the specific statute and a list of coding instructions. The Cohen's kappa agreement was 79 percent and the kappa was 0.891 (statistically significant at $p > 0.000$).

31. Joint Resolution for the Authorized Use of Military Force of 2001, Public Law 107–40, *U.S. Statutes at Large* 115 (2001): 224.

32. Authorization for Use of Military Force against Iraq Resolution of 2002, Public Law 107-243, *U.S. Statutes at Large* 116 (2002): 1498.

33. Barack Obama, "Remarks on Proposed Legislation Submitted to the Congress to Authorize the Use of Military Force against the Islamic State of Iraq and the Levant (ISIL) Terrorist Organization," February 11, 2015, *U.S. Government Publishing Office*; available at www.gpo.gov/fdsys/pkg/DCPD-201500092/pdf/DCPD-201500092.pdf.

34. Barack Obama, "Letter from the President-Authorization for the Use of United States Armed Forces in Connection with the Islamic State of Iraq and the Levant to the Congress of the United States," February 11, 2015, *The White House*; available at www.whitehouse.gov/the-press-office/2015/02/11/letter-president-authorization-use-united-states-armed-forces-connection.

35. In cases where it was impossible to determine the specific year, the year is missing from the spreadsheet.

36. A logistic regression model was used to conduct the analysis for the results presented in Table 4.3.

CHAPTER FIVE

1. Statement by Senator Barack Obama at a campaign rally on August 26, 2007.

2. Executive Order No. 13491, "Ensuring Lawful Interrogations," 74 *Federal Register* 4893 (January 27, 2009); Executive Order No. 13492, "Review and Disposition of Individuals Detained at Guantanamo Bay Naval Base and Closure of Detention Facilities," 74 *Federal Register* 4897 (January 27, 2009); and Executive Order No. 13493, "Review of Detention Policy Options," 74 *Federal Register* 4901 (January 27, 2009).

3. Alpert 2010.

4. Executive Order No. 13499, "Further Amendments to Executive Order No. 12835, Establishment of the National Economic Council," 74 *Federal Register* 6979 (February 11, 2009); and Executive Order No. 13500, "Further Amendments to Executive Order No. 12859, Establishment of the Domestic Policy Council," 74 *Federal Register* 6981 (February 11, 2009).

5. Executive Order No. 12272, "Foreign Service Retirement and Disability System," 46 *Federal Register* 5853 (January 21, 1981); and Executive Order No. 12273, "Central Intelligence Agency Retirement and Disability System," 46 *Federal Register* 5854 (January 21, 1981).

6. Executive Order No. 13409, "Establishing an Emergency Board to Investigate a Dispute between Southeastern Pennsylvania Transportation Authority and Its Locomotive Engineers Represented by the Brotherhood of Locomotive Engineers and Trainmen," 71 *Federal Register* 38511 (July 7, 2006).

7. Trade Act of 1974 Section 202, Presidential Action after Investigations, Public Law 93-618, *U.S. Statutes at Large* 88 (1975): 1978.

8. The United States International Trade Commission investigation was transmitted to the president on December 12, 1978, and was established on its own motion but was initiated as an outgrowth of information collected in conjunction with prior investigations.

9. U.S. Congress, House Committee on Ways and Means Subcommittee on Trade, "Importance of Trade Negotiations in Fighting Protectionism: Active U.S. Involvement, Testimony of Ambassador Barshafsky," USTR, 106th Congress, 1st session, 1999.

10. Executive Order No. 13116, "Identification of Trade Expansion Priorities and Discriminatory Procurement Practices," 64 *Federal Register* 16333 (April 5, 1999). Trade

expansion priorities and Super 301 equivalent to Title VII were allowed to lapse and were not instated until this order.

11. Proclamation 4991, "Suspension of the Application of Column 1 Rates of Duty of the Tariff Schedules of the United States to the Products of Poland," October 27, 1982.

12. *FEA v. Algonquin Sng. Inc.*, 426 U.S. 548, 559 (1976).

13. The immigration accord, the only significant agreement between the Reagan administration and the Castro government, was worked out in December 1984. It provided for the repatriation to Cuba of 2,700 Cuban criminals and mental patients who came to this country as part of the 1980 boatlift from the Cuban port of Mariel. In return, the United States agreed to resume processing the emigration from Cuba of 3,000 former political prisoners and to once again issue normal immigration visas to as many as 20,000 Cubans a year (Gwertzman 1986).

14. Ronald Reagan, "Address to the Nation on National Security," February 26, 1986.

15. Proclamation 5517, "Suspension of Cuban Immigration," 51 *Federal Register* 30470 (August 22, 1986).

16. Executive Order No. 12205, "Prohibiting Certain Transactions with Iran," 45 *Federal Register* 24099 (April 9, 1980); Executive Order No. 12513, "Prohibiting Trade and Certain Other Transactions Involving Nicaragua," 50 *Federal Register* 18629 (May 2, 1985); and Executive Order No. 12917, "Prohibiting Certain Transactions with Respect to Haiti," 59 *Federal Register* 26925 (May 24, 1994).

17. Gerald Ford, "Address to a Joint Session of the Congress, August 12, 1974" (1974).

18. George H. W. Bush, "Inaugural Address, January 20, 1989." *Public Papers of the Presidents of the United States: George Bush* 1 (1989): 2–3.

19. Appendix A includes a discussion of the process used to search for congressional hearings that relate to the topic or subject of a unilateral order and were held before the order was issued by the president.

20. The CS-NOMINATE scores represent an approximate positioning of each member in each chamber on a liberal–conservative ideological scale. The scores range from –1 for conservatives to +1 for liberals. Keith T. Poole, DW NOMINATE Data; available at http://voteview.ucsd.edu/dwnl.html.

21. These models allow us to (1) utilize a dichotomous variable arrangement (where $y_i = 1$ if $y_i^* > 0$ and $y_i = 0$ if $y_i^* \leq 0$) and (2) determine the probabilistic effect of the key independent variables on the dependent variable (Agresti 2002). That is, because the models require a dependent variable to be binary, these models can test the above propositions regarding under what conditions a preemptive order was issued. The model is briefly summarized as follows: $\Pr(y = 1 \mid x) = \exp(\alpha + \beta x_1 + \ldots + \beta x_n) / 1 + \exp(\alpha + \beta x_1 + \ldots + \beta x_n)$, where x_n is the total number of independent variables described earlier. Alternative specifications (such as an ordered logit and count models) revealed substantially similar findings.

22. Given the nature of these orders, it might be expected that ones that address defense, emergencies, foreign aid, or foreign trade are more likely to engender a command order from the president. This proved to be correct in models, which truncated the sample based on policy areas, the results were substantially similar. Because the results were fundamentally the same, we have omitted these results for purposes of presentation.

23. U.S. Congress, House Committee on Energy and Commerce Subcommittee on Energy and Power, "Global Warming," 103rd Congress, 1st session, 1993.

24. U.S. Congress, House Committee on Science, Space and Technology Subcommittee on Space, "Global Change Research Program: Key Scientific Uncertainties," 103rd Congress, 1st session, 1993.

25. Executive Order No. 12843, "Procurement Requirements and Policies for Federal Agencies for Ozone-Depleting Substances," 58 *Federal Register* 21881 (April 23, 1993); Executive Order No. 12844, "Federal Use of Alternative Fueled Vehicles," 58 *Federal Register* 21885 (April 23, 1993); and Executive Order No. 12845, "Requiring Agencies to Purchase Energy Efficient Computer Equipment," 58 *Federal Register* 21887 (April 23, 1993).

26. Regulatory Reform Act, S. 1080 97th Congress, 1st session, 127 *Congressional Record* 7938 (1981); The Senate passed S. 1080 on March 24, 1982, by a 94–0 vote. Regulatory Reform Act: Hearings on H.R. 2327 House Committee on the Judiciary Subcommittee on Administrative Law and Governmental Relations of the, 98th Congress 1st session 312 (1983); and U.S. Congress, Senate Committee on the Judiciary Subcommittee on Administrative Practice and Procedure, "Regulatory Reform Act," 98th Congress, 1st session, (1983) 548.

27. Executive Order No. 12498, "Regulatory Planning Process," 50 *Federal Register* 1036 (January 8, 1985).

28. U.S Congress, House Committee on the Judiciary, Subcommittee on Administrative Law and Governmental Relations of the House, "Regulatory Reform Act: Hearings on H.R. 2327," 98th Congress, 1st session, 1983, 312; Regulatory Reform Act, S 1080, 97th Congress, 1st session, 127 *Congressional Record* 7938 (1981); the Senate passed S. 1080 on March 24, 1982, by a 94–0 vote; U.S. Congress, Senate Committee on the Judiciary, Subcommittee on Administrative Practice and Procedure, "The Regulatory Reform Act Hearing on S. 1080," 98th Congress, 1st session, 1983, 548.

29. Barack Obama, "Statement of Administration Policy: H.R. 3590—Sportsmen's Heritage and Recreational Enhancement (SHARE) Act of 2013," February 3, 2014; Barack Obama, "Statement of Administration Policy: H.R. 2954—Public Access and Lands Improvement Act," February 5, 2014; Barack Obama, "Statement of Administration Policy: H.R. 4012—Secret Science Reform Act of 2014," November 17, 2014; Barack Obama, "Statement of Administration Policy: H.R. 4795—Promoting New Manufacturing Act," November 17, 2014; and Barack Obama, "Statement of Administration Policy: H.R. 5781—The California Emergency Drought Relief Act of 2014," December 5, 2014.

30. Executive Order No. 12727, "Ordering the Selected Reserve of the Armed Forces to Active Duty," 55 *Federal Register* 35027 (August, 27, 1990); Laws of the United States of America including Sections 121 and 673(b) of Title 10 of the U.S.C. 10 USC § 12304, "Selected Reserve and Certain Individual Ready Reserve Members; Order to Active Duty Other Than during War or National Emergency."

31. U.S. Congress, Senate Committee on Foreign Relations, "U.S. Policy toward Iraq: Human Rights, Weapons Proliferation, and International Law," 101st Congress, 2nd session, 1990; U.S. Congress, House Committee on Foreign Affairs Developments in the Middle East, June 20, 1990, July 31, 1990; Joint Committee on Economic Hearing on Economic Outlook at Midyear July 12, 1990, August 2, 1990; and U.S. Congress, House Committee on Foreign Affairs, "Sanctions against Iraq," 101st Congress, 2nd session, 1990.

32. In alternatively specified count models (rather than the logit model presented here), the substantive effects are nearly identical (although the statistical significance is not always the same).

33. In alternative models, we included both divided government and divided government interacted with each of the interbranch conditions. Neither divided government nor the interacted terms were statistically significant.

34. When run separately, the size of the majority party in the Senate had no substantive or statistically significant effect, whereas the majority party in the House had a small negative and statistically significant effect. The pooled measure is therefore largely driven by the effect of the size of the majority in the House.

CHAPTER SIX

1. Barack Obama, "Statement of Administration Policy: H.R. 527—Regulatory Flexibility Improvements Act of 2011," November 29, 2011; and "Statement of Administrative Policy: H.R. 3010—Regulatory Accountability Act of 2011," November 29, 2011.

2. Barack Obama, "Statement of Administrative Policy: H.R. 10—Regulations from the Executive in Need of Scrutiny Act of 2011," December 6, 2011.

3. Executive Order No. 13610, "Identifying and Reducing Regulatory Burdens," 77 *Federal Register* 28469 (May 14, 2012).

4. Minimum Wage Fairness Act S. 1737 and Fair Minimum Wage Act of 2013 H.R. 1010, 113th Congress, 1st session.

5. The six-month moratorium was first issued by Secretary of the Interior Salazar on May 27, 2010, after the April 20 explosion of British Petroleum's Deepwater Horizon drilling rig in the Gulf of Mexico.

6. *Hornbeck Offshore Services LLC v. Salazar*, 696 F. Supp. 2d 627 (E.D. La. 2010).

7. Reversing President Obama's Offshore Moratorium Act of 2011, H.R. 1231, 112th Congress, 1st session.

8. Barack Obama, "Statement of Administration Policy: H.R. 1231—To Amend the Outer Continental Shelf Lands Act to Require That Each 5-year Offshore Oil and Gas Leasing Program Offer Leasing in the Areas with the Most Prospective Oil and Gas Resources, to Establish a Domestic Oil and Natural Gas Production Goal, and for Other Purposes," May 10, 2011.

9. Barack Obama, "The President's Weekly Address," May 14, 2011.

10. Executive Order No. 13580, "Interagency Working Group on Coordination of Domestic Energy Development and Permitting in Alaska," 76 *Federal Register* 41989 (July 12, 2011).

11. American Energy and Infrastructure Jobs Act of 2012, H.R. 7, 113th Congress, 2nd session.

12. Barack Obama, "Statement of Administration Policy: H.R. 7—American Energy and Infrastructure Jobs Act of 2012," February 14, 2012.

13. Executive Order No. 13604, "Improving Performance of Federal Permitting and Review of Infrastructure Projects," 77 *Federal Register* 18887 (March 22, 2012).

14. Intelligence Oversight Act of 1976, S. 2865, 94th Congress, 2nd session. Introduced by Senator Frank Church, Chairman of the Church Investigation Committee.

15. U.S. Congress, Senate Committee on Governmental Affairs, Intelligence Oversight Act: Hearings on S. 2865, 94th Congress 2nd session, 1976.

16. Executive Order No. 11905, 41 *Federal Register* 7703 (February 19, 1976).

17. Gerald Ford, "Special Message to the Congress Proposing Legislation to Reform the United States Foreign Intelligence Community," February 18, 1976.

18. Executive Order No. 12532, "Prohibiting Trade and Certain Other Transactions Involving South Africa," 50 *Federal Register* 36861 (September 10, 1985).

19. The Anti-Apartheid Act of 1985, H.R. 1460, 99th Congress, 1st session; the Anti-Apartheid Act of 1985, S. 635, 99th Congress, 1st session; and the Anti-Apartheid Act of 1985, S. 995, 99th Congress, 1st session.

20. On August 1, 1985, the House passed the conference report (Record Vote No. 288: 380–48) and it was considered in the Senate on September 9, 1985, but on September 10, 1985, the motion to proceed to consideration of the measure was tabled in the Senate. See *Congressional Quarterly Weekly* August 1985 and *Congressional Quarterly Annual* 1985.

21. Ronald Reagan, "Remarks and a Question and Answer Session with Reporters on Signing the Executive Order Prohibiting Trade and Certain Other Transactions Involving South Africa, September 9, 1985," Public Papers of the President, American Presidency Project; available at www.presidency.ucsb.edu/ws/index.php?pid=39073&st=&st1=.

22. Omnibus Budget Reconciliation Act of 1993, Public Law 103-66, *U.S. Statutes at Large* 107 (1993): 312.

23. Executive Order No. 12857, "Budget Control," 58 *Federal Register* 42181 (August 6, 1993); and Executive Order No. 12858, "Deficit Reduction Fund," 58 *Federal Register* 42185 (August 6, 1993).

24. William Clinton, "Remarks on Signing the Executive Orders on Budget Control and the Deficit Reduction Fund, August 4, 1993," Public Papers of the President, American Presidency Project; available at www.presidency.ucsb.edu/ws/index.php?pid=46956&st=&st1=.

25. Executive Order No. 12348, "A Resolution Regarding the Management of the U.S. Assets," 47 *Federal Register* 8547 (March 3, 1982); and S. 231, 97th Congress.

26. Jimmy Carter, "Federal Paperwork Reduction Message to the Congress," November 30, 1979; Jimmy Carter, "Remarks on Signing Executive Order 12174, November 30, 1979," Public Papers of the President, American Presidency Project, available at www.presidency.ucsb.edu/ws/index.php?pid=31759&st=&st1=; Executive Order No. 12174, 44 *Federal Register* 69609, (December 4, 1979); and U.S. Congress, Senate Subcommittee on Federal Spending Practices and Open Government of the Senate Committee on Governmental Affairs, Paperwork and Redtape Reduction Act of 1979: Hearings on S. 1411, 96th Congress, 1979, 1037.

27. The procedure for determining if an order related to a bill on Congress's agenda is presented in Appendix A.

28. After the initial coding, a second coder was given the text of the order and the text of the specific legislation that matched the topic of the order that had gone "furthest" in the legislative process after a hearing. The correlation between the two coded responses was .762. The Cohen's kappa agreement was 88.06 percent, and the kappa was .761 (statistically significant at $p > .000$).

29. *Congressional Quarterly Almanac* 1993 (Washington, DC: Congressional Quarterly), 241–246.

30. The methods used for calculating the variables are explained in Chapter Five, in the section on Data and Methods.

31. In models run but not shown here, the inclusion of these control variables did not affect the results, but the fit of the model was not as good when they were included.

32. Gerald Ford, "Veto of a Milk Price Support Bill," January 30, 1976.

33. A joint resolution to provide for quarterly adjustments in the support price for milk, S.J. Res. 121, 94th Congress, 1st session. Vetoed by the president. The veto override failed in the Senate on February 14, 1976.

34. In models run individually for proclamations and executive orders, the results for the proclamations are substantially the same and similar in terms of statistical significance. But, because of a small n, none of the coefficients for proclamations was statistically significant, although the signs on the coefficients were largely in the same direction as in Table 6.2.

35. In models run (but not shown here) interactions between presidential agenda and the interbranch and intrabranch gridlock in columns 2 and 3 demonstrated a substantially similar effect.

36. William Clinton, "Address before a Joint Session of Congress on Administration Goals," February 17, 1993.

37. William Clinton, "Message to Congress on the National Emergency with Respect to Cuba," March 1, 1996; Proclamation No. 6867, "Declaring a National Emergency and Invocation of Emergency Authority Relating to the Regulation of the Anchorage and Movement of Vessels," 61 *Federal Register* 8843 (March 5, 1996); and the Cuban Liberty and Democratic Solidarity Act of 1996, Public Law 104-114, *U.S. Statutes at Large* 110 (1996): 785.

38. In alternative models that included control variables for sponsorship data in each model, the results were similar.

39. In alternative models, we included both divided government and divided government interaction with each of the interbranch conditions. Neither divided government nor the interacted terms were statistically significant. The results were the same as Table 6.2 for the interbranch measures.

40. Memorandum from Dan Tate to Frank Moore, "re: Federal Judgeship Bill Proposed Executive Order. March 1, 1978. Judgeships (Active): Executive Order (District Court Standards and Guidelines)," 2/78-1/79, CF, O/A 438. Staff Offices Counsel Lipshutz, Box 29, Jimmy Carter Presidential Library.

41. H.R.7843, An Act to Provide for the Appointment of Additional District and Circuit Judges, and for Other Purposes. 95th Congress, 2nd session.

42. Executive Order 12059, "United States Circuit Judge Nominating Commission," 43 *Federal Register* 20949, May 16, 1978.

43. Under the Federal Land Policy and Management Act of 1976, the Department of the Interior was required to review public lands for wilderness classification within fifteen years after enactment; Federal Land Policy and Management Act of 1976, Public Law 94-579, *U.S. Statutes at Large* 90 (1976): 2743.

44. Executive Order No. 12444, "Continuation of Export Control Regulations," 48 *Federal Register* 48215 (October 14, 1983).

45. Bassett 2014.

CHAPTER SEVEN

1. Question posed by Speaker of the House John Boehner (R-OH) to members of the House of Representatives on July 30, 2014. Shortly afterwards, members of the House voted 225–201 in favor of H.R. 676, authorizing Boehner to move ahead with the suit against the executive branch for giving employers a one-year reprieve on enforcing a requirement under the Affordable Care Act that they offer health coverage or pay a penalty.

2. Patient Protection and Affordable Care Act, Title IV—Prevention of Chronic Disease and Improving Public Health, Subtitle A—Modernizing Disease Prevention and Public Health Systems, Sec. 4001. National Prevention, Health Promotion and Public Health Council, Public Law 111-148, *U.S. Statutes at Large* 124 (2010): 119.

3. Executive Order No. 13544, "Establishing the National Prevention, Health Promotion, and Public Health Council," 75 *Federal Register* 33983 (June 16, 2010).

4. *J. W. Hampton Jr. and Co. v. United States*, 276 U.S. 394, 402 (1928); *Frischer and Co., Inc v. Tariff Commission* (1930) and *Frischer and Co., Inc. v. Elting* (1932); *Norwegian Nitrogen Products Co. v. United States*, 288 U.S. 294, 308 et. seq. (1933); and *United States v. George S. Bush & Co.*, 310 U.S. 371 (1940).

5. *Chevron U.S.A. Inc. v. Natural Resources Defense Council*, 467 U.S. 837 (1984); *United States v. Mead*, 533 U.S. 218 (9th Cir. 2001); *National Cable & Telecommunications Assn. v. Brand X Internet Services*, 545 U.S. 967, 980 (2005); and *City of Arlington v. FCC*, 11-1545 (2013).

6. *United States v. Curtiss-Wright Export Corporation*, 299 U.S. 304, 316 (1936); and *In re Neagle*, 135 U.S. 1 (1890).

7. U.S. Department of the Treasury, "CISADA: The New Iran U.S. Sanctions," The Financial Provisions; available at www.treasury.gov/resourcecenter/sanctions/Programs/Documents/CISADA_english.pdf.

8. Executive Order No. 13574, "Authorizing the Implementation of Certain Sanctions Set Forth in the Iran Sanctions Act of 1996, as Amended," 76 *Federal Register* 30505 (May 25, 2011).

9. Executive Order No. 13449, "Protection of Striped Bass and Red Drum Fish Populations," 72 *Federal Register* 60531 (October 24, 2007).

10. Clean Diamond Trade Act, H.R. 1584, Public Law 108-19, *U.S. Statutes at Large* 117 (2003): 631.

11. Executive Order No. 13312, "Implementing the Clean Diamond Trade Act," 68 *Federal Register* 48249 (August 13, 2003).

12. North America Free Trade Agreement Implementation Act, H.R. 3450, Public Law 103-182, *U.S. Statutes at Large* 107 (1993): 2057; Proclamation 6641 (December 15, 1993); and Executive Order No. 12889, 58 *Federal Register* 69681 (December 30, 1993).

13. The Executive Salary Cost of Living Adjustment Act of 1975, H.R. 2559, Public Law 94-82, *U.S. Statutes at Large* 89 (1975): 419; and Executive Order No. 11883, "Adjustments of Certain Rates of Pay and Allowances," 40 *Federal Register* 47091 (October 8, 1975).

14. Department of Defense Authorization Act of 1986, S. 1160, Title VIII: Military Family Act of 1985, Public Law 99-145, Signed by the President, November 8, 1985.

15. Executive Order No. 12568, "Employment Opportunities for Military Spouses at Nonappropriated Fund Activities," 51 *Federal Register* 35497 (October 6, 1986).

16. Executive Exchange Program Voluntary Services Act of 1986 H.R. 3002, Public Law 99-424, *U.S. Statutes at Large* 100 (1986): 964; and Executive Order No. 12574, "President's Commission on Executive Exchange," 51 *Federal Register* 42199 (November 24, 1986).

17. Reorganization Act of 1977 S. 626, Public Law 95-17, *U.S. Statutes at Large* Signed 91 (1977): 29.

18. Executive Order No. 11814, "Activation of the Energy Resources Council," 39 *Federal Register* 36955 (October 16, 1974).

19. Gerald Ford, "Remarks on Signing the Energy Reorganization Act of 1974, October 11, 1974." Public Papers of the President, American Presidency Project; available at www.presidency.ucsb.edu/ws/index.php?pid=4451.

20. Executive Order No. 13228, "Establishing the Office of Homeland Security and the Homeland Security Council," 66 *Federal Register* 51812 (October 10, 2001).

21. George W. Bush, "Address before a Joint Session of the Congress on the United States Response to the Terrorist Attacks of September 11," September 20, 2001.

22. George W. Bush, "Message to the Congress Transmitting Proposed Legislation to Create the Department of Homeland Security," June 16, 2002; and Homeland Security Act of 2002, Public Law 107-296, *U.S. Statutes at Large* 116 (2002): 2135.

23. Executive Order No. 13284, "Amendment of Executive Orders, and Other Actions, in Connection with the Establishment of the Department of Homeland Security," 68 *Federal Register* 4075 (January 28, 2003); and Executive Order No. 13286, "Amendment of Executive Orders, and Other Actions, in Connection with the Transfer of Certain Functions to the Secretary of Homeland Security," 68 *Federal Register* 10619 (March 5, 2003).

24. Intelligence Reform and Terrorism Prevention Act of 2004, Public Law 108-458, *U.S. Statues at Large* 118 (2004): 3638.

25. Executive Order No. 13383, which amended Executive Orders 12139 and 12949 in light of the establishment of the Office of Director of National Intelligence, 70 *Federal Register* 41933 (July 20, 2005). Remarks on signing the Executive Order, December 17, 2004.

26. Barack Obama, "Statement on Signing the Fraud Enforcement and Recovery Act of 2009," May 20, 2009.

27. Executive Order No. 13519, "Establishment of the Financial Fraud Enforcement Task Force," 74 *Federal Register* 60123 (November 19, 2009).

28. President William J. Clinton, "Remarks on Signing the Government Performance and Results Act of 1993 and an Exchange with Reporters," August 3, 1993.

29. John Kamensky, "The U.S. Reform Experience: The National Performance Review," Presentation Notes, Plenary Session, Conference on Civil Service Systems in Comparative Perspectives, April 6, 1997.

30. Executive Order No. 12862, "Setting Customer Standards," 58 *Federal Register* 48257 (September 14, 1993).

31. Barack Obama, "Statement of Administrative Policy: S. 365—Budget Control Act of 2011," August 1, 2011. On August 2, 2011, President Obama signed the Budget Control Act of 2011, Public Law 112-25, *U.S. Statutes at Large* 125 (2011): 240.

32. Executive Order No. 13589, "Promoting Efficient Spending," 76 *Federal Register* 70863 (November 15, 2011).

33. Special Foreign Assistance Act of 1986 S. 1917, Public Law 99-529, *U.S. Statutes at Large* 100 (1986): 3010; Section 204 directs the president to use the president's authorities under the International Emergency Economic Powers Act to assist Haiti in its efforts to recover Haitian assets that Haiti alleges were stolen by Jean Claude Duvalier or his associates.

34. Executive Order No. 12588, Action against certain assets of disputed title, 52 Federal Register 8859 (March 20, 1987). Jean-Claude and Michèle Duvalier departed from Haiti on February 7, 1986.

35. In his statement on signing S. 1917, the Special Foreign Assistance Act, President Reagan noted that he would have had to object "to such a provision if it mandated the specific actions to be taken by the Government because such a mandate would unrea-

sonably detract from the flexibility necessary to formulate and conduct a sound foreign policy." October 24, 1986.

36. An Act to Authorize Appropriations for the Department of Energy for National Security Programs for Fiscal Year 1980, and for Other Purposes, S. 673, Public Law 96-164, *U.S. Statutes at Large* 93 (1979): 1259.

37. Executive Order No. 12192, "State Planning Council on Radioactive Waste Management," 45 *Federal Register* 9727 (February 13, 1980).

38. A legislative history was created for each unilateral order as part of this research. This enabled us to classify all the orders that met the criteria for Direct Action, Legislative Process, and Executing Law.

39. In alternative models using a count model, the results are substantially similar. One exception is the divided government measure, which is not statistically significant in the count models. But divided government is significant in the models in Table B.1 in Appendix B.

40. A factor that we do not address directly is the influence of legislative productivity on the number of unilateral orders issued to implement law. The topic of congressional action and presidential response is found in Appendix B.

41. Foreign Intelligence Surveillance Act of 1978, Public Law 95-511, *U.S. Statutes at Large* 92 (1978): 1783.

42. Jimmy Carter, "Foreign Intelligence Surveillance Act of 1978 Statement on Signing S. 1566 into Law, October 25, 1978." Public Papers of the President, American Presidency Project; available at www.presidency.ucsb.edu/ws/?pid=30048.

43. Executive Order No. 12139, "Foreign Intelligence Electronic Surveillance," 44 *Federal Register* 30311 (May 25, 1979).

44. Executive Order No. 12949, "Foreign Intelligence Physical Searches," 60 *Federal Register* 8169, (February 13, 1995); and Foreign Intelligence Surveillance Act of 1978, Public Law 95-511, *U.S. Statutes at Large* 92 (1978): 1783 as amended by Intelligence Authorization Act for Fiscal Year 1995, H.R. 4299, Public Law 103-359, *U.S. Statutes at Large* 108 (1994): 3423.

45. A paired *t*-test, which compares the mean of the two samples, demonstrates that, of those orders classified as implement, there is a significant difference in those signing statements "for" or "against" legislation. Thus, the differences are different than zero (*t*-statistic = −15.6).

CHAPTER EIGHT

1. "Ann O'Leary to Bruce Reed," April 10, 2000, Papers of Bruce Reed, Domestic Policy Council, William Clinton Presidential Library, Box 109.

2. Ibid.

3. Yoo, John. Memo on Presidential War Powers; retrieved on May 11, 2012, from www.justice.gov/olc/warpowers925.html.

4. U.S. Congress, House, Subcommittee on Commercial and Administrative Law of the Committee on the Judiciary, House of Representatives, *Congressional Limitation of Executive Orders*, 106th Congress, 1st session, 1999.

5. Executive Order No. 10924, "Establishment and Administration of the Peace Corps in the Department of State," 26 *Federal Register* 1789 (March 2, 1961).

6. Proclamation No. 4771, "Registration under the Military Selective Service Act," 45 *Federal Register* 45247 (July 2, 1980).

7. Department of Defense Appropriation Authorization Act of 1980, Public Law 96-107, *U.S. Statutes at Large* 93 (1979): 815.

8. House Joint Resolution 521, Public Law 96-282, *U.S. Statutes at Large* 94 (1980): 552.

9. Jimmy Carter, "Registration under the Military Selective Service Act Remarks on Signing Proclamation 4771, July 1, 1980," Public Papers of the President, American Presidency Project; available at www.presidency.ucsb.edu/ws/index.php?pid=44696.

10. Philip Rucker, "Obama's 7 State of the Union Talking Points. No. 6: 'The Pen and Phone' strategy." *The Washington Post*, January 27, 2014; available at www.washingtonpost.com/blogs/the-fix/wp/2014/01/27/obamas-7-state-of-the-union-talking-points-no-6-the-pen-and-phone-strategy/.

APPENDIX A

1. President Carter addressed the need for the protection of Alaska lands in an interview and question-and-answer session with editors and news directors on January 13, 1978; his State of the Union address, also on January 19, 1978; his remarks on signing into law H.R. 3454, Endangered American Wilderness Act of 1978 on February 24, 1978; and his message to Congress transmitting the Council on Environmental Quality Report on February 28, 1978.

2. *ProQuest® Congressional* allows the reader to explore Congress in action with the most comprehensive online resource available for congressional publications and legislative research. It includes the U.S. Serial Set Digital Collection, the Congressional Research Digital Collection, the Congressional Hearings Digital Collection, and the Congressional Record Permanent Digital Collection. The database includes congressional hearings on a particular topic, congressional publications and hearings related to a bill, legislative histories, voting records, committee information, and the full text of key regulatory and statutory resources.

Bibiliography

Aberbach, Joel D., and Bert A. Rockman. 2000. *In the Web of Politics: Three Decades of the U.S. federal Executive.* Washington, DC: Brookings Institution.

Agresti, Alan. 2002. *Categorical Data Analysis.* New York: Wiley.

Ainsworth, Scott H., Brian M. Harward, and Kenneth W. Moffett. 2012. "Congressional Responsiveness to Presidential Signing Statements." *American Politics Research* 40(6): 1067–1091.

Alpert, Ed. 2010. "Gulf Coast Rebuilding Office Closing This Month," *Times-Picayune*, July 30.

Andres, Gary. 2005. "Polarization and White House/Legislative Relations: Causes and Consequences of Elite-Level Conflict." *Presidential Studies Quarterly* 35(4): 761–770.

Arnhart, Larry. 1979. "The God-Like Prince: John Locke, Executive Prerogative, and the American Presidency," *Presidential Studies Quarterly* 9(2): 121–130.

Ashabranner, Brent. 1971. *A Moment in History: The First Ten Years of the Peace Corps.* Garden City, NJ: Doubleday & Company.

Bailey, Jeremy D. 2004. "Executive Prerogative and the 'Good Officer' in Thomas Jefferson's Letter to John B. Colvin." *Presidential Studies Quarterly* 34(4): 732–754.

———. 2007. *Thomas Jefferson and Executive Power.* Cambridge, UK: Cambridge University Press.

Bailey, Jeremy D., and Brandon Rottinghaus. 2013. "The Development of Unilateral Power and the Problem of the Power to Warn: Washington through McKinley." *Presidential Studies Quarterly* 43(1): 186–204.

Baker, Peter, and Coral Davenport. 2014. "Using Executive Powers, Obama Begins His Last Big Push on Climate Policy." *New York Times*, May 31.

Balleck, Barry J. 1992. "When the Ends Justify the Means: Thomas Jefferson and the Louisiana Purchase." *Presidential Studies Quarterly* 22(4): 679–696.

Barilleaux, Ryan J., and David Zellers. 2010. "Executive Unilateralism in the Ford and Carter Presidencies." In *The Unitary Executive and the Modern Presidency*, edited by Ryan J. Barilleaux and Christopher S. Kelley. College Station: Texas A&M University.

Bassett, Laura. "Obama to Sign Executive Orders on Equal Pay." *The Huffington Post*, April 6, 2014; available at www.huffingtonpost.com/2014/04/06/obama-equal-pay_n_5100361.html.

Bawn, Kathleen. 1995. "Political Control Versus Expertise: Congressional Choices about Administrative Procedures." *American Political Science Review* 89(1): 62–73.

———. 1997. "Choosing Strategies to Control the Bureaucracy: Statutory Constraints, Oversight, and the Committee System." *Journal of Law, Economics, and Organization* 13(1): 101–126.

Belco, Michelle H., and Brandon Rottinghaus. 2009. "Presidential Proclamation 6920." *Presidential Studies Quarterly* 39(3): 605–618.

———. 2014. "In Lieu of Legislation: Executive Unilateral Preemption or Support during the Legislative Process." *Political Research Quarterly* 67(2): 413–425.

Bendor, Jonathan, Ami Glazer, and Thomas Hammond. 2001. "Theories of Delegation." *Annual Review of Political Science* 4: 235–269.

Bendor, Jonathan, and Adam Meirowitz. 2004. "Spatial Models of Delegation." *American Political Science Review* 98(2): 293–310.

Best, Richard A. 2004. *Proposals for Intelligence Reorganization, 1949–2004.* (CRS Report No. RL32500). Washington, DC: Congressional Research Service. Available at http://fas.org/irp/crs/RL32500.pdf.

Binder, Sarah. A. 1997. Minority Rights, Majority Rule: Partisanship and the Development of Congress. New York: Cambridge University Press.

———. 1999. "The Dynamics of Legislative Gridlock, 1947–96." *American Political Science Review* 93(3): 519–533.

———. 2003. *Stalemate: Causes and Consequences of Legislative Gridlock.* Washington, DC: Brookings Institution Press.

Black, Ryan C., Anthony J. Madonna, Ryan J. Owens, and Michael S. Lynch. 2007. "Adding Recess Appointments to the President's 'Tool Chest' of Unilateral Powers." *Political Research Quarterly* 60(4): 645–654.

Boehner, John. 2014. "Speaker Boehner to President Obama: This Is Not How American Democracy Works." Press Release, November 20, Available at www.speaker.gov/press-release/speaker-boehner-president-obama-not-how-american-democracy-works.

Bond, Jon R., and Richard Fleisher. 1990. *The President in the Legislative Arena.* Chicago and London: University of Chicago Press.

Bowles, Paul. 2005. "Globalization and Neoliberalism: A Taxonomy and Some Implications for Anti-Globalization." *Canadian Journal of Development Studies/Revue Canadienne D'études Du Développement* 26(1): 67–87.

Brandt Patrick T and John T. Williams. 2001. "A Linear Poisson Autoregressive Model: The Poisson AR(p) Model." *Political Analysis* 9(2): 164–184.

Brinkley, Douglas. 2007. *Gerald R. Ford.* New York: Times Books.

Bush, George W. 2010. *Decision Points.* New York: Crown Publishers.

Calabresi, Steven G., and Saikrishna B. Prakash, 1994. "The President's Power to Execute the Laws." *Yale Law Journal* 104 (541): 635–663.

Calabresi, Steven G., and Christopher S. Yoo. 2008. *The Unitary Executive: Presidential Power from Washington to Bush.* New Haven, CT: Yale University Press.

Calmes, Jackie. 2011. "Jobs Plan Stalled, Obama to Try New Economic Drive." *New York Times*, October 23.

Calvert, Randall L., Mathew D. McCubbins, and Barry R. Weingast. 1989. "A Theory of Political Control and Agency Discretion." *American Journal of Political Science* 33: 588–611.

Cameron, Charles M. 2000. *Veto Bargaining: Presidents and the Politics of Negative Power.* New York: Cambridge University Press.

Cameron, Charles M., and Jee-Kwang Park. 2008. "A Primer on the President's Legislative Program." In *Presidential Leadership: The Vortex of Power*, edited by Bert A. Rockman and Richard W. Waterman. New York and Oxford, UK: Oxford University Press.

Canes-Wrone, Brandice, William G. Howell, and David E. Lewis. 2008. "Toward a Broader Understanding of Presidential Power: A Reevaluation of the Two Presidencies Thesis." *Journal of Politics* 70(1): 1–16.

Carey, Robert G. 1970. *The Peace Corps.* New York: Praeger Publishers.

Carter, Jimmy. 1982. *Keeping Faith: Memoirs of a President.* Toronto: Bantam Books.

———. 2010. *White House Diary.* New York: Farrar, Straus and Giroux.

Cash, Robert B. 1963. "Presidential Power: Use and Enforcement of Executive Orders." *Notre Dame Lawyer* 39: 44–55.

Christenson, Dino P., and Douglas L. Kriner. 2015. "Political Constraints on Unilateral Executive Action." *Case Western Reserve Law Review* 65(4): 897–931.

Cohen, Jeffrey E. 2012. *The President's Legislative Policy Agenda, 1789–2002.* New York: Cambridge University Press.

Conley, Richard S. 2011. "The Harbinger of the Unitary Executive? An Analysis of Presidential Signing Statements from Truman to Carter." *Presidential Studies Quarterly* 41(3): 546–569.

Cook, Corey. 2002. "The Permanence of the 'Permanent Campaign': George W. Bush's Public Presidency." *Presidential Studies Quarterly* 32(4): 753–764.

Cooper, Joseph, David W. Brady, and Patricia A. Hurley. 1977. "The Electoral Basis of Party Voting: Patterns and Trends in the U.S. House of Representatives." In *The Impact of the Electoral Process,* edited by Louis Maisel and Joseph Cooper. Beverly Hills, CA: Sage Cooper.

Cooper, Philip J. 1986. "By Order of the President: Administration by Executive Order and Proclamation." *Administration and Society* 18: 233–262.

———. 1997. "Power Tools for an Effective and Responsible Presidency." *Administration and Society* 29(5): 529–556.

———. 2002. *By Order of the President: The Use and Abuse of Executive Direct Action.* Lawrence: University Press of Kansas.

———. 2005. "George W. Bush, Edgar Allan Poe, and the Use and Abuse of Presidential Signing Statements." *Presidential Studies Quarterly* 35(3): 515–532.

———. 2014. "Playing Presidential Ping-Pong with Executive Orders." *Washington Post,* January 31.

Corwin, Edward S. 1957. *The President: Office and Powers: 1787–1957.* New York: New York University Press.

Crenson, Matthew and Benjamin Ginsberg. 2007. *Presidential Power: Unchecked and Unbalanced.* New York: W. W. Norton.

Cronin, Thomas E. 1989. *Inventing the American Presidency.* Lawrence: University Press of Kansas.

Cunningham, Noble E. 1963. *The Jeffersonian Republicans in Power: Party Operations 1801–1809.* Chapel Hill: University of North Carolina Press.

Dahl, Robert. 1967. *A Preface to Democratic Theory.* Chicago: University of Chicago Press.

Deering, Christopher J., and Forrest Maltzman. 1999. "The Politics of Executive Orders: Legislative Constraints on Presidential Power." *Political Research Quarterly* 52(4): 767–783.

Deering, Christopher J., and Steven S. Smith. 1997. *Committees in Congress.* Washington, DC: Congressional Quarterly Press.

Dickinson, Matthew J. 1996. *Bitter Harvest: FDR, Presidential Power and the Growth of the Presidential Branch.* Cambridge, UK: Cambridge University Press.

———. 2008. "The Politics of Persuasion: A Bargaining Model of Presidential Power." In *Presidential Leadership: The Vortex of Power*; edited by Bert Rockman and Richard Waterman. New York: Oxford University Press.

Dickinson, Matthew J., and Jesse Gubb. 2016. "The Limits to Power without Persuasion." *Presidential Studies Quarterly* 46(1): 48–72.

Dodds, Graham G. 2006. "Executive Orders from Nixon to Now." In *Executing the Constitution: Putting the President Back into the Constitution*, edited by Christopher S. Kelley. Albany: State University of New York Press.

———. 2013. *Take Up Your Pen: Unilateral Presidential Directives in American Politics.* Philadelphia: University of Pennsylvania Press.

Durrant, Jeffrey O. 2007. *Struggle over Utah's San Rafael Swell.* Tucson: University of Arizona Press.

Edwards, George C. III, and Andrew Barrett. 2000. "Presidential Agenda Setting in Congress." In *Polarized Politics: Congress and the President in a Partisan Era*, edited by Jon R. Bond and Richard Fleisher. Washington, DC: Congressional Quarterly Press.

Edwards, George C. III, Andrew Barrett, and Jeffrey Peake. 1997. "The Legislative Impact of Divided Government." *American Journal of Political Science* 41(2): 545–563.

Epstein, David, and Sharyn O'Halloran. 1994. "Administrative Procedures, Information and Agency Discretion." *American Journal of Political Science* 38: 697–722.

———. 1999. *Delegating Powers: A Transaction Cost Politics Approach in Policymaking under Separate Powers.* Cambridge, UK: Cambridge University Press.

Erickson, Paul. D. 1985. *Reagan Speaks: The Making of an American Myth.* New York: New York University Press.

Eshbaugh-Soha, Matthew. 2005. "The Politics of Presidential Agendas." *Political Research Quarterly* 58: 257–268.

Farley, Robert, 2010. "Stupak Revises Abortion Stance on Health Care Bill, Citing Obama's Executive Order," *Tampa Bay Times*, March 23,

Fatovic, Clement. 2009. *Outside the Law: Emergency and Executive Power.* Baltimore: Johns Hopkins University Press.

Fenno, Richard F. Jr. 1958. "President–Cabinet Relations: A Pattern and a Case Study." *American Political Science Review* 52(2): 388–405.

Fine, Jeffrey A., and Adam L. Warber. 2012. "Circumventing Adversity: Executive Orders and Divided Government." *Presidential Studies Quarterly* 42(2): 256–274.

Fiorina, Morris. 1982. "Legislative Choice of Regulatory Forms: Legal Process or Administrative Process?" *Public Choice*: 39: 33–61.

———. 1986. "Legislator Uncertainty, Legislative Control, and the Delegation of Legislative Power." *Journal of Law, Economics, and Organization* 2: 33–51.

———. 1996. *Divided Government.* Boston: Allyn and Bacon.

Fisher, Louis, 1978. *The Constitution between Friends: Congress, the President, and the Law.* New York: St. Martin's Press.

———. 1997. *Constitutional Conflicts between Congress and the President*, fourth edition. Lawrence: University Press of Kansas.

———. 1998. *The Politics of Shared Power: Congress and the Executive.* fourth edition. College Station: Texas A&M University Press

———. 2000. *Congressional Abdication on War and Spending.* College Station: Texas A&M University Press.

———. 2003. *Nazi Saboteurs on Trial: A Military Tribunal and American Law*, second edition. Lawrence: University Press of Kansas.

———. 2005. "Item Veto: Budgetary Savings," (CRS Report RS22155). Washington, DC: Congressional Research Service.

———. 2007. *Constitutional Conflicts between Congress and the President*, fifth edition). Lawrence: University Press of Kansas.

———. 2010. "The Unitary Executive: Ideology Versus the Constitution." In *The Unitary Executive and the Modern Presidency*, edited by Ryan J. Barilleaux and Christopher S. Kelley. College Station: Texas A&M University.

Fleishman, Joel L., and Arthur H. Aufses. 1976. "Law and Orders: The Problem of Presidential Legislation." *Law and Contemporary Problems* 40(3): 1–45.

Genovese, Michael A. 2010a. "Foundations of the Unitary Executive of George W. Bush." In *The Unitary Executive and the Modern Presidency*, edited by Ryan J. Barilleaux and Christopher S. Kelley. College Station: Texas A&M University.

———. 2010b. *Presidential Prerogative: Imperial Power in an Age of Terrorism*. Stanford, CA: Stanford University Press.

Gibson, Tobias Tandy. 2006. "The Office of Legal Counsel and the Presidency: The Legal Strategy of Executive Orders." PhD dissertation. Washington University in St. Louis.

Gilligan, Thomas W., and Keith Krehbiel. 1987. "Collective Decision-Making and Standing Committees: An Informational Rationale for Restrictive Amendment Procedures." *Journal of Law, Economics and Organization* 3: 287–335.

Gleiber, Dennis W., and Steven A. Shull. 1992. "Presidential Influence in the Policymaking Process." *Western Political Quarterly* 45(2): 441–467.

Goldsmith, Jack. 2007. *The Terror Presidency: Law and Judgment inside the Bush Administration*. New York: W. W. Norton and Co.

———. 2012. *Power and Constraint: The Accountable Presidency after 9/11*. New York: W. W. Norton.

Goldsmith, William M. 1974. *The Growth of Presidential Power*. New York: Chelsea House Publishers.

Gomez, Brad T., and Steven A. Shull. 1995. "Presidential Decision Making: Explaining the Use of Executive Orders." Paper presented at the Annual Meeting of the Southern Political Science Association, Tampa, Florida, November 2–4.

Grant, J. Tobin, and Nathan J. Kelly. 2008. "Legislative Productivity of the U.S. Congress, 1789–2004." *Political Analysis* 16(3): 303–323.

Gwertzman, Bernard, 1986. "Cuba, in Immigration Concession, Said to Drop Ban on a U.S. Radio," *New York Times*, July 9.

Hamilton, Alexander. 2003. *The Federalist Papers*, edited by Clinton Rossiter. New York: New American Library.

Hamilton, Alexander (Pacificus), and James Madison (Helvidius). 2007. *The Pacificus–Helvidius Debates of 1793–1794*, edited and introduction by Morton J. Frisch. Indianapolis: Liberty Fund.

Hart, James. 1925. *The Ordinance Making Powers of the President of the United States*. Baltimore: Johns Hopkins University Press.

Healy, Gene. 2008. *The Cult of the Presidency: America's Dangerous Devotion to Executive Power*. Washington, DC: Cato.

Hebe, William. 1972. "Executive Orders and the Development of Presidential Power." *Villanova Law Review* 17: 688–712.

Howell, William G. 2003. *Power without Persuasion: The Politics of Direct Presidential Action.* Princeton, NJ, and Oxford, UK: Princeton University Press.

———. 2005. "Unilateral Powers: A Brief Overview." *Presidential Studies Quarterly* 35(3): 417–439.

Howell, William G., S. Adler, C. Cameron, and C. Riemann. 2000. "Divided Government and the Legislative Productivity of Congress, 1945–1994." *Legislative Studies Quarterly.* 25(2): 285–312.

Howell, William G., Saul P. Jackman, and Jon Rogowski. 2013. *The Wartime President: Executive Influence and the Nationalizing Politics of Threat.* Chicago: University of Chicago Press.

Howell, William G., and Douglas Kriner 2008. "Power without Persuasion: Identifying Executive Influence." In *Presidential Leadership: The Vortex of Power,* edited by Bert A. Rockman and Richard W. Waterman. New York: Oxford University Press.

Howell, William G., and David Lewis. 2002. "Agencies by Presidential Design." *Journal of Politics* 64(4): 1095–1114.

Howell, William G., and Kenneth R. Mayer. 2005. "The Last One Hundred Days." *Presidential Studies Quarterly* 35(3): 533–553.

Howell, William G., and Jon C. Pevehouse. 2005. "Presidents, Congress, and the Use of Force." *International Organization* 59(1): 209–232.

Huber, John D., and Charles R. Shipan. 2002. *Deliberate Discretion? The Institutional Foundations of Bureaucratic Autonomy.* Cambridge, UK: Cambridge University Press.

Huetteman, Emmarie. 2014. "Aides Say Obama Is Willing to Work with or without Congress to Meet Goals." *New York Times,* January 26.

Jacobs, Lawrence R., and Robert Y. Shapiro. 2000. "Conclusion: Presidential Power, Institutions and Democracy." In *Presidential Power: Forging the Presidency for the Twenty-First Century,* edited by Robert Y. Shapiro, Martha Joynt Kumar, and Lawrence R. Jacobs. New York: Columbia University Press.

James, Frank. 2012. "With DREAM Order, Obama Did What Presidents Do: Act without Congress." *NPR,* June 15.

James, Scott C. 2009. "Historical Institutionalism, Political Development, and the Presidency" In the *Oxford Handbook and the American Presidency,* edited by George C. Edwards III and William G. Howell. New York: Oxford University Press.

Joachim, David S. 2014. "Obama Orders Rule Changes to Expand Overtime Pay." *The New York Times,* March 13.

Johnson, Alexandra D., Meredith Gibbons, and Tobias T. Gibson. 2010. "Rethinking Unilateral Powers in the Obama Administration." *PRG Newsletter.* Presidency Research Group American Political Science Association.

Johnson, Jeh Charles. 2014. *Memorandum on Exercising Prosecutorial Discretion with Respect to Individuals Who Came to the United States as Children and with Respect to Certain Individuals Who Are the Parents of U.S. Citizens or Permanent Residents.* Washington, DC: Department of Homeland Security. Available at www.dhs.gov/sites/default/files/publications/14_1120_memo_deferred_action.pdf.

Jones, Charles O. 2005. *The Presidency in a Separated System,* second edition. Washington, DC: Brookings Institution Press.

Kagan, Elena. 2001. "Presidential Administration." *Harvard Law Review* 114(8): 2246–2385.

Kelley, Christopher S. 2007. "The Law: Contextualizing the Signing Statement." *Presidential Studies Quarterly* 37(4): 737–748.

Kelley, Christopher S., and Bryan Marshall. 2008. "The Last Word: Presidential Power and the Role of Signing Statements." *Presidential Studies Quarterly* 38(2): 248–267.

Kennedy, Joshua B. 2014. "Signing Statements, Gridlock, and Presidential Strategy." *Presidential Studies Quarterly* 44(4): 602–622.

Kerwin, Cornelius M. R. 2003. *Rulemaking: How Government Agencies Write Law and Make Policy.* Washington, DC: Congressional Quarterly Press.

Kiewiet, D. Roderick, and Mathew D. McCubbins. 1988. "Presidential Influence on Congressional Appropriations Decisions." *American Journal of Political Science* 32(3): 713–736.

———. 1991.*The Logic of Delegation: Congressional Parties and the Appropriation Process.* Chicago: University of Chicago Press.

Kim, Clare, 2014, "Boehner: Minimum Wage Raise Affects 'No One,'" *MSNBC,* January 28,

King, Gary, and Lyn Ragsdale. 1988. *The Elusive Executive: Discovering Statistical Patterns in the Presidency.* Washington, DC: Congressional Quarterly Press.

Kingdon, John. 2003. *Agendas, Alternatives, and Public Policies.* New York: Longman.

Kleinerman, Benjamin A. 2005. "Lincoln's Example: Executive Power and the Survival of Constitutionalism." *Perspectives on Politics* 4: 801–816.

———. 2009. *The Discretionary President: The Promise and Peril of Executive Power.* Lawrence: University Press of Kansas.

Korte, Gregory. 2014. "Obama Issues 'Executive Orders by Another Name.'" *USA Today,* December 17.

Krause, George A., and David B. Cohen. 1997. "Presidential Use of Executive Orders, 1953–1994." *American Politics Quarterly* 25: 458–481.

Krause, George A., and Brent M. Dupay. 2009. "Coordinated Action and the Limits of Presidential Control over the Bureaucracy: Lessons from the George W. Bush Presidency." In *President George W. Bush's Influence over Bureaucracy and Policy: Extraordinary Times, Extraordinary Powers,* edited by Colin Provost and Paul Teske. New York: Palgrave.

Krehbiel, Keith. 1991. *Information and Legislative Organization.* Ann Arbor: University of Michigan Press.

———. 1995. "Cosponsors and Wafflers from A to Z." *American Journal of Political Science* 39(4): 906–923.

Krehbiel, Keith, and Daniel Kessler. 1996. "Dynamics of Cosponsorship." *American Political Science Review* 90(3): 555–566.

———. 1998. *Pivotal Politics: A Theory of U.S. Lawmaking.* Chicago: University of Chicago Press.

Kroger, Gregory. 2003. "Position Taking and Cosponsorship in the U.S. House." *Legislative Studies Quarterly* 28(2): 225–246.

Krutz, Glen S., and Jeffrey S. Peake. 2009. *Treaty Politics and the Rise of Executive Agreements: International Commitments in a System of Shared Powers.* Ann Arbor: University of Michigan Press.

Langston, Thomas S., and Michael E. Lind. 1991. "John Locke & the Limits of Presidential Prerogative." *Polity* 24(1): 49–68.

Laski, Harold J. 1940. *The American Presidency.* New York: Harper and Brothers.

Lewis, David E. 2003. *Presidents and the Politics of Agency Design*. Stanford, CA: Stanford University Press.

Light, Paul. 1999. *The President's Agenda: Domestic Policy Choice from Kennedy to Clinton*, third edition. Baltimore: Johns Hopkins University Press.

Lindsay, James. 1994. "Congress, Foreign Policy, and the New Institutionalism." *International Studies Quarterly* 38(2): 281–304.

Liptak, Adam. 2014. "As Obama Vows to Act on Climate Change, Justices Weight His Approach." *New York Times*, February 19.

Long, J. Scott, and Jeremy Freese. 2006. *Regression Models for Categorical Dependent Variables Using STATA*. College Station: STATA Press.

Lowande, Kenneth. 2014. "After the Orders: Presidential Memoranda and Unilateral Action." *Presidential Studies Quarterly* 44(4): 724–741.

Lowery, Wesley. 2014. "Senate Republicans Block Minimum Wage Increase Bill." *The Washington Post*, April 30.

Lugar, Richard G. 1988. *Letters to the Next President*. New York: Simon and Schuster Trade Division.

Lupia, Arthur, and Mathew McCubbins. 1994. "Learning from Oversight: Police Patrols and Fire Alarms Reconsidered." *Journal of Law, Economics and Organization* 10(1): 96–125.

Madison, James. 1906. *The Writings of James Madison, Comprising His Public Papers and His Private Correspondence*, volume 6, edited by Gaillard Hunt. New York: G. P. Putnam's Sons.

———. 1911. "James Madison's Notes of the Constitutional Convention." In *The Records of the Federal Convention of 1787*, volume 1, edited by Max Farrand. New Haven, CT: Yale University Press.

Mansfield, Harvey C. 1989. *Taming the Prince: The Ambivalence of Modern Executive Power*. New York: The Free Press.

———. "Hyperlink http://scholar.harvard.edu/harveym 2003." In *Never a Matter of Indifference; Sustaining Virtue in a Free Republic*, edited by Peter Berkowitz. Stanford, CA: Hoover Institution Press.

Marlow, Melanie M. 2011. "President Obama and Executive Independence." In *The Obama Presidency in the Constitutional Order: A First Look*, edited by Carol McNamara. Blue Ridge Summit, PA: Rowman & Littlefield.

Marshall, Bryan W. 2011. "Congress and the Executive: Unilateralism and Legislative Bargaining." In *New Directions in Congressional Politics*, edited by Jamie L. Carson. New York: Routledge.

Marshall, Bryan W., and Patrick J. Haney. 2010. "Aiding and Abetting: Congressional Complicity in the Rise of the Unitary Executive." In *The Unitary Executive and the Modern Presidency*, edited by Ryan J. Barilleaux and Christopher S. Kelley. College Station: Texas A&M University.

Marshall, Bryan W., and Richard L. Pacelle Jr. 2005. "Revisiting the Two Presidencies: The Strategic Use of Executive Orders." *American Politics Research* 33(1): 81–105.

Martin, Lisa. 1999. "The President and International Commitments: Treaties as Signaling Devices." *Presidency Studies Quarterly* 35(3): 440–465.

Mason, Jeff. 2014. "Republicans Decry Obama Plans to Bypass Congress to Advance Agenda." *Chicago Tribune*, January 26.

Mayer, Kenneth R. 1999. "Executive Orders and Presidential Power." *The Journal of Politics* 61(2): 445–466.

———. 2001. *With the Stroke of a Pen; Executive Orders and Presidential Power.* Princeton, NJ, and Oxford, UK: Princeton University Press.

———. 2009. "Going Alone: The Presidential Power of Unilateral Action." In *The Oxford Handbook of the American Presidency,* edited by George C. Edwards III and William G. Howell. New York: Oxford University Press.

Mayer, Kenneth R., and Kevin Price. 2002. "Unilateral Presidential Powers: Significant Executive Orders, 1949–99." *Presidential Studies Quarterly* 32(2): 367–386.

Mayhew, David R. 1991. *Divided We Govern.* New Haven, CT, and London: Yale University Press.

McCarthy, Nolan M., and Keith T. Poole. 1995. "Veto Power and Legislation: An Empirical Analysis of Executive and Legislative Bargaining from 1961–1986." *Journal of Law, Economics and Organization* 11: 282–312.

McCubbins, Mathew. 1985. "The Legislative Design of Regulatory Structure." *American Journal of Political Science* 29(4): 721–748.

McCubbins, Mathew, and Arthur Lupia.1994. "Who Controls? Information and the Structure of Legislative Decision Making." *Legislative Studies Quarterly* 19: 361–384.

McCubbins, Mathew, Roger G. Noll and Barry R. Weingast. 1987. "Administrative Procedures as Instruments of Political Control." *Journal of Law, Economics and Organization* 3: 243–277.

———. 1989. "Structure and Process; Politics and Policy: Administrative Arrangements and the Political Control of Agencies." *Virginia Law Review* 75:431–482.

McCubbins, Mathew, and Talbot Page. 1987. "A Theory of Congressional Delegation." In *Congress: Structure and Policy,* edited by Mathew McCubbins and Terry Sullivan. Cambridge, UK: Cambridge University Press.

McCubbins, Mathew, and Thomas Schwartz. 1984. "Congressional Oversight Overlooked: Fire Alarms vs. Police Patrols." *American Journal of Political Science* 28(1): 165–179.

Meacham, Jon. 2012. *Thomas Jefferson: The Art of Power.* New York: Random House.

Milkis, Sidney, and Michael Nelson. 1993 *The American Presidency: Origins and Development 1776–1993.* Washington, DC: Congressional Quarterly Press.

Mitnick, Barry M. 1973. "Fiduciary Rationality and Public Policy: The Theory of Agency and Some Consequences." Paper presented at the 1973 Annual Meeting of the American Political Science Association. New Orleans.

———. 1975. "The Theory of Agency: The Policing 'Paradox' and Regulatory Behavior." *Public Choice* 24: 27–42.

Moe, Terry M. 1985. "The Politicized Presidency." In *The New Direction in American Politics,* edited by John E. Chubb and Paul E. Peterson. Washington, DC: The Brookings Institution.

———. 1987. "An Assessment of the Positive Theory of Congressional Dominance." *Legislative Studies Quarterly* 12: 475–520.

———. 1990. "The Politics of Structural Choice: Toward a Theory of Public Bureaucracy." In *Organization Theory: From Chester Barnard to the Present and Beyond,* edited by Oliver E. Williamson. New York: Oxford University Press.

———. 1994. "Presidents, Institutions, and Theory." In *Researching the Presidency: Vital Questions, New Approaches*, edited by George C. Edwards III, John Kessel, and Bert Rockman. Pittsburgh: University of Pittsburgh Press.

———. 1998. "The Presidency and the Bureaucracy: The Presidential Advantage." In Michael Nelson, *The Presidency and the Political System (Fifth Edition)*, edited by Michael Nelson. Washington, DC: Congressional Quarterly Press.

———. 2005. "Power and Political Institutions." *Perspectives on Politics* 3(2): 215–233.

Moe, Terry M., and William Howell. 1999. "The Presidential Power of Unilateral Action." *Journal of Law, Economics and Organization* 15(1): 132–179.

Moe, Terry M., and Scott A. Wilson. 1994. "Presidents and the Politics of Structure." *Law and Contemporary Problems* 57(2): 1–44.

Morgan, Ruth P. 1970. *The President and Civil Rights: Policy Making by Executive Order.* New York: St. Martin's Press.

Moynihan, Donald P. 2003. "Public Management Policy Change in the United States 1993–2001." *International Public Management Journal* 6(3): 371–394.

Nathan, Richard P. 1983. *The Administrative Presidency* (second edition). New York: Wiley.

Nather, David. 2014. "The Politics of Obamacare Delays." *Politico*, February 21.

Neighbors, William D. 1964. "Presidential Legislation by Executive Order." *University of Colorado Law Review* 37: 105–118.

Neustadt, Richard E. 1990. *Presidential Power and the Modern Presidents: The Politics of Leadership from Roosevelt to Reagan* (third edition). New York: The Free Press.

O'Halloran, Sharyn. 1994. *Politics, Process, and American Trade Policy.* Ann Arbor: University of Michigan Press.

Ouyang, Yu, and Richard W. Waterman. 2015. "How Legislative (In)Activity, Ideological Divergence, and Divided Government Impact Executive Unilateralism: A Test of Three Theories." *Congress & Presidency* 42(3): 317–341.

Pastor, Robert, 1980, *Congress and the Politics of United States Foreign Economic Policy, 1929–1976,* Berkeley: University of California Press.

Perrow, Charles. 2007. *The Next Catastrophe: Reducing Our Vulnerabilities to Natural, Industrial, and Terrorist Disasters.* Princeton, NJ: Princeton University Press.

Peterson, Mark A. 1990. *Legislating Together: The White House and Capitol Hill from Eisenhower to Reagan.* Cambridge, MA: Harvard University Press.

Pildes, Richard H., and Samuel Issacharoff. 2004. "Between Civil Libertarianism and Executive Unilateralism: An Institutional Process Approach to Rights during Wartime." *Theoretical Inquiries in Law* 5(1): 1–45.

Pious, Richard M. 2006. "Public Law and the 'Executive' Constitution." In *Executing the Constitution: Putting the President Back into the Constitution*, edited by Christopher S. Kelley. Albany: State University of New York Press.

———. 2009. "Prerogative Power and Presidential Politics." In the *Oxford Handbook on the American Presidency*, edited by George C. Edwards III and William G. Howell. New York: Oxford University Press.

———. 2011. "Prerogative Power in the Obama Administration: Continuity and Change in the War on Terrorism." *Presidential Studies Quarterly* 41(2): 263–290.

Poll, Richard Douglas, David E. Miller, Eugene E. Campbell, and Thomas G. Alexander 1989. *Utah's History.* Logan : Utah State University Press.

Polsby, Nelson W. 1964. *Congress and the Presidency.* Englewood Cliffs, NJ: Prentice-Hall.

Ponder, Daniel E. 2005. "Presidential Leadership in a Fractured State: Capacity, Autonomy, and the American State." *International Journal of Public Administration* 28(5-6): 531–546

Poole, Keith T., and Howard Rosenthal. 1991. "Patterns of Congressional Voting." *American Journal of Political Science* 35(1): 228–278.

———. 1997. *Congress: A Political-Economic History of Roll Call Voting*. Oxford, UK: Oxford University Press.

Posner, Eric A., and Adrian Vermeule. 2010. *The Executive Unbound: After the Madisonian Republic*. New York: Oxford University Press.

Ragsdale, Lyn. 2009. *Vital Statistics on the Presidency: George Washington to George W. Bush*. Washington, DC: CQ Press.

Reeves, Andrew, and Jon C. Rogowski. 2016. "Unilateral Powers, Public Opinion, and the Presidency." *Journal of Politics* 78(1): 137–151.

Rice, Gerald T. 1985. *The Bold Experiment: JFK's Peace Corps*. Notre Dame, IN: University of Notre Dame Press.

Rossiter, Clinton. 1956. *The American Presidency*. New York: Harcourt, Brace and Company.

———. 1960. *The American Presidency*, revised edition. New York: Harcourt Brace and Co.

Rottinghaus, Brandon. 2015. "Assessing the Unilateral Presidency: Constraints and Contingencies." *Congress and the Presidency* 42(2): 287–292.

Rottinghaus, Brandon, and Jason Maier. 2007. "The Power of Decree: Presidential Use of Executive Proclamations, 1977–2005." *Political Research Quarterly* 60(2): 338–343.

Rottinghaus, Brandon, and Adam Warber. 2015. "Unilateral Orders as Constituency Outreach: Executive Orders, Proclamations, and the Public Presidency." *Presidential Studies Quarterly* 45(2): 289–309.

Rucker, Philip. 2013. "Obama Responds to Heckler on Immigration Reform: 'It Won't be as Easy as Shouting.'" *The Washington Post*, November 25.

Rucker, Philip, and Ed O'Keefe. 2013. "Obama's Far-Reaching Gun-Proposals Face Uncertain Fate in Divided Congress." *New York Times*, January 16.

Rudalevige, Andrew. 2002. *Managing the President's Program: Presidential Leadership and Legislative Policy Formulation*. Princeton, NJ, and Oxford, UK: Princeton University Press.

———. 2005a. *The New Imperial Presidency: Renewing Presidential Power after Watergate*. Ann Arbor: University of Michigan Press.

———. 2005b. "The Structure of Leadership: Presidents, Hierarchies, and Information Flow." *Presidential Studies Quarterly* 35(2): 333–360.

———. 2011. "Executive Orders and Their Formulation: Persuasion or Command?" Paper presented at the 2011 Annual Meeting of the Midwest Political Science Association, Chicago.

———. 2012. "The Contemporary Presidency: Executive Orders and Presidential Unilateralism." *Presidential Studies Quarterly* 42(1): 138–160.

———. 2014. "The Letter of the Law: Administrative Discretion and Obama's Domestic Unilateralism." *The Forum* 12(2): 29–59.

Sala, Brian. 1998. "In Search of the Administrative President: Presidential 'Decree' Powers and Policy Implementation in the United States." In *Executive Decree Authority*, edited by John Carey and Matthew Shugart. Cambridge, UK: Cambridge University Press.

Savage, Charlie. 2007. *Takeover: The Return of the Imperial Presidency and the Subversion of American Democracy.* New York: Little, Brown and Company.

———. 2012. "Shift on Executive Power Lets Obama Bypass Rivals." *New York Times,* April 23: CLXI.

———. 2015 *Power Wars: Inside Obama's Post-9/11 Presidency.* New York: Little, Brown, and Company.

Schramm, Susan Slavin. 1981. *The Politics of Executive Orders.* Unpublished PhD Dissertation, George Washington University, Washington, DC.

Schlesinger, Arthur M. Jr. 1973. *The Imperial Presidency.* New York: Houghton Mifflin.

Gary J. Schmitt, "Thomas Jefferson and the Presidency," 1989. In *Inventing the American Presidency*, edited by Thomas E. Cronin. Lawrence: University Press of Kansas.

Scigliano, Robert. 1989. "The President's Prerogative Power." In *Inventing The American Presidency*, edited by Thomas E. Cronin. Lawrence: University Press of Kansas.

Sessions, Jeff. 2014. "Senator Sessions Reacts: We Must Stop Emperor Obama." *USA Today*, November 20.

Shabecoff, Philip, 1981. "Reagan Order on Cost–Benefit Analysis Stirs Economic and Political Debate," *New York Times*, November 7.

Shafie, David. 2013. *Eleventh Hour: The Politics Of Policy Initiatives in Presidential Transitions.* College Station: Texas A&M University Press.

Shane, Peter M. 2009. *Madison's Nightmare: How Executive Power Threatens American Democracy.* Chicago: University of Chicago Press.

Shear, Michael. 2014b. "Obama, Citing a Concern for Families, Orders Review of Deportations." *The New York Times*, March 13.

———. 2014a. "Obama, Daring Congress, Acts to Overhaul Immigration." *The New York Times*, November 20.

Shear, Michael, and Jennifer Steinhauer. 2013. "Obama Willing to Use Executive Orders on Guns." *The New York Times*, January 14.

Shugart, Matthew Soberg, and John M. Carey. 1992. *Presidents and Assemblies: Constitutional Design and Electoral Dynamics.* New York: Cambridge University Press.

Shull, Steven A. 1993. *A Kinder, Gentler Racism? The Reagan–Bush Civil Rights Legacy.* Armonk, NY: M. W. Sharp.

———. 1997. *Presidential--Congressional Relations: Policy and Time Approaches.* Ann Arbor: University of Michigan Press.

———. 2006. *Policy by Other Means: Alternative Adoption by Presidents.* College Station: Texas A&M Press.

Shull, Steven A., and Thomas C. Shaw. 1999. *Explaining Congressional–Presidential Relations: A Multiple Perspective Approach.* Albany: State University of New York Press.

Sollenberger, Mitchel A., and Mark J. Rozell. 2012. *The President's Czars: Undermining Congress and the Constitution.* Lawrence: University Press of Kansas.

Spence, David B. 1999. "Managing Delegation Ex Ante: Using Law to Steer Administrative Agencies." *The Journal of Legal Studies* 28(2): 413–459.

Spiliotes, Constantine J. 2000. "Conditional Partisanship and Institutional Responsibility in Presidential Decision Making." *Presidential Studies Quarterly* 30(3): 485–513.

Spitzer, Robert. 1993. *President and Congress: Executive Hegemony at the Crossroads of American Government*. New York: McGraw-Hill.

Stimson, James. 1999, *Public Opinion in America: Moods, Cycles, and Qwings*, second edition. Boulder, CO: Westview Press.

Stupak, Bart. 2012. "Bart Stupak on Contraception Mandate, Statement of Former Congressman Bart Stupak Regarding HHS Contraception Mandate," Democrats for Life Panel Discussion, September 4. Available at www.democratsforlife.org/index .php?option=com_content&view=article&id=773:bart-stupak-on-contraception-mandate&catid=24&Itemid=205.

Sullivan, George. 1964. *The Story of the Peace Corps*. New York: Fleet Publishing.

Sundquist, James L. 1981. *The Decline and Resurgence of Congress*. Washington, DC: The Brookings Institution.

Sunstein, Cass R., and Lawrence Lessig, 1994. "The President and the Administration." *Columbia Law Review* 94(1).

Taft, William Howard. 1916. *Our Chief Magistrate and His Powers*. New York: Columbia University Press.

Thomas, George. 2000. "As Far as Republican Principles Will Admit: Presidential Prerogative and Constitutional Government." *Presidential Studies Quarterly* 30(3): 534–552.

Treverton, Gregory F., and Pamela Varley. 1992. *The United States and South Africa: The 1985 Sanctions Debate*. Washington, DC: Institute for the Study of Diplomacy.

Tulis, Jeffrey. 1988. *The Rhetorical Presidency*. Princeton, NJ: Princeton University Press.

U.S. Congress. 1957. House of Representatives. Committee on Government Operations. *Executive Orders and Proclamations: A Study of the Use of Presidential Powers*. 85th Congress, 1st session, December.

Vladeck, Stephen I. 2004, "Note, Emergency Power and the Militia Acts," *Yale Law Journal* 114 (149): 176–180.

Volden, Craig. 2002. "A Formal Model of the Politics of Delegation in a Separation of Powers System." *American Journal of Political Science* 46(1): 111–133.

Walsh, Daniel C. 2012. *An Air War with Cuba: The United States Radio Campaign against Castro*. Jefferson, NC: McFarland and Company.

Warber, Adam L. 2006. *Executive Orders and the Modern Presidency: Legislating from the Oval Office*. Boulder, CO: Lynne Rienner Publishers.

———. October 2014. "Public Outreach, Executive Orders, and the Unilateral Presidency." *Congress & the Presidency* 41(3): 269–288.

Waterman, Richard W. 1989. *Presidential Influence and the Administrative State*. Knoxville: University of Tennessee Press.

———. 2009a. "The Administrative Presidency, Unilateral Power, and the Unitary Executive Theory." *Presidential Studies Quarterly* 30(1): 5–9.

———. 2009b. "Assessing the Unilateral Presidency." In the *Oxford Handbook of the American Presidency*, edited by George C. Edwards III and William G. Howell. New York: Oxford University Press.

Waterman, Richard W., and Kenneth J. Meier. 1998. "Principal–Agent Models: An Expansion?" *Journal of Public Administration Research and Theory* 8(2): 173–202.

Weisman, Jonathan. 2014. "Boehner Doubts Immigration Bill Will Pass in 2014." *New York Times*, February 6.

Weko. Thomas J. 1995. *The Politicizing Presidency: The White House Personnel Office, 1948–1994.* Lawrence: University of Kansas Press.

Whittaker, William. 2005. *Congress, the Davis-Bacon Act: Suspension* (CRS Report No. RL 33100). Washington, DC: Congressional Research Service. Available at www .opencrs.com/rpts/RL33100_20050926.pdf.

Whittington, Keith E., and Daniel P. Carpenter. 2003. "Executive Power in American Institutional Development." *Perspectives on Politics* 1(3): 495–513.

Wildavsky, Aaron. 1966. "The Two Presidencies." *Trans-Action* 4(2): 7–14.

Wilmerding, Lucius. 1952. "The President and the Law." *Political Science Quarterly* 67(3): 321–338.

Yoo, John. 2005. *The Powers of War and Peace: The Constitution and Foreign Affairs after 9/11.* Chicago: University of Chicago Press.

———. 2009. *Crisis and Command: The History of Executive Power from George Washington to George W. Bush.* New York: Kaplan Press.

Young, Laura D. 2013, "Unilateral Presidential Policy Making and the Impact of Crises." *Presidential Studies Quarterly* 43(2): 327–351.

Index

executive orders (*continued*)
Executive Order 13514, 120;
Executive Order 13519, 151–52;
Executive Order 13535, 4–5, 10–11,
144–45; Executive Order 13544,
144; Executive Order 13563,
121; Executive Order 13574,
147; Executive Order 13589, 153;
Executive Order 13610, 121;
Executive Order 13626, 5, 10–11;
Executive Order 13657, 18–19,
21–22; Executive Order 13658, 2–3,
19; Executive Order 13689, 108,
109; of Ford, 44, 49, 50, 99, 125–26,
148; regarding intergovernmental
relations, 45–46; of Kennedy, 70,
177–78; number of, 43–44; of
Obama, 2–3, 4–5, 5, 10–11, 18–19,
19, 21–22, 42, 54, 66, 92–94,
108, 109, 121, 124, 125, 141–42,
144–45, 151–52, 153, 181–82; vs.
proclamations, 34, 36, 40, 43, 44,
45, 46, 47, 48, 54–55, 64, 67–71; of
Reagan, 8, 26–27, 41–42, 44, 49,
50, 54, 63, 70, 98, 107–8, 126, 127,
131, 148, 149, 153, 193n6; review
process, 63; of Franklin Roosevelt,
40–41, 60, 61; by source of authority,
67, 69–71, 77–79; over time, 41,
69–71; after vetoes, 24, 131, 133,
140; during war, 41, 46, 69, 77,
78
executive power: expansion of, 7, 14,
16, 172–76, 180; meanings of, 6
executive prerogative, 14, 58, 60,
61–64, 167, 169, 172
Executive Salary Cost of Living
Adjustment Act of 1975, 148
Export Administration Act of 1979,
47, 140–41
export controls, 44, 46–47

"Family Fairness" program, 196n2
Family Medical Leave Act (FMLA), 171
Farley, Robert, 191n13
Fatovic, Clement, 62, 175
Federal Code, 43

Federalist Papers: Federalist 37, 17;
Federalist 47, 10, 17, 61; *Federalist*
48, 17; *Federalist* 51, 61; *Federalist*
69, 17; *Federalist* 70, 32, 96
Federal Land Policy and Management
Act of 1976, 204n43
Federal Property and Administrative
Services Act, 66–67
Federal Register, 43, 194n1
Federal Reserve Act, 38
Feldman, Martha, 123
Fenno, Richard F., Jr., 80
Financial Crisis Inquiry Commission,
151, 152
Fine, Jeffrey A., 9, 31, 73, 170
Fiorina, Morris, 30, 81, 83
first term: first half, 28; second half,
29, 78, 102, 104, 106, 108, 134,
137, 155, 156
Fisher, Louis, 17, 43, 61, 62, 83, 122,
146, 198n27
Fleisher, Richard, 118
Fleishman, Joel L., 7, 10, 24, 82
Ford, Gerald, 42–43; adaptive orders,
157; budget policy, 148; command
orders, 99, 100–101; dairy policy,
133; and Energy Research and
Development Administration
(ERDA), 149; executive orders,
44, 49, 50, 99, 125–26, 148;
implementation orders, 148, 157;
inflationary impact statement, 44;
intelligence policy, 125–26; Nixon
pardon, 43, 44; number of orders
during legislative process, 49; number
of orders issued in executing law,
49; number of orders using direct
action, 49, 50; oath of office, 195n16;
oil embargo policy, 99; preemptive
orders, 125, 128; Proclamation
4311, 43; Proclamation 4423, 133;
proclamations, 43, 44, 133; relations
with Congress, 51, 100–101, 128,
148, 149; routine orders, 100;
State of the Union Address of
1975, 148; supportive orders, 128;
total number of orders, 43–44

Moe, Terry M. (*continued*)
on delegation of authority, 81;
on modern presidents, 95; on
presidential advantages, 120
Moffett, Kenneth W., 151
Morgan, Ruth P., 9
most favored nation status (MFN), 47
Moynihan, Donald P., 152
Murray, Patty, 182
Mutual Security Act, 177

Napolitano, Janet, 196n2
Nathan, Richard P., 9, 70, 98, 111
Nather, David, 147
National Competitiveness Act, 25
National Economic Council, 94
National Environmental Policy
Act (NEPA), 57, 124
National Information
Infrastructure Act, 25
National Park Service, 40
National Performance Review (NPR),
152
National Security Council
Staff, 18–19, 21–22
National Wildlife Refuge System, 48
negative binomial models,
74, 75, 77, 198n24
Neighbors, William D., 7, 18, 118
Nelson, Michael, 39, 61
Neustadt, Richard: on Constitutional
Convention of 1787, 32; on power
as unilateral vs. persuasive,
32; *Presidential Power*, 1; on
presidential bargaining, 7, 118,
180; on presidential power,
180–81; on presidents as clerks/
administrators, 1, 7, 18, 25,
145–46; on presidents as leaders,
1, 18, 146; on routine orders, 94
New Deal, 37, 40–41, 69
Nixon, Richard, 8, 93, 125; import
policy, 35; pardon, 43, 44;
proclamations regarding wage and
price controls, 35; resignation, 43,
101, 195n16; Watergate scandal,
43

No Child Left Behind Act, 4
Noll, Roger G., 59, 82
North American Free Trade
Agreement, 148

Obama, Barack: adaptive orders, 151–52,
153; as administrator, 4–5, 6, 18–19,
21–22, 108, 144; Arctic policy, 108,
109; campaign promises, 53, 92–93;
command orders, 108, 109; detention
and interrogation policy, 42;
education policy, 4; efficient spending
policy, 153; energy policy, 119–20;
environmental policy, 125; equal-pay-
for-women policy, 141–42; executive
memoranda of, 42; Executive Order
13490, 42; Executive Order 13491,
42; Executive Order 13504, 93–94;
Executive Order 13512, 94; Executive
Order 13514, 120; Executive Order
13519, 151–52; Executive Order
13535, 4–5, 10–11, 144–45; Executive
Order 13544, 144; Executive
Order 13563, 121; Executive Order
13574, 147; Executive Order 13589,
153; Executive Order 13610, 121;
Executive Order 13626, 5, 10–11;
Executive Order 13657, 18–19,
21–22; Executive Order 13658, 2–3,
19; Executive Order 13689, 108, 109;
executive orders, 2–3, 4–5, 5, 10–11,
18–19, 19, 21–22, 42, 54, 66, 92–94,
108, 109, 121, 124, 125, 141–42,
144–45, 151–52, 153, 181–82; on
executive privilege, 66; Guantanamo
Bay promise, 92–93; Gulf Coast
recovery policy, 93–94; gun control
policy, 181–82, 187; health care
policy, 4–5, 6, 10–11, 143, 144,
171–72, 174, 204n1; immigration
policy, 3–4, 56–57, 64, 174, 196n2;
implementation orders, 147; as
independent, 2–4, 6, 19, 144–45,
151–52; Iraq policy, 86; minimum
wage policy, 2–3, 19, 53–54, 66–67;
on national minimum wage, 2;
national monuments policy, 37; oil

CPSIA information can be obtained
at www.ICGtesting.com
Printed in the USA
LVOW11*1454130417
530731LV00007B/181/P